A Harp in the Stars

for the lights, supported by a lyric
Figure Foundation

A HARP in the STARS

An Anthology of Lyric Essays

Edited by RANDON BILLINGS NOBLE

University of Nebraska Press * Lincoln

Acknowledgments for the use of copyrighted
material appear on pages 279–80, which
constitute an extension of the copyright page.

Library of Congress Cataloging-in-Publication Data
Names: Noble, Randon Billings, editor.
Title: A harp in the stars: an anthology of lyric
essays / edited by Randon Billings Noble.
Description: Lincoln: University of Nebraska Press,
[2021] | Includes bibliographical references.
Identifiers: LCCN 2021016970
ISBN 9781496217745 (paperback)
ISBN 9781496229205 (epub)
ISBN 9781496229212 (pdf)
Subjects: LCSH: American essays—21st century. |
BISAC: LITERARY COLLECTIONS / Essays
Classification: LCC PS689 .H37 2021 | DDC 814/.608—dc23
LC record available at https://lccn.loc.gov/2021016970

Designed and set in Minion Pro by L. Auten.

Contents

Introduction

RANDON BILLINGS NOBLE

> Late Middle English (in the sense 'bring [a person] into a place
> or group'): from Latin *introducere*, from *intro-* 'to the inside'
> + *ducere* 'to lead'

Where to begin?

In 1993, when Deborah Tall first used the term *lyric essay*?

Or back in the late 1500s, when Montaigne used the word *essay* to describe what he had been writing?

Or at the turn of the tenth century, when Sei Shonagon wrote her pillow book full of what we might now call list or nonce or flash essays?

Or further back, with the ancient Greeks, and the invention of the lyre that eventually gave us the word *lyric*?

> ORIGIN late 16th century: from French *lyrique* or Latin *lyricus*,
> from Greek *lurikos*, from *lura* 'lyre'

Lurikos, lura, lyre. To the ear, "lyre" and "liar" sound the same, which I resist because I do not condone lying in essays, lyric or otherwise. But mythology tells us that the origins of the lyre come from a kind of lie.

Hermes, the gods' messenger and something of a trickster, stole Apollo's sacred cattle. Taking off the cattle's feet, he reattached them backward to hide their tracks as he drove them to a secret cave. When Apollo could not find them, he was furious. Hermes tried to deny his theft but ultimately confessed. In atonement, he gave Apollo a new way to make music: the lyre. First made of a tortoise shell, reeds, and gut, it evolved into a U-shaped instrument, similar to a harp, with a crossbar and seven strings. It was played alone or as an accompaniment to songs or poems. Music to sweeten a story.

Apollo accepted the gift (or payment, really) and became the god of music. Later he taught Orpheus how to play the lyre. Orpheus became the best musician and poet known to humankind. He charmed trees, rocks, and rivers. While sailing with the Argonauts he overpowered the Sirens with his songs, allowing the ship and its crew to pass safely on their quest to find the Golden Fleece. And when his wife died, he sang his way into the dark underworld to retrieve her. His music was so powerful it could almost—almost—raise the dead.

Lyric essays have the same power to soothe, to harrow, to persuade, to move, to raise, to rouse, to overcome.

Like Orpheus and his songs, lyric essays try something daring. They rely more on intuition than exposition. They often use image more than narration. They question more than answer. But despite all this looseness, the lyric essay still has the responsibilities of any essay: to try to figure something out, to play with ideas, to show a shift in thinking (however subtle). The whole of a lyric essay adds up to more than the sum of its parts.

But the lyric essay is slippery. There's no widespread agreement on what it is or what to call it. When Montaigne first started writing his *essais*, he was just essaying—trying out new lines of thought. Only later would the idea—and the name—of "essay" stick.

And when Sei Shonagon was noting observations in her pillow book she wasn't thinking about whether her lists and notes would be considered essays, lyric or otherwise. But by the 1990s, a thousand years after she had written them, excerpts were anthologized in books like Philip Lopate's *The Art of the Personal Essay*, and they became, indeed, essays—lyric essays.

Around this same time the *Seneca Review*, edited by John D'Agata, published an anthology called *We Might As Well Call It the Lyric Essay*. Deborah Tall had used the term *lyric essay* in an email to D'Agata, who quickly took up the term and popularized it. He also stretched it—perhaps too far—to include poems and some fictions. The last line of the introduction to his anthology is "We might as well call it the lyric essay because we need as many terms as there are passions for the form."

With this I agree. Lyric essays require a kind of passion, a commitment to weirdness in the face of convention, a willingness to risk confusion, a comfort with outsider status. When I'm writing a lyric essay, I'm not worried about what it is or what to call it. But when I started teaching lyric essays, I needed to put words to the form, to try to define it, to make it at least a little more accessible and understandable—even as I kept running into contradictions in my own thinking. Sometimes I enjoyed the lyric essay's elusiveness; other times I felt like I was the one following the backward hoofprints. But the lyric essay's wily capaciousness is among its strengths.

I came to define a lyric essay as

a piece of writing with a visible / stand-out / unusual structure
that explores / forecasts / gestures to an idea in an unexpected way

But about that visible / stand-out / unusual structure, those gestured-to ideas: lyric essays are tricky. If you try to mount one to a spreading board, it's likely to dodge the pin and fly away. If you try to press one between two slides, it might find a way to ooze down your sleeve. And if you try to set it within a taxonomy, it will pose the same problems as the platypus—a mammal, but one that lays eggs; semiaquatic, living in both water and on land; and venomous, a trait that belongs mostly to reptiles and insects. It will run away if on land—its gait that of a furry alligator—or swim off in the undulating way of beavers. Either way it can threaten you with a poisoned spur before it ripples off.

Despite its resistance to categorization, there are broad forms of the lyric essay that are worth trying to define. In this anthology you will find four of them.

Flash Essays

ORIGIN Middle English (in the sense 'splash water about'): probably imitative; compare with *flush* and *splash*

I've defined flash essays as being one thousand words or fewer. They are short, sharp, and clarifying. The shortest ones illuminate a moment or a realization the way a flash of light can illuminate a scene. Longer ones may take a little more time but regardless of their length, the meaning of the essay resonates more strongly than its word count might suggest.

Nels P. Highberg's "This Is the Room Where" unpacks decades of life in one room and one sentence. "The Sound of Things Breaking" by Ru Freeman centers around a broken plate but encompasses infinitely larger questions of loss and identity. And Marsha McGregor's "On Beauty Interrupted" stumbles upon a grisly sight on a forest floor that redefines our very notion of beauty.

Lightning flashes, as do cameras, flares, signals, and explosions; all show a brief moment in a larger scene. A small syringe can deliver a powerful drug. A capsule can too—unless it dissolves in a glass of water to reveal a paper flower. Regardless of their content, flash essays are imitative of their form. They give the reader a splash of a moment and leave us flushed with emotion and meaning.

Segmented Essays

> ORIGIN late 16th century (as a term in geometry): from Latin *segmentum*, from *secare* 'to cut'

Segmented essays are divided into segments that might be numbered or titled or simply separated with a space break.

These spaces—white space, blank space—allow the reader to pause, think, consider, and digest each segment before moving on to the next. Each section may contain something new, but all still belong cogently to the whole. Sarah Einstein's essay "Self-Portrait in Apologies" is comprised of a series of apologies to wronged parties from ex-boyfriends to ancestors. Lia Purpura writes about sparrows, fires, and open space—all united under a single "Loss Collection." And the hurts in Sayantani Dasgupta's "The Boys of New Delhi: An Essay in Four Hurts" add up to reveal the lingering effect of a certain kind of pain but also the new understanding that follows.

Segmented essays are also known as

Fragmented
(ORIGIN late Middle English: from French, or from Latin *fragmentum*, from *frangere* 'to break')

Paratactic
(ORIGIN mid-19th century: from Greek *parataxis*, from *para-* 'beside' + *taxis* 'arrangement'; from *tassein* 'arrange')

Collage
(ORIGIN early 20th century: from French, literally 'gluing')

Mosaic

(ORIGIN late Middle English: from French *mosaïque*, based on Latin *musi(v)um* 'decoration with small square stones', perhaps ultimately from Greek *mousa* 'a muse')

How you think of an essay may influence how you write it. Citrus fruits come in segments; so do worms. Each segment is part of an organic whole. But a fragmented essay may be broken on purpose and a collage or mosaic deliberately glued together.

Braided Essays

ORIGIN Old English *bregdan* 'make a sudden movement', also 'interweave', of Germanic origin; related to Dutch *breien* (verb)

Braided essays are segmented essays whose sections have a repeating pattern—the way each strand of a braid returns to take its place in the center.

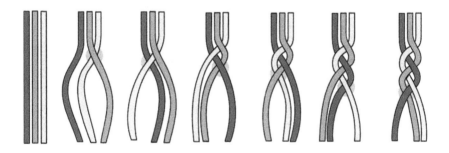

Each time a particular strand returns, its meaning is enriched by the other strands you've read through. In this anthology, Elissa Washuta's braided essay "Apocalypse Logic" weaves together the United States' history of treaties and betrayal, the 2016 election, Chinuk Wawa, and her own family's history; by the end of the essay you have a new understanding of the destructive pressure whiteness imposes on Native American life. Aimée Baker's "Beasts of the Fields" starts with an infestation of rats and weaves in seasonal cycles and her brother's increasing distance and decline to reveal how some threats are nearly impossible to eradicate once they take hold.

You can braid hair for containment or ornamentation. You can braid fibers into a basket to carry something or into a rope to tie something. Maybe it's something you want to hold fast. Or maybe it's to tense a kite against the wind—to fly.

Hermit Crab Essays

> ORIGIN Middle English: from Old French *hermite*, from late Latin *eremita*, from Greek *erēmitēs*, from *erēmos* 'solitary'
>
> ORIGIN late 16th century (referring to hawks, meaning 'claw or fight each other'): from Low German *krabben*

Hermit crab essays, as Brenda Miller named them in *Tell It Slant*, borrow another form of writing as their structure the way a hermit crab borrows another's shell. Laurie Easter uses a word-search puzzle as the form for her essay about a missing friend, "Searching for Gwen." The footnotes to "Informed Consent" tell more of the story behind Elizabeth K. Brown's participation in a study on families of alcoholics. And a bottle of body wash is the surprising container for Dorothy Bendel's "Body Wash: Instructions on Surviving Homelessness."

These extraliterary structures can protect vulnerable content (the way the shell protects the crab), but they can also act as firm containers for content that might be intellectually or emotionally difficult, prodigious, or otherwise messy.

In life hermit crabs aren't hermits at all; they're quite social. And in a way hermit crab essays are too, because they depend on a network of other extraliterary forms of writing—recipes, labels, album notes—and what we already know of them.

I've always thought that a hermit crab's front looks like a hand reaching out of the shell, a gesture that draws the onlooker inwards. Instead of a needing a shell that protects, the content of a hermit crab essay might lie in wait—like the pellets in a shotgun shell or a plumule of a seed—ready to burst beyond the confines of the form and take root in the reader's mind.

But some of these forms overlap. Sandra Beasley's "Depends on Who You Ask" is a flash essay that's also segmented; its diptych structure gives you the needed space to understand each part until you realize what the essay as a whole is really about. Tyrese L. Coleman's "Why I Let Him Touch

My Hair" is both flash and a kind of braid, with the scene that leads up to the hair-touching acting as the repeated strand. A lyric essay can be many things at once, the way a square is also a rectangle, a parallelogram, a quadrilateral. One shape, but many ways of naming it.

Near the end of this book is another kind of overlap:

Craft Essays

> ORIGIN Old English *cræft* 'strength, skill', of Germanic origin; related to Dutch *kracht*, German *Kraft*, and Swedish *kraft* 'strength'. *Craft* (sense 3 of the noun), originally in the expression *small craft* 'small trading vessels', may be elliptical, referring to vessels requiring a small amount of 'craft' or skill to handle, as opposed to large oceangoing ships.

These craft essays are also lyric essays. They are separated out for easy reference but also because they are united by content (they all think overtly about lyric essays) even though they express that content in a variety of lyric forms. They are like small trading vessels that bring new ways of thinking about the essay from one port to another.

And because there are so many ways of thinking about essays—lyric essays in particular—I've asked *all* the contributors of this anthology to share their thoughts in the very last section of the book.

Meditations

> ORIGIN mid-16th century: from Latin *meditat-* 'contemplated', from the verb *meditari*, from a base meaning 'measure'; related to **mete**

Here you will find a wide range of thinking about the lyric essay: how it can leap, search, wander, hint at, unravel, excavate, and create; how it can both replicate and explain trauma; how it comes from or leaves behind fiction and poetry; how it acts like a panther, an iceberg, an on-ramp, an artichoke; how it's defined and how it can never be defined; how it tries and how it delivers; how it sings and how it plays.

Orpheus's lyre accompanied him through all sorts of adventures. It traveled with him as deep as the underworld and after his death was sent by Zeus to live among the stars. You can see its constellation—Lyra—in the summer months if you live in the Northern Hemisphere, the winter months if you live in the Southern. This feels like an apt metaphor for the lyric essay: The stars are there, but their shape is what your mind brings to them.

It is my hope that writers, readers, students, and teachers will both learn and take pleasure from the surprising, beautiful, wily, and diverse lyric essays that follow.

A Harp in the Stars

Gyre

DIANE SEUSS

When I was a schoolgirl, now and then a delicious state would come over
me. It was unpredictable, and there was nothing I could do to bring it
on, though it visited me more than once when I was plugging my ears to
block out the teacher's reading to us out loud from one of the Little House
books, which I loathed for the plodding cadence of their prose. The state
cannot be adequately described, but I'll try. There was a kind of slowing
down of everything in me and all things outside of me, a slowing down
that helped me hear the earth turning on its axis, or not turning, but grinding, like its gears needed oil, but the sound was pleasing, maybe because
it had a correlative within me, in my mind and in my gut, something I
related, years later, to Yeats's phrase "the widening gyre." I now think of
it as pre-sexual, or sexual before sex's melding to any association with
dirtiness, like a metal key, the kind we once used to tighten roller skates,
was set into a slot in my body-mind and slowly spun, screwing something
tighter, or loosening something, making me deeper or more shallow.
After a time, whatever it was, I couldn't reclaim it, until today, now that
I'm on the other side of life. I was walking the dog down a shaded alley
and had just passed something for which I feel an affinity—a rusty gate,
separated now from the fence whose entrances and exits it served—that
had been half-consumed by the twisted trunk of an old maple. Then a
tractor rumbled by. Nothing extraordinary—just a small lawn tractor, a
green two or three notches darker than that of spring grass. The driver,
a man with a reddish beard, smiled at us, nothing furtive or lascivious,
just one human being to another, I assume because I held the dog off to
the side and kept him still, yielding to the tractor's slow black wheels. It
surprised me to feel it after all these years, the turning of that rusty metal
key, the tightening or loosening of my spine, the spinning, as the galaxy
spins, or so they taught me in astronomy class, which I eventually failed.

The feeling now was not as forceful as it was then—diluted, maybe, by time, or more focused, but smaller, as when looking through the wrong end of a telescope. Still, I felt it, or remembered feeling it, the slowing down, the grinding spin, the clicking increments of a pleasurable turning of rusty gears, tooth by tooth by tooth. Maybe it is less the thing itself than the remembering of the thing, as when I recall the girl I was and spring's arrival. I was so young I didn't remember it ever having come before. Its delicacies hit me like the blows of a hammer, or the hammering pleasures of a crowd of sweat bees adorning me with the ministrations of their tiny stingers. I won't know spring that way again, but I remember knowing it, and someday I will remember the remembering, and then I'll remember the remembering of the remembering, the dark dreamy wheel of memory's mechanism, rounding a wide curve.

Immortal Wound

JERICHO PARMS

Actias luna (Linnaeus, 1758)

Montpelier, Vermont

To think I almost missed it—the small incongruity that lay on the sidewalk beneath the lamplight of Main Street. Though difficult to see, when I crouched down, the form of a Luna moth at first appeared in its stunning wholeness as if it might merely be at rest. But when it didn't rouse as I approached, nor budge when I drew a finger to its wing, I knew the moth was dead.

Nearby, lovers stumbled from the bar, clutching one another through the back pockets of their jeans. As their whispers receded down the street, I knelt, pinching carefully, and placed the moth in my hand. Yellow margins accentuated the hind wings' curving tails. Purple lined the top of the forewings—a pale purple, like drowned lips or hypothermic skin. At four and a half inches, its pale green tissue-paper wings filled my palm, which grew clammy, a little smitten, in the summer night—and, indeed, it *was* summer again, and the air was swollen and my skin was lonely and I was wishing New England had fewer churches and more sky.

When I felt a sudden stir, I thought there might still be life in the moth, that she was not in fact dead but *dying*. But it was just the wind stiffening her wings. I feared then, with the moth's lightness, that the same wind might take those wings, that I might lose her. The late-night chill made it hard to tell if the warmth in the cradle of my hand sprang from the moth's underbelly or my own budding grief.

Just then, I envied Woolf her day moth zigzagging against a windowpane; I envied Dillard the candlelight that singed her moth's wings, its body burning like cinder through the night. I envied these women, each witness to the moment of their moth's expiration, each in her expressive brevity embalming those dying wings.

The death of a moth is a common occurrence—consequence of destined wanderings and genetic attraction. Still, what cruel mystery is a Luna, royal silk moth of the deciduous forest, found dead outside a small-town bar? And what justice could I offer but to notice the thin scratch just below the eye of her left wing, like a run in a stocking scarring the otherwise smooth, unblemished surface?

In the pool of night, the moth grew translucent, more blue-green than yellow-green, pearly under the moon. Six legs curled beneath the cotton-like abdomen; two feathery antennae vibrated in the air. We are entering rigor mortis, I thought. But again, it was the breeze cutting between us— between her drying form and my pulsing palm. Her wingtips bobbed in the air to form the letter V. I wanted to whisper into the shape of those wings—*I feel certain that I am going mad again*, or *You have given me the greatest possible happiness*—and then close them gently like a vintage coin purse I once inherited. But I wouldn't trouble her with such things. Too many other questions surfaced as I studied her form: Had she died young? Did she mate and deposit her bounty of eggs? What led her here, now? The flickering glow of the drive-through ATM, the two-screen theater's starlit marquee, the neon draft signs in the windows of the dimly lit bar? Had she tried this once before? How long did she lie there before being found?

What most lingers is the silence of the moth's death—or, rather, her after-death. I can't attest to her body jerking in spasm *like a flame-faced virgin*. I can't say she exhibited a *superb last protest* as if overpowered by a mean antagonist. I do imagine her body falling (because I have a thing about falling bodies), her wings flapping like pages of a book and then waving until they looked like wings again. Instead, for me she simply appeared, as if discarded, misplaced, dropped like a folded dollar bill that might have been tucked somewhere and then slipped away like a clue—a lead in a case gone cold—leaving mystery the sole widow of death.

Perhaps we are all insects of longing and luminous dreams: dusky sallow, common house moth, *Actias luna*—strong fliers seeking to mate at midnight, feeding on birch leaves, spinning silk into papery cocoons. Haven't we all fed on the strange beauty of our findings, spun such strangeness into stories, secrets, silence, to insulate and cosset the great uncertainties that leave us stripped, bare? Don't we live to glide along invisible currents, swearing we will find somewhere on earth, some familiar light that knows us? Insisting on nocturnal promise, we are drawn to the spotlights that blind us just as surely as a glaring headlight might steer us off-course or the taillight of a lover driving steadily away can forever burn.

Ever since that night, that moth, that familiar bruised purple, that summer blue, I've been thinking about instinct and ardor. The way they lure and misguide us as eagerly as life and death collide. Wedded like Vegas lovers to the conniving bulb of light, to the forgiving kerosene of the heart, we go down dancing, or blazing, or in a moment unobserved, as if it never came to pass, as if it never even happened at all.

Vide

SARAH MINOR

L'appel du vide ("the call of the void") is a French expression describing the temptation some feel to jump from a high precipice. A French man who I once met in Italy likened the sentiment to a siren's song. He said some claim that a fear of heights is not about a fear of falling, but rather the fear that one might suddenly be compelled to throw themselves over an edge. It seems then that people fear not the height, but *l'appel du vide* itself—what the void might call out of them.

If I lift my elbow as high as my earlobe, I can cover the boat and everyone in it with my left thumb and block them from view. If my wrist lies parallel with this rock ledge, it must be level with the spans of gulls rising on thermals in the distance and the surface of the ocean some sixty feet below. If from here I can see that the horizon is an oval, then it never was a line.

For three summers we, the children of the two-piece mothers, spent our weekends practicing water breathing at the bottom of the neighborhood pool. Some older kids had told at least one of us that gas exchange could happen straight through our skin, so we ritually pressed ourselves against tiles of a temperature just below human. We tried until our eyes got heavy in their goggles, until the pool filters got loud in our ears. Only one kid had to be rescued, though I admit it was twice in the same afternoon, and soon I could swim the length of the pool in one breath. I got bored of the breath-holders then, or else we were forcibly disbanded. I got interested in moving through water and held my tongue out to taste the chlorine.

Below, our boat leans into a loose tongue of waves, toward the grotto and away again. The surface of the ocean is dented aluminum. When I grimace I can see through my lids into a sky that looks hazy with rain. My toes are blue from clenching the ledge, this open mouth's philtrum—its cupid's bow, its bones volcanic. It's been a dozen minutes and the captains have abandoned their rudders, barnacled and trailing rust. The low boats jostle in wait. If I'm the first to try this jump in two months, as they say, if I am the first woman in six ... *"If you can't do it climb back down already!"* my man shouts into the sky, because I've dragged us both this far from home and we have this game of riling each other up when it matters. It's an old game, and not a nice one, and I only know when we're playing when no one else is playing with us. I know he's been working hard at kinder persuasions this summer we've been abroad, following a caravan of farm work across olive groves, but right now I can't see any real difference with the nettles biting my ankles.

I learned about snorkel breath the year my dad sent us out along the edge of the Atlantic reef where he'd learned to walk. We kept our eyes on the sharp urchins marching in fishnet light. Then I looked up to round the jetty and found myself sailing into a swimming animal my exact size. I stiffened when her forehead hit mine for a fraction of a second before she flicked away, shuddering, as if to make us both forget. My hair folded in her wake. *"That*

I know that for seven weeks we've been sleeping upright on night trains, working cracked fields for one bed and two meals a day, in the earth

shark is a Nurse!" said
my father's face above
the water, *"She doesn't
bite!"* But I wasn't thinking
teeth—just that up close, her
eyes didn't turn in their sockets.

together like a weighted machine. From here I can see Naples spewing garbage and smoking in the wind. A hot breeze peels a swallow from my throat. I know that in ten days we plan to haul brown boxes across the same threshold and I don't think I can get out of it anymore.

Later, after the hurricanes, dad smuggled my sister
and I out onto the beaches lined with red flags, SWIMMING
PROHIBITED. We sprinted out in thin one-pieces, scrambling
into water intent on emptying itself. He taught us to yell
"Granddaddy—over!" or *"Little Uncle—under!"* depending on the
shape of a swell before it broke. The goal was to lay perpendicular
inside a barrel just before the whitecap split. We learned when
to roll ourselves into those cavities and then pull free, and
the brackish Atlantic shot us evenly, like harpoons.

The leathered men below start to jeer in Italian. They lift sets of fingers to signal their bets. The chains wound in their chest hair are blinding. To them I am bar soap, girl, American. And from up here I'm starching them individually, trying to throw my limbs from this rock.

After four summers we'd all been pummeled by the surf,
but no one had felt a catch at the beach break. That
line between rock and wave where the water pulls
and falls at the same time. At the end of a
long day indoors we were angry with my
father in the way children can be when
they recognize a woman who isn't
their mother but who may try to   Later,
be soon. The rain broke and we   at the
ran across the dunes when the   bottom of
sky was flat and closing. I dared   the Rillito
my sister to get in, and then   River, I'll find
swam hard ahead of her   a dead bat on
until the waves around my   its back. It will be
shoulders were matte like   an eccentric place
those tapping the sky. I felt   to wind up on a first
the sandbar and stood up,   date, though not
feeling accomplished, and   eccentric, in Tucson, for
then the water in front   the pair of us to stand on a
of me kept rising.   dry riverbed in September.
The animal will lie
open faced, its wings gathering the

Our Italian host and captain is gesturing expressively and repeating the English necessary to those who deal in tourists. *"Hey!"* he calls, *"Andiamo!"* again. The sun is printing a ring into my forehead. I know could plant myself here indefinitely if I could just stop swaying. I know I could tumble forward, eyes closed, but they say if I hit flatfooted I'll split both insteps. If I don't tuck my chin, the neck will snap. If I look down into the water, the eyes might burst on contact. Our attractive French companion is at my man's shoulder, shading his nose against the sun glinting off all the Lycra not encasing me: *"Let's go!"* A gull circles and cries.

I lean into the void, down the grotto's throat, past the sea and spackled shoulders and this man announcing that he knows more than I've let him, that soon his books will lean their backs hard against mine. I clench the muscles that bind my eyes to my face and the small ones encasing my toes. In swimming we would call this a pencil jump—a long one.

As the wave hit it pulled me from
the bar and under it. I laced fingers
around the back of my neck like dad
showed us when we were small. I felt
the sand in my gums and opened
my eyes to the water revolving. It
felt like entering a vacuum, but
more familiar, like day-
dreaming in class,
or dozing in
the heat.

shadow of a bridge suspending
Campbell Avenue above us and sending
traffic across the deep wash that funnels
water during spring monsoons. In dry seasons
like these, the Rillito will become a sunken
highway where coyotes and javelina packs slip
below the long city at night, running parallel with
tumbled mountains to the north. Like them, Mexican
free-tailed bats find the wash in the wake of habitat
destruction, taking sanctuary in the structures left behind.
The bat at our feet will look hammerheaded, about a
handsbreadth from ears to toes. It will fall out of the expansion
joints that rumble around the anxious colony all slung up and

In the air I tilt forward and
cannot right myself. The
fall is so slow I nearly
open my eyes to see
where I've traveled.
Then the water
zips me into a
column and my
intestines

Next, my hands
snaked out as from
under a pulled rug
as the wave spit
me onto the
shore. Foam
lapped as I
coughed and
sour water
came out of
my mouth.
There was
a swath of
weed in
my hair
and a
sizzling
behind my
nose. My
sister yelled
that it was
too rough,
she was going
in *to tell.* And
when we came in
dripping my
father was cooking
dinner. He thought we
wanted attention—we
did. So when I
couldn't explain
how I had finally
breathed water,
I said I felt cold
and went to bed.

twittering inside Campbell and the man beside me will look up into
the concrete cells and guano will darken and stink up the sand. We'll
be on the brink of something I'm not ready for. The sun will sit low as
the bats prepare to leave for mosquitoes and the night. I'll have spent
the previous month pushing heavy furniture in slow circles around the
low adobe house that the last man and I had shared and all the rooms
will feel sharp-edged and out of order. I'll have packed away our photos
of the ocean. At night I'll lay on the cool kitchen tiles in watery, digital
light and stare up into the ceiling cracks. I'll try to rustle something new
from myself, something to merit a new body. But there will be nowhere
to walk under the natural drought and the unblinking sky, and I'll find
that it is hard to become submerged in the desert. So I'll eat a hotdog
beside a man in a baseball cap and drive with him to watch a colony
of bats let go from a dry bridge at sunset. I won't really know, then,
that this is a date.

We'll move toward the banks, careful not to brush against one
another. He'll have jeans on, despite the heat. Here and there in the
wash, spined branches brought by old water and wound with trash
will sit piled like the skeletons of old waves. Beads of sweat will catch
on the man's cotton neckline. We'll read the signs of old water lines
stacking up the banks where silence will fit us more easily and I'll
regret wearing a dress.

Quickly then, the sun halves itself along a ridgeline. Light
drains from the top of the sky and a sound like a glass rim being rubbed
signals a smudge developing below the expansion beams and the bridge.
The shards that billow out from under it will spool themselves into an
eddy between columns, gaining speed as we make disgusted noises with
our breath. At first, only a ribbon will dart away like a black leak in the
structure. Then long loops will pull out from beneath and catch into the sky
as if tracing a current on the surface of a much higher river pulling
westward, with us at its very bottom. Against the light we'll be able to see
individual wings among them. Bats smaller and more numerous than any
coordinated school of herring I've seen hiding together in the shape of their
maker. I'll be reminded then about a bit from Jamaica Kincaid that I still
haven't read yet, as she quotes Charles Kingsley in the opening lines of
"Wingless": *"You would have been very cold sitting there on a September night
without the least bit of clothes on your back, but Tom was a water baby, and
therefore felt cold no more than a fish."* And for long minutes, the stream of
bats will spread out and still will not separate from the bridge. It will lean
slowly north and then south again, making waves of the ribbon stretching
so far we'll lose sight of its beginning. And we'll sway imperceptibly, taking
that in. Then the man will lift the brim of his hat and point to a trail where
the shyest will be dusting out last, groggy and uncoordinated. We'll stare after
them a while, stalling, until all that's left to do is climb out.

bristle back. I
stay there a
while, fastened,
as the light
around me dims.

Unless a person
has drowned, the
scalp surfaces first.
But somewhere above
me there's a
commotion. *"Hey!"*
says our captain
as he claps my cold
back. Our French
companion winks. *"Good
form—You go through the
seabed? Your man here
was concerned."* His
referent holds
my elbow.
*"Well, you got me
this time,"*
he says.

Satellite

SARAH PERRY

Sometime during the years I was entangled in a transpacific love, I was sitting at an oak desk in a library. The light was waning and the big leafy tree that stretched up and shadowed half of the window was taking on the darker green of dusk. I was worn out, slumped and looking mute at the bit of sky beyond those leaves. Just then I saw a bright, orangey chunk of light make its way across the air: a satellite catching the last rays of sunlight, racing around the world.

I thought of my boyfriend on the near shore of a far land. I considered the geometry of the arcs between us—surface of earth, of water, the path drawn by the globe's spin, that drawn by the satellite. If he were looking up, could he have seen that satellite soon after me? Could it pass through the night that lay between us and emerge into his morning, once again angling fiery light into tired eyes?

I took out a pen. I drew diagrams on my notebook, trying to find the shape of time between us, a complex thing made of motion and mass, dependent on the attraction of bodies. I held my breath to make perfect circles, to keep my hand from shaking as I carved deep arcs in the thin cardboard cover. One dot for him. One dot for me. Square of satellite bigger than each of us, riding an imaginary hoop.

It's easy to forget that orbits are ellipses, that distances are more variable than they seem. Again and again, I scribbled out one attempt and tried once more, laying down clean lines against the void, until I ran out of space. The size of the darkness between us remained the largest unknown. Because I couldn't figure out the proof, I decided to trust the fantasy, and because I trusted, I never tested it. I never called him and asked him to look at the horizon, for a message from me.

Woven

LIDIA YUKNAVITCH

I can't remember the name of the bar, but I remember I was twenty-two, and I was having the time of my life on Halloween night with my then-girlfriend in Greenwich Village. At twenty-two we could drink like beautiful androgynous unafraid fish. Young badass women in love in the bohemian capital of the world. That's how it felt to me, anyway. She was a student at New York University. I wasn't anything, having flunked out of college. We had plans that spanned continents. Youth foreshortens everything—faces, lives.

Partway through a shit-ton of cheap vodka shots she got up on our rickety little wooden bar table and danced. When I say "danced" I mean punched the air like a boxer. So I climbed up on my chair and "danced" just underneath her, and she started laughing uncontrollably, pointing, pointing at my midsection, because my skirt was tucked up into my neon-blue tights enough that my neon-blue butt was showing. I guess I'd made a miscalculation the last time I'd used the bathroom. We laughed that kind of deep-throated about-to-be-women laugh. The laugh of girls before their voices thin out and tighten from the exhaustion of womanhood.

In fact—and it's only because I'm old and no longer give a crap that I can tell you this—I laughed so hard I made a little unstoppable poop in those neon-blue tights. Like a perfectly round deer turd.

It was a night I wanted never to end.

Or, I wish with all my heart that the story ended there.

Mythic youth.

But that's not where the story ended.

*

When I was four years old my Lithuanian grandmother told me a folk-tale about the water spirit Laume. I'd accidentally locked myself in my grandparents' bathroom and gone into hysterics when I couldn't get out. My father was furious at my ineptitude. His yelling nearly broke the door down. This is the story she told me once I was liberated.

Laume came from transcendental waters, and her spirit lives in all waters, even in baths and showers, in rivers, streams, oceans, the rain, and in toilets. She is the guardian of all children, the not yet born, the newly born, the orphaned, the forgotten, even the dead. If there is a child coming into the world, she can foresee it. If a child is mistreated, she will sometimes take him and raise him herself. If a child is lost, she protects him while gathering information about the usefulness of the parents. If parents are mishandling a child, she will transform him into whatever lesson they need to learn.

Above all she values sincerity, and next industriousness on the part of mothers, particularly the women's work of weaving.

Laume rewards those who work hard; she also punishes severely those who seek reward without an attention to hard work and those in pursuit of self-aggrandizement.

Go look underneath your pillow to see if she has left you treasure.

I walked upstairs to the bedroom.

My whole body shook. I stood in the bedroom a long minute with my eyes closed, waiting for hands on my shoulders. I looked around for my father there in the dark, because that's the life I had, a father there in the dark, but he wasn't anywhere.

I looked underneath my pillow.

There was a star woven from straw.

*

Laume takes many forms and inhabits many tales. One of the most famous Laumes was a fisherman's daughter, Egle, queen of the serpents. One day Egle finds a large eel in her clothes after swimming in the Baltic Sea. The eel takes her clothing and only returns it when she promises to marry him. When she accepts, the eel becomes a handsome young man named Zilvinas. They live underwater together and have three children, two sons and a daughter. After a time, Egle longs to visit her parents and siblings on land.

Zilvinas is terrified that Egle's former family will reject her. But though he is worried, he agrees to let her go and bring their children. Zilvinas instructs Egle to call to him: "If you are alive and well, come back to me in a milky wave; if you are dead, in a bloody wave."

When she arrives to visit her earthly family, Egle's brothers, jealous of her freedom, torture her sons to death; her daughter, smitten with one of the earth brothers, betrays the secret call and lures Zilvinas to shore, where he is murdered. When Egle returns to the lip of the water, she sees a bloody wave and learns that her earth brothers have betrayed her. She curses herself and her daughter, turning them into trees forever.

Many infant girls in Lithuania have the names of trees.

*

In the ninth year of our eleven-year marriage, my second husband emerged from our kitchen pointing a gun at me. I haven't written much about this, at least not literally. I don't ever talk about it. It's a bit like a little malformed myth still lodged between my heart and my rib cage.

In America, it's tricky to describe violence without it turning into entertainment.

A Sig Sauer P229 9-mm handgun. Statistically, the most popular handgun in the United States.

I'd just entered the house after work. The kitchen light was on, but not the living room light, so he was backlit. The whole house smelled like Jameson. I stood in the dark. My car keys were still in my hand. He crossed the space between us. When he was maybe three feet away, he stopped. The gun was pointed at my chest. The air in my lungs concrete. I walked the rest of the distance between us, until the gun was between my breasts. That's how I know he was crying.

I stared at my second husband.

Nothing moved in the house except our breathing.

"Stop loving me," he finally said, the gun heavy enough for me to feel my sternum ache.

As if love was killing him.

Stop loving me.

"No," I said, and I closed my eyes and put my arms around him and pressed in. I waited for the possible death moment between a man and a woman.

Walking straight into violence was nothing new to me. I'd learned how to walk deliberately and unflinchingly into violence from my father, like so many other children do in this country.

In fact, in this country we raise all of our children on one form of violence or another. And so my question is not "Why did you walk into that violence?"

My question is "Where does my love come from that I walk through male violence to find it?"

*

Laumes are the oldest spirits of Lithuanian mythology. The images of these spirits may have developed during the historical Mesolithic period, just after the Ice Age. Laume first appeared in the form of animals, like goats, bears, or mares. Later she took on a half-human appearance, usually bird claws for feet, the lower body of a she-goat, and large stone nipples. Later still she was represented as a beautiful and supernatural water woman-creature, with fair hair and skin the color of the moon. Laumes were both benevolent and dangerous. They could tickle men to death and then eat their bodies. They could protect women and children or punish them brutally.

Laumes lived near lakes, abandoned bathhouses, rivers, swamps, or other waterways. Laumes liked to gather near water under the new moon at night and dance. They could cause rain and storms and hail by singing and dancing and swimming.

Anyone who knows me knows why I am attracted to Laumes. I am a child of the waters. But then so are all of us, before the breach.

*

I had a recurring dream for twenty years that I would have three sons.

I did not have three sons, and I'm fifty-two, so it's not looking likely. What I did have was a daughter, who died, and one son, sun of my life. But I did have three husbands.

Maybe dreams don't mean a goddamned thing.

Or maybe they mean everything.

They say you marry a man who is like your father. My father, the artist-turned-architect, molested and abused us. He was big. Angry. Loud-fisted. Marked us forever—three little women, making for their lives.

My first husband was gentle as a swan. A painter with long fingers and eyelashes. You can see what I was shooting for. I almost self-immolated next to his passivity.

My second husband, another painter, used harsh lashing strokes on the canvas. He was big and loud, but made softer by alcohol and art. Except when he wasn't. The gun of him. Sig Sauer.

My third husband, father of my son, is big and loud and a filmmaker. But there is the gentleness of a cellist in his hands and eyes.

So sometimes I wonder if my dream was meant to show me not three sons but three husbands. Take my second husband, for instance—the one who pressed the gun of him to me—he was a lot like a child. I wonder if Laume came and took my baby daughter, who died right before I met him, and replaced her with a man-child. This is kind of how we get through our lives: we tell ourselves stories so that what's happening becomes something we can live with. Necessary fictions.

Maybe I had some hard lessons to learn about the difference between doing good work and trying too hard to be a woman.

Woman. Like anyone even knows what that is still.

Or violence. Maybe this is a story about violence.

Or maybe I'm still looking for a way to forgive myself for that failure of womanhood. Two marriages gone busto. Jesus, woman. I keep waiting to feel like a failure.

I wonder what would happen if I didn't know what this story was about.

I think this might be a children's story.

*

It is said that Laume was a silken-haired sky goddess who lived in the clouds. One myth claims that she fell in love with a beautiful young man down on earth and that they had a son. Laume descended to earth from the sky to feed her son with her breasts. But when the highest god found out about the son and the sacrilegious love, he killed the boy and scattered his remains between the stars in the sky, and he cut Laume's breasts. Stone pieces of them can still be found on earth in the form of sea-creature fossils.

You would not believe how many sea-creature fossils I've collected over the years. Tons of them. I don't know why. Crustaceans and sea spiders. Conglomerate rocks with pieces of hermit crab fossilized in them. Fish from the desert hills. Ammonites. It's a wonder to see something so clearly meant for movement in water captured swirling in stone. Like a petrified snapshot. Or like history's motion arrested.

*

I'm going to try it again.

When I was twenty-two I spent Halloween night in Greenwich Village. I drank vodka in a Russian bar with my girlfriend at the time. A huge middle-aged Russian man and his male friends said drunk fat Russian things to us all night, not a word of which we understood, and we laughed, they laughed, and we toasted, and things seemed strangely okay, like when you are young. I kept yelling, "I'm Lithuanian!" to the Russian men, like that was something. Later in life I'd learn what an idiotic thing that was to be yelling. But at the time it seemed everyone, even the moon, was laughing and drunk.

At midnight a giant parade of costumed people passed the bar, and so we joined them and walked for miles together. There were animals: goats, bears, horses, unicorns, centaurs. There were bird claws for feet, the lower bodies of she-goats, large, extended tin foil breasts and exaggerated codpieces, and all sorts of witches, fairies, and mermaids. It was one of the happiest nights of my life. We were two girl-women in love; we were walking with an army of people in Halloween costumes more vivid and outrageous than reality would ever be. Fear was not anything about us.

Later on, we found ourselves a few alleys away from her crappy dorm room. We were stumble-walking, arm in arm. We kissed and teetered along and laughed. I put my hand up her shirt. Then I saw her head lurch forward in a not-right way, and she made a sound—or something did—like someone smashing a pumpkin with a bat. Something hard at my back, and then my side imploding.

Two men had come up behind us. One hit her in the skull with a baseball bat, another stabbed me in the lower back and side with a knife. My girlfriend dropped to her knees, her head hitting the pavement. I saw her body perfectly balanced, head and knees keeping her perched upright, blood everywhere. I saw the two men laughing and yelling. I saw their shaved heads. I saw stars before I passed out. The last thought I remember thinking: *Skinheads.*

There is language enough to describe it, but going there is beyond language, so mostly I don't. I don't know how to belong to the story in a way that doesn't betray it. I don't even want to be in the story, the one in which a woman I loved was left partially paralyzed.

But mostly I don't tell the story because I didn't stay with her happily ever after forever and ever.

I've noticed the scar at my back and side has softened over the years. It's so tiny you can barely see it. Receding with age and fat, I suppose. Or the guilt of wanting more life.

*

A woman was harvesting a flowerbed and had taken her child with her. She was so busy with her work that the child slept through the day.

The woman went home in the evening to milk the cows and make dinner. She served her husband, who asked her, "Where's my son?" With terror she whispered, "I have forgotten him!" She ran as fast as she could to the place where she had left her son, and she heard Laume speak: "Hush, forgotten child." The mother asked Laume for her child back. The fairy said, "Come, come, dear woman, take your child, we have done nothing to him. We know that you work very hard, at many jobs, and that you didn't want to leave your child behind."

The Laumes went on to shower the babe with treasures, enough gifts to raise several children on. The mother went home with her precious baby and with her gifts; she was greeted with great joy.

Another woman, hearing of this good fortune, was taken over by jealousy. She thought, "I shall do the same as her and also be showered in gifts." The next evening, at dusk, she took her child, left him in the fields, and went home. When, after dinner, she returned to the field, she heard the Laumes: "Hush, you left your child in greed." And the child screamed with great pain, for he was being pinched mercilessly. The Laumes continued their torture until the mother approached. Then they tossed the child at her feet. The babe was dead.

*

When my infant daughter died, spilling out with our shared waters, the story breached. Every story I have ever told has a kind of breach to it, I think. You could say that my writing isn't quite right. That all the beginnings have endings in them.

*

Violence doesn't only exist in men.

Think of mother violence, for example. When my son was in grade school I had hysterically violent thoughts. I was afraid he'd be bullied. I actually pictured the moment—I saw myself stride across the school grounds, pick a bully child up by his ankles, hold him upside down, shake the shit out of him, and fling him in a dumpster. I thought all the way through "Mamma has to go to jail."

My Lithuanian grandmother cut the tip off my father's tongue as a boy.

*

After I became a mother and married for the third time, I had a skinhead in my writing class. I know he was a skinhead not from the way he looked, though that's exactly what he looked like: the nineties version of a London skinhead. I know he was a skinhead because he came to my office and told me. He asked not to have to do group work. I'm embarrassed to say that made me laugh. I also remember thinking: *You are a brutal abomination* and *Not long ago this guy was just a boy, just his mother's son—what happened?*

His writing was impeccable. He completed every assignment. His theses were not Hitleresque. He was oddly polite and courteous. I gave him a C, only because I could, whether or not I should have. If he'd challenged the grade, he'd have won. In many ways he was the best writer in the class.

What is a teacher? A mother?

*

Another Laume is a goddess of the home and a warm hearth. If you do not tend to your family and fire well, she burns your house down. With everyone inside. The word for fireplace in Lithuanian has come to be understood as "family relations."

*

In my twenty-third year of teaching college, on a day we were discussing violence as a theme, something repressed inside me lurched, and I told my Halloween-night story to the class. I mean it shot out of my mouth before I could stop it.

Sig Sauer–like.

I lifted up my shirt and showed them my scar. It was one of the more unprofessional teaching moments of my career, though it would certainly not be the last. So much shame came out of my mouth. The shame of a daughter whose body was written by her father. The shame of leaving a woman I loved. The shame of failed marriages and motherhoods.

At the end of the story I also told them what I'd learned about our attackers. They weren't skinheads. They'd been marines. My then-girlfriend would be neurologically damaged and partially paralyzed for the rest of her life. The marines spent three months—ninety whole days—in jail. One was dishonorably discharged.

Everyone got quiet. I thought maybe the story was over, and my intention was to get us all writing and out of the well of overly personal pathos I'd let us fall into, but then a Latino man in the class, his neck covered in tattoos, stood up. All I knew from his writing was that he'd been a gang member. That he'd made mistakes and gone to jail. That he was writing A+ ideas with C+ skills. That his parents were undocumented workers. That he had four sisters. But I learned that day that he'd also been on three tours of duty for our country before he'd turned twenty-two. I also learned that the military had begun relaxing tattoo restrictions in 2004. He stood up and said, "I apologize on behalf of marines." His sentence was perfect. The air in the room vacuumed.

He walked the length of the room, straight at me. I braced myself for the moment—I wasn't sure how much longer I could keep from crying. Briefly it occurred to me that I might die if he got any closer, closer than three feet away. Then he did a regular human thing. He hugged me. He said it again. This time in my ear, and his breath made the hairs on my neck shoot up. "I apologize on behalf of marines."

But that's not what I heard. I heard, "You don't have to punish yourself for love."

I didn't die like I thought I might. From his random compassion, I mean. I wasn't a very good teacher. I don't know what I was. I gave him an A in the class, in the end. That day we wrote stories about the small violences in our daily lives.

*

In one story, Laume takes all the children away from their parents in a particular village because they sent their eldest boys to war. The mothers become barren and the fathers can no longer hold any food down, and thus they die. The village fades from history because the parents did not take care of their children.

*

You know, stories change, just like the lives we've lived and selves we've inhabited. Nobody's been the same person twice. I mean really. It's the people walking around acting and sounding especially self-assured and whole who worry me the most.

I like hearing the world's stories about itself. That's partly why I teach world literature. It helps me feel less incarcerated by the world, or my past, or my mistakes and confusions. It helps me remember I'm not just American. I'm not just a woman. A mother. A teacher. A wife. I find value in thinking in stories. Aren't we all woven through with stories? Isn't that how we think of our lives, how we survive them? Now, when someone hurts me, I remember that they are only living the terms of their own fictions—sometimes desperately—so their selves don't unravel.

I like that idea. A woven person.

Little misshapen stars made of straw.

Re: Sometime after 5:00 p.m. on a Wednesday in the Middle of Autumn

DANIEL GARCIA

after Jaquira Díaz

If the first step is admitting powerlessness, then you should know I told everyone what a bastard you are, but I told my therapist I love you, not because I came to believe I could turn everything over to something larger than myself, but because the bus that goes to the apartments on Inman Street where we lived in the same complex that summer when you raped me (there, I said it; I finally found the word) is on a different side of campus now, and I know this because, whenever I wait for the bus that goes to the station by my house, I look away from the dark afternoon sky and see the old bus putter by with the half-faded digital signboard that says Centre Place in nothing but right angles and start after it; and how, during that summer, days before the gutting, the sweltering heat carried you across the distance between us, even though I didn't recognize your silhouette until you stepped on, sober for once; how we hadn't seen each other in nearly a year; how I was afraid because I didn't know where we'd gone in all that time, because your eyes found me first, as if you thought I was there waiting for you, because you looked so stupid and sexy with your hair sticking out like a crown of wild thorns while wearing that brown long-sleeve shirt and cargo pants that should've been a jumpsuit for how profusely you were sweating, because I almost admitted in front of God and everybody, *that's the man I fell in love with*, except I didn't have the word then (*love*, I mean), because you asked to sit next to me wearing all that apology on your face and we both knew I'd forgive you for my shortcomings—how you said you'd fuck me if I was a girl—but more importantly, cariño, if God is God, how could God make you leave knowing I tilted my head up to that starless gore that only changes when all the light has been ripped out of it and prayersobbed *si tú no vuelves*

no se que voy a hacer no se que voy a hacer fuck you fuck you fuck you
with my fists against your door night after night, not knowing you were
elsewhere until that last time, sometime after the gutting, at sunset's cusp,
when I saw the boxes in the bed of the pickup and knew they were your
things but how could they be without you (yours, I mean), and what did
that say about me; how the man you got your eyes from said *rehab* when
I walked up and asked; how I said you knocked me around *a couple times,*
and saw (I'm sorry, cariño, let me make amends don't be angry I'm sorry
I'm so sorry) his eyes, fresh with injury, must've known everything then:
not that I was wrong for admitting where your palms had been but that I
wanted only for God to will I be carried back to you alongside the boxes,
that you kissed me first, that I called fifty times the night you took off,
drunk and alone and laughing, that I wasn't girl enough to get fucked but
girl enough to be assaulted that night on campus in the music building
where you ripped out the last of my boyhood, that I didn't cry, that we
laid in your bed ten months after, the backs of my thighs fresh with shame
from where your fingers had been, my leg nestlecurled around yours, that
I didn't cry then either but cried in bed when the thrashing thing in my
throat awakened because I'd found the word months and months later,
que siempre sea la voluntad de Dios que tú y yo podamos permanecer así,
because I knew his eyes, hands, shoulders and face weren't yours but
were close enough to tell me that this was the closest my eyes would ever
get to hold a you softer with time, one I'd never spend my life with, that
I'd christen today and every day my soles don't chase the bus down as a
victory even though they aren't; that if, just before I would step on, ride
across town, and carry myself across the distance between us, I might
glimpse the door to an unempty apartment if I surrender just so, a door-
knob spinning before I can raise my fist, a you on the other side, waiting.

Searching for Gwen

LAURIE EASTER

Word List														
GWEN	M	A	G	L	A	M	A	N	K	P	O	L	F	N
MISSING	Y	E	W	F	T	J	M	O	I	W	Q	O	R	C
ELUSIVE	P	O	E	T	R	Y	U	I	G	Y	U	S	H	O
POSSIBILITIES	R	Q	N	D	Y	O	A	T	C	N	V	A	X	N
TRAUMA	O	J	C	K	T	R	R	C	D	Z	N	U	B	F
INTIMATE	S	E	R	R	I	E	T	I	M	G	U	H	S	L
DEVOTION	E	S	A	E	U	G	R	D	E	R	P	E	M	I
ADDICTION	H	P	T	K	R	O	A	D	F	E	I	R	G	C
RELAPSE	A	A	I	A	G	N	E	A	T	T	E	M	P	T
ADVENTURES	R	L	V	E	N	V	H	X	I	L	M	N	G	E
TWEAKER	R	E	E	W	O	P	E	L	U	S	I	V	E	D
INSIDIOUS	O	R	G	T	C	C	I	N	T	I	M	A	T	E
ATTEMPT	W	D	I	V	N	B	Z	M	L	Y	R	I	C	H
CHANGED	I	O	E	F	I	N	S	I	D	I	O	U	S	O
AMALGAM	N	A	S	S	U	J	H	S	R	E	H	A	B	M
HARROWING	G	Q	S	O	N	L	Y	S	E	U	L	C	Q	E
INCONGRUITY	Z	O	A	L	M	Y	K	I	M	E	M	O	I	R
CONFLICTED	P	L	Y	A	D	V	E	N	T	U	R	E	S	I
SOLACE	V	H	O	C	H	A	N	G	E	D	L	O	V	E
CLUES	L	I	F	E	N	O	N	F	I	C	T	I	O	N
FOUND														

1. My friend has disappeared. The search poster says she was last seen on March 2, 2017. The font is a large block print in white on bright red. A warning. Her sweet face looks out from the page. This photo grips me like a fist squeezing my heart as soon as I see the poster the first time. I am reminded of how she used to look—bright blue eyes; smooth, shiny, rosy skin; straight white teeth, smiling. But this is not the sole cause of my reaction. Neither is the thought that that face could have come to harm. The squeezing heart-grip is because I know this photo. I took it. In my house. She is sitting on my couch, smiling at me through the lens. We were celebrating "Second Thanksgiving" in January, when my younger daughter was home from college for winter break, four years earlier. What this search poster photo doesn't show is that next to her on the couch sits her then six-year-old son. He grins, looking sideways from the camera, toward someone else. His head leans against his mother's arm, her hand resting against his hair.

   A couple weeks before this search poster was released, I had received a text from GWEN's sister seeking information and help in finding her. Gwen's family, who live on the east coast, hadn't heard from her for more than two weeks. She wasn't answering her phone, and her voicemail box was full. In an ordinary situation, it could be rationalized that a grown adult might be busy and late in returning calls. But her life is not ordinary. Such rationalizations could not be justified. Her family notified authorities and have since hired a private investigator. She is currently listed as MISSING.

2. Some missing people are never found. They come to nefarious ends and either remain lost and unseen or their remains are found. Some people don't want to be found. They hide. From the law, from people they owe money to, from abusive ex-boyfriends. They hide out of fear or shame or because they are out of their minds. They are like smoke sifting through a screen—ELUSIVE.

3. My imagination leaps in appalling bounds. Could she have been abducted? Is she the victim of human trafficking? Did her ex-boyfriend kill her in a drug-induced rage and dispose of her body? Did the stress of losing custody of her son and the havoc of a life destroyed by methamphetamine spur her to suicide? Is she holed up

in an abandoned house, alone or with other addicts? Did she suffer a seizure, heart attack, or stroke from overdosing? Is she slipping past us on the rural highway, unsuspected in someone else's rig, close yet unreachable? Or could she be in rehab? The ideal scenario, but not likely. So many POSSIBILITIES.

4. Her family flew to Oregon to meet with the state police and private investigators. They held a meeting—to share and gather information that may lead to Gwen's whereabouts—outside on an eighty-five-degree day at the community land in our small town. This is the land where my children once attended an alternative school, where I taught cooking, quilting, and crafts, that after much hard work and effort, failed to secure its charter. The land where my missing friend once taught my young daughters belly dancing and a father (of a boy) complained it was improper. The land I walked fourteen years prior as school pictures were being taken on a similar afternoon, yet one not so hot, while a different friend's fifteen-year-old son was alone at home and hanged himself from a tree. This is the land I normally avoid because it holds memories deep in its soil the way a healed flesh wound holds scar tissue from TRAUMA.

5. Here is the nature of my relationship with Gwen: when my twelve-year-old daughter was in the pediatric intensive care unit at Doernbecher Children's Hospital in Portland, and I was at my most vulnerable because I didn't know if my daughter would live or die, I made one phone call to a friend. She was the one. INTIMATE.

6. When this same daughter was two years old, she used to follow my friend around our property as Gwen worked transplanting, watering, or weeding in our nursery. My daughter's refrain then was "Only my Gwen." An announcement. A claiming. I know this feeling. I feel it too. No matter how many people love her, no matter how many close relationships she has had, I will always think of her as "only my Gwen." DEVOTION.

7. This is what happens when you smoke methamphetamine: It releases an onslaught of dopamine, producing a rush of intense pleasure, followed by a prolonged sense of euphoria that lasts between six and twelve hours. The amount of dopamine released is twelve times that

of activities like sex or ingestion of alcohol or nicotine or certain foods. Dr. Richard Rawson, associate director of UCLA's Integrated Substance Abuse Programs, says, "methamphetamine produces the mother of all dopamine releases." After the drug wears off, depression counters the previous experience of pleasure and euphoria, inciting repeated use of the drug to avoid turbulent crashes. Such behavior leads to ADDICTION.

8. Once, a few years before Gwen disappeared, she called and said, "Will you come get all the alcohol out of my house? I need it out of here. *Now.*" I didn't hesitate. She loaded me up with bottles of hard liquors, liqueurs, wine, and prescription pills not prescribed to her. I promptly placed them in the back of my car. We sat for a long time, discussing her addiction. I said, "Maybe you should go to AA," knowing that if she didn't get help, her newfound sobriety would likely be brief. She balked. "Oh, no. I could never do that," she said. I offered to take her. She said she'd think about it.

A month later, she called. "Hey, Lore, I'd like to get my bar back," she said.

"Your bar?" I said. *What the fuck?* I thought. "I gave it away."

"You gave it away? But I just gave it to you to hold for a little while."

"No, you didn't."

"What about the pills? Do you still have those?"

"No," I said. "I threw them in the garbage."

A few months after that, at her birthday party, she was so drunk, she floated naked in the hot tub, not buoyant above the water, but mostly submerged. Ophelia in the river before she drowned. RELAPSE.

9. It wasn't always fractures and chaos. There were times of sweetness and fun. A trip to Bandon by the sea, Gwen newly pregnant, me seeking a reprieve from motherhood. When the VW bus we were driving broke down in Winston, rather than canceling our excursion, we left the vehicle at an auto repair shop and rented a car. We stayed at the Sea Star Hostel, ate fish and chips in the sunshine along the wharf with the seagulls, searched for agates on the beach. We trespassed on an abandoned blueberry farm for sale along Highway 1, where the blueberry bushes stood high above our heads, and drove

far up Elk River Road until we found the perfect emerald swimming hole, down a steep trail, a hidden oasis. There was an overnight at the Greensprings Inn, soaking together in the Jacuzzi tub, singing as she played the guitar, and pulling her son on a sled in the snow the next morning. There was the Oregon Country Fair. By day we sold velvet and lace halter tops, shawls, skirts, and dresses we had designed and sewn together. By night we roamed the oak tree paths arm in arm in the dark so as not to lose one another. There was the trip to Arcata for her birthday to see Rickie Lee Jones in concert at Humboldt State University. We stopped at the Smith River along the way, stripped off our clothes and plunged into the icy green water. We lay on our backs bobbing above the rocks, water sluicing over and around our curves until our pale skin turned watermelon. Later, after the concert, we drove to Patrick's Point, where we had set up a tent on the bluff above the ocean, and climbed into our sleeping bags, huddling together in the dark, all warmth and closeness, crashing waves and minty breath as we drifted into sleep. ADVENTURES.

10. I ran into her ex-husband the day Gwen was summoned to an emergency court hearing because he had filed for temporary sole custody of their son. I was out walking with my family at a local nature preserve. Their son was subdued and walked away from us, downcast. He had just learned he would not be seeing his mother for a while. "She's been making poor choices and hanging out with the wrong people," her ex said. "I never would have thought she'd become a tweaker." He did not say she had become a meth user. In fact, he did not know this as certainty. But everything implied it. The way her once good looks had faded from bright and lively to gaunt and strung out. The way her mood could swing and she'd surge into sudden rage and violence, like the episode that provoked the emergency hearing. The way she couldn't seem to maintain a steady home, work, or previous years-long friendships. TWEAKER implied meth.

11. Methamphetamine is made from pseudoephedrine (decongestant found in cold medicine) and other highly toxic ingredients, which can include acetone (nail polish remover or paint thinner), lithium (used in batteries), toluene (used in brake fluid), hydrochloric acid (used to make plastic), red phosphorus (found in matchboxes, road

flares, and other explosives), sodium hydroxide (lye), sulfuric acid (used in drain and toilet bowl cleaner), and anhydrous ammonia (found in fertilizer and counter top cleaner).

This is what chronic smoking of meth does to a body and brain:

The outward physical effects include drastic weight loss, malnutrition, insomnia and sleep deprivation, dental decay, elevated body temperature and dehydration, sores and abscesses, and an aged appearance. The unseen effects can be irreversible damage to major organs such as the heart, lungs, liver, and kidneys. An overdose of meth can cause convulsions, heart attack, stroke, or death. Methamphetamine is a central nervous system stimulant that is neurotoxic. Chronic meth use damages the brain and causes chemical changes. Effects include psychotic symptoms: paranoia, hallucinations, delusions, and self-absorption; aggression and violence due to a lack of impulse control; impaired thinking and judgment; memory loss; decreased attention span; anxiety; mood swings; reduced inhibition; compulsive motor actions like twitching or scratching; and an increased risk of stroke and Parkinson's disease.

Many words describe how meth affects a life. Its signature, though, its defining characteristic is that meth is INSIDIOUS.

12. Her Facebook posts turned dark and desperate, describing in text with pictures how her on-again-off-again boyfriend had trashed her rental and her car. One day, after she had been evicted and was living out of her car and a string of motels (when she could afford it), her rambling Facebook post read like a suicide note, addressed to her son as a goodbye letter, saying how tired she was and she just needed to close her eyes and dream of her son in a peaceful sleep. Alarm bells rang in my brain. I immediately called her phone but got no answer, so I messaged her on Facebook, pleading for a response, then I started calling motels. The first motel I called wouldn't confirm if she was staying there. Against policy. I began asking every clerk I called for her room, and when they asked me for the room number, I feigned ignorance. They all came back saying there was no one by that name at their motel. That's when I called the sheriff, but without knowing her location, there was nothing they could do. About an hour later, she messaged me back, telling me where to find her, and said, "Please don't send the cops here."

She answered the motel door in a tank top and underwear, her hair stringy and hanging in her face, which looked ashen and haggard with dark patches under her eyes, an expression of part shame, part relief at seeing me. The room was freezing because the air conditioner blasted on high, and the air smelled of an unfamiliar toxic chemical I could barely stand to breathe. I pulled a chair close to the bed to face her and said, "I'm here to help you, but you have to be honest with me. If you're not, I'll know it, and I'm outta here."

I quizzed her, and she confessed to everything: using meth for nearly two years, how and when she started, having smoked it prior to my arrival, as well as prior to writing her distressing Facebook post. She said she couldn't keep track of time. Not in the way regular people lose track and are late to an appointment, but in the way time shapeshifted so that she wasn't sure what was actual and what was imagined. Whole chunks of time disappeared, and she didn't know what had happened. She warned me she could "go from zero to a hundred" in an instant—one moment she'd be fine; the next she'd be enraged. And then she described an episode (one I had already heard about from another person's perspective) with such clarity and accuracy (and conflicting with the other person's account) that I felt certain she was fabricating the facts. Not lying directly. I think she truly believed what she was saying. It was more like her fabrication was the product of delusion. I expressed no doubt. This was a reconnaissance mission. My intention was to save her, not alienate her. ATTEMPT.

13. We went out for dinner at the G Street Bar & Grill. She was in good spirits and mostly acted like her normal self (although an extremely hyped-up version), but as the evening passed, there was an obvious lack of balanced relating. It felt like she could *hear* my voice but wasn't really *listening* to what I had to say. She showed no interest in the changes in my life since we had last seen each other sixteen months before. After dinner, we sat in the car in the parking lot, and a family walked by, a baby sitting on the man's shoulders. I said, "You know I'm a grandma now." She made no remark other than an insulting joke I can't remember now and then started talking about something else. One might think she, who had lost custody of her

son, didn't want to talk about grandchildren because in contrast to her loss, it was too painful. Maybe some of that floated beneath the surface. Her behavior, though, didn't express that much care, thought, or reflection. It revealed dissonance between the person I used to know and the one sitting beside me. That was the defining moment. I realized my old friend was gone. In her place sat a dysfunctional woman who had lost the ability to reason and care about others. By the time we got back to the motel, she was growing confused, agitated, and angry. I left her in the parking lot, searching through the back of her car, muttering to herself in an incoherent repetition, an edge of violence rising in her body. A person CHANGED.

14. The vernacular used to refer to addiction and those who struggle with it has changed. Terms such as "meth addict" and "substance abuser" have become "person with a meth [or substance] use disorder." Such terminology is believed to be person centered and avoids characterizing one by his or her addiction. The transition away from substance "abuse" is meant to abate the negative moral judgments associated with the word. At the meeting on the community land with Gwen's family, her sister reminded everyone that the last couple of years of Gwen's struggle is only a blip in the timeline of her life. We, who have known her for longer than two years, know the essence of her being—devoted mother; talented musician and belly dancer; healing and intuitive massage therapist; pirate radio DJ spinning Bluegrass Tendencies; loving sister, daughter, and friend. A person is not one thing or another—addict or responsible adult—she is an AMALGAM.

15. I said I would be her touchstone; she could call me when she needed grounding. I would help her focus, come up with strategies for recovery, and (hopefully) implement them. She called, agitated and struggling to make a to-do list. She couldn't think straight. She couldn't remember what she needed to write down. She said, "Just hearing the sound of your voice helps." "Do you want me to come?" I asked. "Yes," she said.

   When I arrived, she was on the phone with an insurance representative, trying to get approval for detox. She put the phone on speaker so I could listen. The woman expressed concern that if she went to detox without a bed waiting for her in a rehab center directly afterward, she would relapse and detox would have been futile. Gwen tried to remain calm. Her sole focus was the upcoming custody hearing. She wanted to show the court she was taking steps to get clean. But the insurance rep wouldn't authorize approval, and this agitated Gwen, who had barely slept and not eaten since the day before. I started writing a to-do list for her—get an evaluation from Options (the local nonprofit providing psychosocial rehab services), find a lawyer, get a new phone charger—when a Domino's delivery guy knocked on the door. Gwen's sister had called in a delivery order in hopes she would finally eat. The insurance phone call had stressed her out, and she could barely hold the sandwich still because she was shaking so bad. She bit aggressively into it. After one bite, she started a pattern of repeated muttering, like the night before. She babbled about needing her son, about wishing her abusive ex-boyfriend were there—if only she could see him and talk to him, everything would be better.

"Well, you can forget that. He's the last thing you need."

I had said the *wrong* thing. A deep, guttural roar erupted out of her. She rose and slammed her fists down hard on the table, inches from where I sat. It rocked from the force. She paced back and forth, tensing her fists, her arms, unadulterated rage hijacking her body. I have been in the presence of rage before. But this rage exploded in unmatched fury and vibrated at a frequency entirely unpredictable. Suddenly I was vibrating too. But with fear. I felt certain she was going to attack me. Then she ran to the bathroom and shut herself inside, yelling in a rush, "Lore, you need to leave, you need to leave, I need you to leave, get out of here, you better get out of here, I need you to get out of here, Lore, now, go, get out of here!" I grabbed my bag and fled. I flew down the stairs, running for what felt like my life, afraid the colossal form of Lyssa, goddess of fury and madness, would swoop upon me in the stairwell and strike me down. HARROWING.

16. As I drove home from the motel, past the lush, spring-green farms and fields, it was hard to reconcile the fact that here, in this place teeming with beauty and life and potential, lurked a pathology of

people in drug-addled discord, an energy so harmful and frightening it hid amid the grass like a viper waiting to strike. INCONGRUITY.

17. Gwen's ex-husband's lawyer called and asked if I would testify against her in court. Until I revealed that Gwen had confessed her meth use to me, they had no confirmation of her addiction, only suspicion and hearsay. The lawyer said my testimony would insure "court-ordered" treatment and put Gwen at the top of an exhaustive list for inpatient treatment. In Oregon, public rehab centers are maxed out. The number of people seeking treatment exceeds the number of beds available. The wait is long. For a person suffering from methamphetamine addiction, such a wait can feel like a lifetime. A lifetime of continued damage to the brain and body. The lawyer said the goal was to get Gwen treatment so she could return to being an active part of her son's life with shared custody. She laid out the protocol: detox; ninety days' inpatient rehab; and then a transition to a halfway house, where she would have support and therapy to reintegrate into living independently a life free of meth. During treatment, she could have access to her son, at first via phone calls and then in person. Court was in a week. I had to make a choice. Would I sacrifice our relationship to help save her life? *Yes, absolutely*, I thought. *Maybe someday she'd forgive me.* Even Gwen's sister supported me in testifying. But then I thought about Gwen's fragile state, the delicate trust she had instilled in me, how she had said, "You're my only friend who isn't a drug addict," and I wasn't sure if I could do it. With my testimony, the temporary full-custody order in favor of Gwen's ex would become permanent. She'd hate me for that. CONFLICTED.

18. Gwen found a lawyer who took her case pro bono, and they settled out of court. She signed an agreement requiring her to get treatment, just as her ex's lawyer had described, and I was relieved of making the decision of whether to betray her. She never went to inpatient rehab. I could have testified against her, and it still wouldn't have insured her recovery. It most likely would have ruined our friendship, though. The last time I saw her she was evicting me from her motel room. It was tense and terrifying and unpredictable. But I knew she loved me. There is that, a bit of SOLACE.

19. When Gwen went missing, her last phone call was to a friend on the East Coast. For Gwen, her phone was her lifeline. She remained tethered to it—until she lost it. She lost multiple phones in the last year leading up to her disappearance. Every time she lost one, she contacted her sister, who paid the phone bill, to get a replacement. After that last phone call, Gwen didn't seek a new phone. The voicemail box filled up, and her family was no longer able to reach her. There were no sightings of Gwen or her car. Three months later, after her family hired a private investigator and the Oregon State Police agreed to take the case, Gwen's car was found in the north end of Grants Pass, behind some motels, adjacent to Interstate 5. Authorities reviewed security footage, but the cameras record over old footage every week or so, so they came up with no new leads. I heard rumor the contents of her vehicle included her phone, laptop, and a tablet. All evidence remains in police custody. Her family continues to ask for prayers and everyone to "keep the faith" in hopes this information will help find her. CLUES.

20. To deal with the fact that Gwen is missing, I have developed a numbness of spirit in her regard. I cannot linger too deeply in the questions of who, what, where, when, why, and how, for if I do, a sinking dread threatens to bury me. Sometimes it does. Temporarily. But then I squash it back into numbness. Numbness allows for hope to thrive. That hope is a seedling that roots itself in a crack of concrete, defying heat, drought, and the soles of shoes in order to grow. This essay is my invocation. It calls upon the missing and transforms her from elusive smoke sifting through a screen to something tangible. I wonder how Gwen might react to it. Gwen the addict would probably go nuts and rail against my words, positioning herself as the victim, blaming me for betraying her confidence and accusing me of an inaccurate portrayal. Gwen the person and friend not addicted to meth might feel some shame. Maybe some regret. Perhaps she would see her story as the story of a thousand others. Perhaps in reading this essay, she would be thankful to have lived through the story and come out the other side. I'm willing to take that gamble. I'm willing to risk her hating me. That would mean I'd see her again one day. That would mean she will be FOUND.

Answer Key

M	A	G	L	A	M	A	N				F		
		W			M	O				O			C
		E			U	I				U		H	O
		N		Y	A	T		N			A		N
				T	R	C	D		N				F
	E		R	I		T	I		G			S	L
	S		E	U			D	E			E		I
H	P		K	R			D			I			C
A	A		A	G		E	A	T	T	E	M	P	T
R	L		E	N	V			I					E
R	E		W	O		E	L	U	S	I	V	E	D
O	R		T	C		I	N	T	I	M	A	T	E
W		I		N	B		M						
I	O			I	N	S	I	D	I	O	U	S	
N			S			S							
G		S	O			S	E	U	L	C			
	O		L			I							
P			A	D	V	E	N	T	U	R	E	S	
			C	H	A	N	G	E	D				
			E										

*Gwen is a pseudonym.

This Is the Room Where

NELS P. HIGHBERG

I keep my keys where I can watch the guy across the street mow his lawn shirtless; where I learned my niece was having her fourth child; where you can find Gary's dogeared, underlined, and deeply annotated copy of "The Federalist No. 10," written by James Madison on November 22, 1787; where I watch *Real Housewives of New York* on the DVR; where I have cried on the phone more often than in any other room of the house; where I listen to that Lizzo album at least once a day; where I store the trophy Tria and I won for Duet Shakespeare Reading junior year of high school; where I emailed Gary's brother a photo of Gary in front of Saint Catherine's Palace outside Saint Petersburg, Russia, fulfilling a dream he had since they first watched *Nicholas and Alexandra* in the seventies; where I read Sylvia Plath out loud all last summer, taking notes for the following semester's teaching; where I masturbated on cam with that guy from Toronto who was into rubber porn; where I (try to) check my blood pressure every day; where we stared at CNN the night of the 2015 terrorist attacks in Paris, having just returned home from some movie I no longer remember; where I filmed YouTube videos unpacking monthly subscription boxes of *kawaii* trinkets from Japan; where we had that insipid fight about the credit card; where our PhDs hang, framed together, side by side; where I perused ads for older, muscular gay male escorts in New York City; where I watched *Clerks* for the first time since Gary and I saw it at the artsy theater back in Ohio the first year we were dating; where some married guy I met on Scruff told me, after the sex was over, I would be cute if I went to the gym; where my husband, Gary, died. Come in.

The Boys of New Delhi

An Essay in Four Hurts

SAYANTANI DASGUPTA

1. Because I Was Twelve

Because no one else "saw" me. Because I felt too big in my skin, my legs concrete pillars and not the statuesque, never-ending sexiness of the girls I envied but couldn't bring myself to admit. In that New Delhi heat, your music store was one with air-conditioning. I am embarrassed to admit that that's what brought me in the first time, and not the quest for any great music.

Remember I wanted to pay you for the Grammy Awards cassette? When I pulled out the forty-rupee note from my jeans, you chuckled. You grasped the money, shook your head, and slid it right back. That brush of your fingers lived in my jeans for days. You smelled of cigarettes and everything my dad disapproved of. You had broad shoulders and an indigo shirt. Every day as I walked up to your store, I knew you watched me through the tinted screen of your door, in full view of your coworkers. Probably you all laughed a bit at my expense too.

You were twenty-seven; your fingertips carried experience. You had thin lips, and I wanted their pinch around mine, the graze of your teeth on my throat. But one day, you disappeared. Your coworker said you got married and moved to a new city. That night, I cried like an eleven-year-old girl and not the twelve-year-old woman I thought I had become.

2. Compatibility

Once, when I was thirteen, I asked my friend, who was fifteen, if he would introduce me to his friends in the neighborhood, you know, boys his age—older, smarter, cool. I asked because I remember feeling pretty good about myself that day. School had been fantastic. The kind teachers had been kind,; the horrid one hadn't shown up. I had even received a certificate for winning a debate. My best friends and I had gathered at our designated spot under the banyan tree during lunch and laughed hysterically over a classmate's new boyfriend. He insisted on showing his love and devotion by giving her soppy nicknames. No way, we had insisted—our future boyfriends were going to be so much cooler than that.

After I returned home from school, I had inaugurated a new black sweater and a purple polka dot skirt. My hair was tousled but just the right amount. There was that slight nip in the air signaling New Delhi's sweet winter was just around the corner.

Spurred by all these good vibes, I made my audacious request. I asked, "Hey, do you think you could introduce me to some of your friends?"

I remember how quickly my friend shook his head, how abruptly he said, "No, I don't think so."

I should have dropped the subject. I should have guessed why he was looking away. Instead, I smoothed my skirt. I touched a black button on my sweater as if it was my lucky charm. I demanded answers. "Why not?"

My friend cleared his throat. He continued to look away. Finally, when he spoke, his voice was so low, I had to lean my head toward him. "I am not sure," he said, "I am not sure you will be *compatible* with any of them."

This time, I nodded. I dropped the subject. I knew what he meant. *Compatibility* was a big word. I was a big girl. Most days, I was ashamed of my body but confident of other aspects of myself, like my sense of humor, my ability to write well, the solid loyalty I offered my friends. But in that moment, all my qualities went away. He *was* older, smarter, more knowledgeable. What did I know of his friends, of boys that were almost young men, and what they found "compatible"?

Today, I am a university professor. I put on a suit of confidence every day, although some days, it struggles to sit properly. Semester after semester, I read essays where students write about all the ways they feel ugly in their skin. I have a hard time associating the harsh words they use for themselves with how I see them in the classroom: confident, stylish, smart. They remind me that underneath our suits, we are all a little beastly.

That friend and I are in touch via the occasional email. He is on to his third marriage now. None of the previous marriages lasted for more than one year, at best two. I wonder if he still closes conversations with words like *compatibility*.

3. Winter Coat

When I was fifteen, I bought a sweater that was red, black, and long. It went past my knees and had shiny black buttons the size of poker chips. I bought it with my allowance one evening when I was wandering through the neighborhood market. In the New Delhi of the 1990s, those markets with their clutch of permanent shops and a revolving array of seasonal vendors were the equivalent of the now-ubiquitous mall.

It was the start of the winter season, and the red and black sweater was hanging from a plastic rope. The vendor selling it had heaped his wares on three rectangular tables. One carried colorful scarves and socks; another, hats of all shapes and sizes; the third, bright, new sweaters. My eyes went straight to the red and black sweater and stayed there. Those two colors were my favorites. I mean, has there ever been a more badass combination than red and black?

So I bought it. Impulsively.

It was a sweater but felt like a coat, the kind men and women wore in American films, the kind you didn't find easily in New Delhi. The hundred rupees felt like a splurge, but the sweater made me feel stylish, like I was on the runway, even though the world had me convinced that there wasn't anything even a tiny bit stylish about my height or girth or face.

A Man in My Life noticed my new sweater. Instead of a smile, his eyes narrowed in displeasure. He nodded curtly. Which only meant one thing. Disapproval-disappointment-waste-of-time-and-money.

So I smiled. A lot. And I talked. A lot. I chattered with Energy and Enthusiasm, the two weapons nervous people use the world over when desperate to win approval. To no avail.

The Man in My Life shook his head. He said I shouldn't wear it because it made me look fatter than I was already. He said I should return it and buy something else, maybe a scarf, or a pair of socks. He even offered to come with me and help me choose.

I refused. Sure, his words wounded, but not enough to make me give up my sweater. I couldn't help it. That combination of red and black did make me feel like a stylish badass.

So the Man in My Life took to reminding me every time we went for walks. Even on days when I had done tremendous things at school, when

I felt tall and regal, he continued to pull me down. He said, "Don't wear it. It makes you look fatter. It accentuates your shortness."

When I try clothes at stores these days and something doesn't fit, I still hear his words loud and clear. Sometimes, my plucky fifteen-year-old self sneaks out and rips away his displeasure. Other days, it hides. It lets his words sting until I leave the dressing room and go back home.

4. Kimbhutkimakar

When I was seventeen, the boy I dated told me he couldn't believe he was with someone of my shape. He called me Kimbhutkimakar. The word doesn't mean anything, neither in English nor in Bengali, our mother tongue, but it exists. It's the name of a monster from *Abol Tabol*, a book of nonsense rhymes, penned by Sukumar Ray. I feel certain that the original intent behind the poems and their accompanying illustrations was to entertain children, not hurt teenage girls with brittle confidence.

When I was a kid, my mother used to read to me those very same nonsense rhymes. I loved them so much I could recite several of them from memory. Kimbhutkimakar too had once been among my favorites. And why not? He had the head of a tusked elephant, a wild bushy mane, a long alligator-like tail, the hind legs of a giant bird, and his back and shoulders were covered in feathers. The poem's first line read, "This disgusting creature . . ."

Now, nearly twenty years later, that boy who once called me Kimbhutkimakar is the father to a little girl. I am friends with him on Facebook, where he routinely posts pictures of his wife and daughter, who link their arms with his and smile straight into the camera. Here's a picture of them eating out. There, they have gone to the movies. Yesterday, they played badminton. Last month, they vacationed in Paris.

I have never met either his wife or their daughter. But I wonder what names he calls them now, what words they don't repeat when they look into the camera, what echoes they will hear all their lives.

The Wait(ress)

AMY ROOST

Six hours north of Vancouver, I sit in the ICU next to my sister-in-law, who is dying. Advanced pancreatic cancer. I'm struggling because I'm not with my tribe, rather with near-strangers who are cut from a foreign cloth.

Across the room sit my husband's two nephews, who both work at a copper mine outside of town. It was recently in the news for "killing" a lake on a First Nation reserve. Their dad can't imagine staying overnight in the hospice with his wife, who has "days left," and yet he stands over her insisting she fight harder because she has everything to live for. I can barely make out my husband, who seems to be blending into the standard-issue hospital wallpaper imprinted with helpless men, past and present.

Me? I stroke the top of a soon-to-be-cold hand, daydreaming of the day I'll take up with the waitress who serves me warm marionberry coffee cake at the Old Town Cafe in Bellingham, Washington. The one with the long salt and pepper hair who—even though I only visit three times a year—remembers that I like extra butter and my coffee black.

Beasts of the Fields

AIMÉE BAKER

Spring

The rats appeared in late spring when the winter gray had yet to shake itself loose from our northern New York valley and everything smelled of rain and mud. They came in from the fields and took hold of our barn that once sheltered the pigs we raised for slaughter. By the time the rats came, though, the barn's only other inhabitants were a dog, an aging cat who slept his afternoons away in faint patches of sunlight, and the mice.

Before that spring arrived, we were used to the skittering of mice in the barn. We listened for the small scrabble of claws against wood, cardboard, and metal scrap as we wrestled rototillers and wheelbarrows from the depths of the barn to ready them for their time in the fields.

When the barn still housed bales of hay my father and uncle cut from the back forty three times a year, there hadn't been any mice. Mother cats would birth their babies deep in the gaps between the bales, and their warm kitten bodies would smell like summer grass long after they grew gangly and began to hunt the mice.

The mother cats and kittens were not gone long before the mice took over. Before that spring, I tried to save the baby mice that would fall from the rafters to the cement floor, their bodies hitting the cement with a sound like splattering rain. When I found them, I'd wrap their bodies in rough-cut pieces of blue gingham flannel and make them beds from cardboard matchboxes. The babies would last for a day, maybe a bit longer if they were unfortunate, as I tried to feed them droplets of milk from a small straw. Someone had to do it, I thought, care for the living creatures who didn't know they were dead yet.

I would have done the same for the rats, those large-bodied beings with their scaled tales that birthed their babies in the walls and steadied themselves among the rafters. But these rats didn't need anyone to save them.

*

In Tanzania an organization breeds giant pouched rats and trains them to detect the smell of explosives in landmines. They're shipped to countries where war has left its mark deep in the earth. The rats are fitted with harnesses and their ears slicked with sunscreen to protect them while they work. In the mornings, their handlers take them to the fields, and every day the rats cover ground, nimbly stepping over thatches of grass and rocks, quickly clearing fields that people had been too scared to farm.

Our rats are more common, brown rats that were once thought to have spread from Norway in cargo ships filled with lumber and now inhabit almost every continent. These are the rats of our stories, the rats of ditches and drains, the rats of disease and death.

If you see one, there are ten more. If you see one, there are fifty more. This is the threat of the brown rat, that somewhere there are untold numbers hiding, the scope of their presence immeasurable. Though brown rats can live to be three years old, most die within their first year, but in this same year, two rats can become fifteen thousand. This is how they live, by becoming something beyond their own bodies.

*

The spring of the rats, my brother barely left his bedroom. The light he bought at a novelty store glowed red from underneath his door like a warning. When we were home alone together, I listened for the sound of his feet scuffling across his clothing-ridden floor. This was how I kept him alive, by listening.

On long, cold days when even his small movements became too much for him, he lay in bed and played music cranked so high the sides of our trailer pulsed with the sounds of death metal. I retreated then to my own room at the other end of the trailer, the music so loud I had to wait until it stopped to reassure myself he was still alive.

"What's wrong with your brother?" friends asked on the days he attended school, and we watched as he skulked past, his eyes cast down and the thick chains he'd attached from his waistband to his wallet slapping against his jeans.

"He's fine," I said. But how do you explain what lives inside someone, the way I knew a dark and heavy thing wanted to claw its way from his body? The way I'd begun to crave silence?

Summer

Summer dawned hot the year the rats came, so hot I closed my bedroom curtains tight before the sun had a chance to get too high. During the day, I would sweat in the heat of my room, a single fan whirring constantly in the window. In summers before, I would have retreated to the barn, sat myself down on the cold and dirty concrete, a sweating glass of water in my hand. But that year, I stayed away, too nervous to be alone out there.

Still, there was work to be done. Weeds to pull. Rocks to pick. Potato bugs to flick into empty tin cans. This is how we spent our weekends, my brother and I pacing the rows of strawberries, tomatoes, beans, potatoes, and peas while my skin turned red and blistered under the sun. Every week it was the same until the weeds got so thick, we couldn't make out our pathways anymore. Each year, at the end of summer, my father would say that the next time we'd start out smaller, grow fewer things, manage the fields better. But during winter, when the seed catalogues arrived in the mail, green and full of promise, my father would forget his vow and begin planning, sketching out rows and rows of vegetables to plant. By the time planting season arrived, he'd turn over the earth with the roto-tiller or, on big years, with the tractor, until the garden space grew large enough to accommodate his plans.

The year before the rats, he built a compost bin, an eight-by-eight-foot wooden structure we threw our food scraps and leaves in. The bin sat on the edge of the field in the space where the grass would grow tall enough it was hard to see the sides of it as the summer trudged on.

"Here, bring this out to the compost," my mother would say after dinner, handing me a metal bowl filled with the day's leavings: potato peels, bits of banana, unfinished cereal.

I'd run from the house until I hit the bin, palms striking rough wood as I quickly shook out the bowl and took off again. I never lingered. This was the place the rats found their meals, and if I listened close enough, I could hear them down in its depths.

*

Rats are easy to find if you know what to look for. You can locate a rat by the oily residue it leaves behind on the walls near its entrance. Or by the trails it makes, its feet following the same pathways over and over as it travels from food source to the safety of its home. Or by the sound of it, the gnawing grate as the rat wears down its teeth on wood and metal.

Brown rats breed heavily starting in the spring and continue through summer, birthing most of their young before cold weather sets in. These rats form families, female rats nestling together in burrows to care for their young. When there are few rats, a male will protect their home, positioning itself as protector of the nests, guarding the small holes the rats use as entrances to the tunnels. They form a community of their own, these rats. Still, over millions of years they've become commensal, their population growing alongside humans, always dependent on what we leave behind, the care we forget to take in securing the things we love.

*

My brother tried to kill himself for the first time that summer. He clambered toward the roof of the trailer and wedged his body through the vent hole that gave access to a cramped attic of sorts, a space between the old tin roof and the new one that would heat up quickly in the summer sun. There was little room up there, with only small pockets between the rafters to hide in. But it was there that my brother slit his wrist with a blade taken from my father's pack of disposable razors, running it horizontally along the skin in lines so straight they looked like they'd been drawn with a ruler. He stayed in his hideaway while blood began to rise up and flow down his arms.

Below, inside the trailer, I waited and listened for the sound that would alert me to where he'd hidden himself. That morning, after our parents had gone to work, I heard him leave. The door slamming shut behind him, quick and hard like a bullet, before his feet clomped out over the deck. Then, for hours, nothing.

By the time my parents got home, the silence felt like lead, a weighty thing pulling me down through the dirt. But before dusk settled over the fields, he abandoned his den and made his way inside, hiding his wrists behind his body while drops of blood fell to the floor. It was my father, a former army medic, who cared for him, opening the starlight blue first-aid kit and wrapping my brother's arms in silence. This is how we cared for ourselves: the amber sting of Betadine, the rolls of pristine white gauze, the tight pull of medical tape.

Fall

In fall my father started sealing any holes he could find in the barn. There were too many between the slatted sides, so he nailed large sheets of Texture 1-11 to the exterior, and briefly our old, weathered barn, looked new again, the siding still bright with the shine of fresh wood. He nailed the siding over the cat door, a small square we'd cut in the broadside of the barn so the cats could come and go as they pleased. With just one elderly tabby, the hole had become a rat highway, funneling them from the wide-open fields into the safety of the dark barn.

Despite these efforts, the rats still came. Along New York's Canadian border, winter comes swiftly. October means thick winter coats over Halloween costumes and snow boots by November. The rats of this borderland know to prepare early, and they began readying for winter. Starting at dusk, they foraged for food and stockpiled their finds.

The rat trail led directly from the barn to the compost bin, a pile of easy helpings. The bin had yet to yield fertile soil like my father had hoped, its size too large to adequately move the contents about, the mix of leaf matter to food waste never quite right. But the idea of it had been there, a means to turn our rocky, dry soil into something more magical, something that would help us produce more food than weeds.

"Here," my father said one late fall day while handing my mother, brother, and me the nearest heavy gardening tools. My mother with a shovel, me with a flat hoe, and my brother with a spade, all with their blades rusted from being left out in the rain too often. We stood between the trailer and the bin, instruments of death ready, while my father took the tractor to the wooden container. Bucket raised, he lifted and then tilted the frame over, the movement of the structure enough to send the rats fleeing for safety. And then, we swung our tools close to the ground, the shovels and hoes thumping against bodies.

*

Brown rats originated along the plains of Mongolia and northern China where they began to live beside human settlements. Though their bones have been found medieval German towns, it's said that they only took hold in Europe after hordes of them swam across the Volga River and into Russia, fleeing an earthquake that struck that region in 1727. Then they made their way into the rest of the continent and filled the streets and sewers. Invaded homes and pits and barns.

For most of recent history, the rats have been there. Men of the Paris slaughterhouses told stories of fallen horse carcasses picked clean by rats in the night, not a shred of flesh left on the bones. And then there's the story of a mine closed off for a season, the shaft filling with so many rats that when it reopened, a careless worker who slipped down into their masses was consumed within minutes.

And just as the rats fight to live, we fight to see them dead. In New York City there were so many rats, men threw them in pits illuminated by gas lanterns and bet on how long it would take for dogs to kill them, the dogs taking the rats between their jaws and shaking them until they were dead. Now terriers and dachshunds patrol those same city streets with their owners looking for a kill, shaking the rats they find just like the pit dogs once did. Every rat killed a victory.

But brown rat colonies are hard to erase. Even with complete eradication of their numbers, rat populations will return and grow within two years. If rats are reduced by any other percentage, their population growth will be slow at first and then hit a period of rapid expansion before reaching peak numbers within a matter of months. In other words, rats are made for survival.

*

That fall, my brother stopped going to school. He'd ride the bus with me for a day or two before skipping four or five days in a row. Over and over, a repeated pattern. When he was there, it felt like his body took up more room than the school could hold. The dusty scent of his cheap cigarettes clinging to his clothes, the oiliness of his long, unwashed hair. The sound of his boots on the tile floor. The sharp slice of his laughter. All of it pulled across my skin like a knife.

On days he stayed home, though, it was the silence that gnawed at me. My father had nailed a screen over the roof vent hole. "To keep out bugs," he said, as though insects were making inroads to our house through the openings and down through our layers of roofs. That screen barrier, we all knew, was too flimsy to offer any security, and so I imagined my brother back up there when no one was home, running a blade across his arms again. How can you count on someone to be alive if you're not there to listen for the breath entering and leaving their lungs?

Winter

The growing season was short and inconsequential that year. Before the snow came, we pulled up tangles of cucumber vines after the frost killed them off, the plants gone yellow with the bursts of cold. The tractor's plow turned under the rest, the fields of vegetables and weeds disappearing down into the dirt.

Where the compost bin had been was just a blank, dark spot by the field, the imprint of the wooden sides still visible on the ground. These were the only signs that the bin was once there, the rats inexplicably gone as well. Perhaps terrified by the sound of the tractor, their disappearing food source, or the sight of the slaughter of some of their own, our barn was once again the home of mice and the occasional chipmunk.

"Where do you think they've gone?" I asked my father, eyeing the tree line where the fields gave way to sumac and grape vines before continuing on into dense woods.

My father stood next to me, breath puffing into the cold, evening air. "Not sure," he said.

"Do you think they'll be back?" I asked. He didn't respond. Whether or not they would survive the winter and return was not a question that had an answer.

*

The only things brown rats need to survive the cold are shelter and a steady source of food. These rats do not hibernate, and their metabolisms are too fast to use fat as a food store. Instead, they continue life much as they do during every other season, finding food, storing food, even breeding in the winter chill.

But in particularly cold winters, weaker rats will not survive. Unable to find warmth and too exhausted to try, they will freeze to death in the night. In cities, people will find their bodies frozen on sidewalks, their corpses rigid with both rigor mortis and the plummeting temperatures. In rural regions, it's harder to find the rats that perished, their bodies hidden beneath winter-weathered grasses or tucked behind wood piles.

*

My brother is gone, not missing exactly, but away from home when he shouldn't be. He's with friends, I know, those dark creatures who slink around the hallways at school. "They're trouble," my father will often say of them. So, that night, when the phone rings, I am ready, just as I always am, for disaster. There's a particular sensation to being prepared for emergencies. It's a full-body tingle and a hardness in your gut. The feeling like you can't get enough air. And for me, a grin and harsh burst of laughter, the kind of sensory response that's unwelcome and suspicious but there nonetheless.

From this night's events, I won't remember what my parents say to me as they leave. I know my brother is in danger somewhere, and it's dark when they both leave in a flurry. I'm left, for the first time, home alone at night. I wait for news in the same way that I will always wait for bad news in the future. Curled stiffly on the couch, frozen with the inability to move. I leave a twenty-four-hour news station playing on the television, as though the voices of strangers will offer comfort. They don't, and I keep track of time by the hard ticking of the clock on the wall.

What is happening elsewhere is that my brother is dying. In a small neighborhood filled with single story ranch homes built in the 1960s, he's lying on someone's lawn, not moving. He has mixed some blend of drugs and drank as much cold medicine as he can stomach, the combination of which he hopes will kill him. It's cold out, the type of night where people settle deeper into their coats, tug on their gloves, and with tears crystalizing on their eyelashes declare the night "bitter" before sliding into their warm cars. This is the kind of night where cold can kill, and my brother is alone on that lawn, no coat or gloves to protect his skin or his organs or his heart that is struggling to beat.

His friends leave him there and return to their party, teenagers uncertain of what to do with a body on the front lawn. Perhaps the music is turned down then, or the curl of nervous whispers makes its way through the crowd. In truth, most of his friends are so drug rattled they forget him. One is sober enough, though, to call our house, but that's the only one my parents need because it sends them stumbling from our home.

When they arrive, my brother is still on the lawn in the snow and when they gather him into the car, they think for a moment he's already dead, his body gone cold and stiff. My father holds him in the backseat trying to revive him while my mother drives to the emergency room of the local hospital. There's no time to wait for an ambulance to arrive. My mother drives so fast that a state trooper tries to stop them, his lights and siren signaling for them to pull over to the side of the road. Instead my parents gesture from the car, their movements frantic enough that he pulls in front of them, lighting the way to the hospital.

By the time my father calls home, I've settled into my brother's death. The house filled only with the ticking clock and the steady drone of the television is my vision of what the future holds. There will be no listening for him, I think, the dull task I've taken up as though caring for something else is what I was meant to do. Without him, there will be no jolt of adrenaline when a door slams or when his fist connects with a wall. No clatter of my own body against the trailer walls as I sidle away from him, his fingers pinching across my skin, mottling my arms, legs, and stomach with dark bruises. No hiss of my own breath when he wraps his fingers around my throat and whispers, "I can kill you if I want." No crying out as he tugs my hair until strands of it rip from my scalp and he asks, "Are you still a virgin?" In their place will be an empty space, one I can fill with silence. Or one I can begin to fill with my own steady breath. The air no longer ratcheting through my lungs, the burn of it like unshed tears.

"He's alive," my father says and even through the phone line I can hear the relief in his voice. The relief that says, "Not this time," as though in prayer. Beyond him, somewhere in the hospital, doctors and nurses are pumping my brother's stomach, forcing him to throw up again and again so that he might live for another night. Live for another day.

"He didn't die?" I ask. I don't listen for my father to say the words again before hanging up the phone, settling the receiver into its cradle with a dull click. The answer is already there. Not this time.

In My Brother's Shadow

TALEA ANDERSON

Sometimes, when my brother and I stand awkwardly at opposite sides of the room, unspeaking, I remember our days as detectives, when we dressed in black sweatshirts festooned with Christmas lights, neon-rimmed sunglasses, and Grandpa's tweed hats, and ran through the Alberta summertime to watch the customers who picked strawberries at our farm. Which is to say, he watched while I—his sister born half blind—eyed the ground at my feet. I played at being Linnaeus with my own lists of things observed close by: smooth pieces of gravel, tent caterpillars, white strips of bark, bluebells hidden in the grass, and purple-headed thistles that matched my own height and wingspan. While he ran and hid, I picked foxtails and combed them out the wrong way to feel their sandpaper edge. I rubbed dandelion heads onto my hands like paint, like spilled sunlight, and smiled to see the yard seeping into me. He ran ahead, all commando, watching Hutterites, neighbors, and church members from behind trees and the shadows under the playhouse where he'd shown me how to throw paper airplanes dive-bombing down to plant somewhere in the yard, plastic soldier figurines taped to their undersides for the ground assault to come. Sometime, two years later, he'd plant a jackknife in the wall of his room and tell me he wanted to be an assassin. I'd stumble back, wondering when my brother grew up and left me behind with my pebbles and sticks and smudgy fingers. Putting that aside—rewind, rewind—I still feel the glow of our shared purpose when I ran invisible in my brother's shadow and copied down license plate numbers for all the unseen perps in the berry patch. For that moment, that sliver of time, we lived in the same world and told the same story about it—the two of us dressed in tweed and neon.

Mash-Up

A Family Album

SARAH VIREN

Track 1

Everything is a cipher. —Vladimir Nabokov, "Signs and Symbols"

Two elderly parents take a trip to see their deranged child in a sanatorium for his birthday and they bring with them a basket of ten fruit jellies, which they have chosen carefully in hopes that they will mean nothing to him. Their son suffers from a condition the doctors call "referential mania." He believes that the world is inscribed with messages specifically about him and his innermost thoughts. It started young, when he was a kid. And, later that night, after their trip to the sanatorium, his mother remembers the earliest signs of his condition as she sits in the living room, passing the pages in an album of photos of her son when he was four, then six, then eight, then ten. Our family albums lined two shelves in our living room; they start in 1978, when my parents married, and end around 2008, when my mom stopped making them. There is one for almost every year and inside my mom has taped little notes, annotating our life: *Sarah at two before the tulips, Sisters together after the bath, Grandma visiting for Christmas.* Each time I went home, I pulled down one or two of those albums from the shelf and looked through the photos, first from nostalgia but later as if I might find a clue between the pages. When did this all start? The mother believes it started after her son got pneumonia, or rather that's when her son's illness *hardened, as it were.* After that, there was no going back, no saving him—though that night, after their visit to the sanatorium, the father wakes up and is suddenly determined to have hope. They will bring their son home again, he says. His plan leaves him flushed and almost happy and he sips a cup of tea noisily, talking about how he and his wife will take turns watching over their son to keep him from harming himself. While they plan, the jellies they never had a chance to give him that day sit unopened on the table before them, telling another story.

Track 2

Here is a counterpoint. —Zadie Smith, "The Embassy of Cambodia"

A young woman from the Ivory Coast works as a nanny and maid for a rich family in one of those quiet British suburbs with lots of brick houses and backyards shut off by walls. Every Monday, she steals free passes to the family's gym from a drawer in the foyer and goes there on her lunch break to swim. On her way to the pool, she passes an embassy behind whose towering wall she always sees the rise and fall of a shuttlecock from a game of badminton that she can imagine taking place but never sees. But I see the game. The shuttlecock zips across Bermuda grass in our Florida backyard that pushes up against swamp. There is a screened porch nearby and palm meadow bushes pop up everywhere on the periphery, and my mom is happy. She tells us she loves badminton. Her laugh is loose. Her movements are sober. My mom calls the shuttlecock a birdie and launches it into the air at my brother and me or at my sister and me on the other side. She is surprisingly good, and the game is surprisingly fun. I am twelve or maybe fourteen and I have a thought that will never be erased: *Our family is perfect,* I think. The family that the Ivory Coast woman works for is cruel and the mother eventually fires her. She has nowhere to go, so she agrees to move in with a Nigerian man she knows, a friend with whom she sometimes talks about the injustice of suffering. While waiting for the bus that will take her to his house, she watches the badminton game one more time from her side of the wall. *Pock, smash. Pock, smash.* The birdie moves back and forth in an uneven rhythm. *As if one player could imagine only a violent conclusion and the other only a hopeful return.*

Track 3

Which was the correct lyric? —Lorrie Moore, "Paper Losses"

A woman marries a man because they are both peaceniks, but many years pass and the man begins building small rockets in their basement and the woman admits she is sort of a hawk. The husband goes down to their basement every night after dinner and stays there for hours, emitting strange smells. He changes. The woman says her husband is like an alien and the basement is his alien pod. The basement in the house where we grew up had wooden stairs leading into darkness, and once, when I was two or maybe three, I pushed my sister down those stairs in her baby walker. The washer and dryer were in that basement and they would shake like they had a cat in them while my mom stacked folded clothes on the counter that ran along the far wall. My sister fell the length of the stairs after I pushed her and only survived because a family friend happened to be working on the banister that day. He looked up and saw her tumbling in her walker and caught her before her head smashed on the tile floor. My mom laughs about it now, saying I tried to kill my baby sister. But when I imagine her falling, I can only think about what might have been. For the couple, the basement was a sign of worse things to come. They eventually agree to a divorce, but first they take a cruise with their kids. While they're visiting one island or another, a resort worker traps a nest of baby sea turtles in a basket for all the tourists to see. He holds them captive for so long that, when he finally releases them, it is too late in the day and they are eaten *one by one* by a frigate bird. If my sister hadn't been caught that day, I would probably feel now that every family problem was my fault. And while that would have harder to bear, it would have been a simpler narrative to tell, one with a clear cause and the following effects.

Track 4

Everything is getting terrible. —Flannery O'Connor, "A Good Man Is Hard to Find"

A family takes a road trip from Atlanta down to Florida. The grandmother sits in the backseat between the two children and hides a cat in the basket in her lap. She wants to go to Tennessee instead and warns the family that an escaped convict called The Misfit is on the loose down near Florida, which is where I am one day in August when the phone rings. "It's mom," my dad says, and I wait, foot pivoted to turn. I am twenty-nine and about to leave on a road trip to Iowa, where I will start grad school in the fall. "Oh, Annie," my dad says after he picks up. He looks at me, but it's unclear whom he's talking to when he says, "She died." He then hands me the phone and my mom tells me that she was alone with her mom, my grandmother, that morning, and, watching her lying there, she suddenly decided to crawl into the bed with her, like the little girl she once was. Lying there, she held her mom and cried and told her that she loved her and that she could leave now. And after a while she realized that her mom had stopped breathing. She had left. The grandmother on the road trip stops breathing after The Misfit shoots her in the chest three times. This, after the family gets lost looking for a plantation that doesn't exist and after the grandmother's cat has gotten loose and caused their car to wreck on the side of the road. Right before she's shot, the grandmother looks at The Misfit and says, "Why, you're one of my babies. You're one of my own children." My dad says that my mom's drinking began when my brother, the baby, moved out of our house. Either that or when things with my sister started to get bad. But I always said my grandmother's death brought on the change. Her father died when she was young and for a long time it was just she and her mom in a Chicago apartment together. So when my grandmother died that August, my mom was suddenly alone as she'd never been before.

Track 5

I'm trying to solve a puzzle. —Harrison Ford, *The Fugitive*

A surgeon comes home at night to find his wife stabbed and dying after being attacked by a one-armed man. The surgeon struggles with the one-armed man, but the man gets away, and the wife dies. The surgeon is convicted of her murder, but he escapes before being sent to death row and spends the rest of the story trying to prove that he is innocent. In the moment we are at now, he has reached the edge of a long storm drain and appears to be caught by the lead investigator in his case. "I didn't kill my wife," the surgeon yells at the detective, his voice echoing in the chamber. "I don't care," the detective yells back. The water trickles and drips. The air-conditioning in the front room where we sit on an orange couch coats our bare skin in ice vapor. My sister recites the lines for both the surgeon and the detective. She speaks for everyone in the story. The surgeon jumps from the storm drain into a waterfall, but he somehow survives. My sister knows every line of the *Godfather* trilogy too. And *Sound of Music*. And *Rent*. Later she will spend several years shut up in an apartment watching and memorizing movies, letting dishes and magazines accumulate around her. Taking drugs that are prescribed and not prescribed. But now she is still so young. She has red hair and a birthmark on her chin the shape of a triangle that mom thought was a piece of paper towel the first time she saw it. She tried to wipe it off. *Out damn spot. Out, I say!* But some things cannot be removed. My sister says, "I didn't kill my wife," and then she says, "I don't care!" I tell her to stop echoing the story I'm trying to watch, and she goes quiet, but I hear her still wanting to speak. The surgeon fights and fights and eventually his truth becomes known. The one-armed man is killed. The world is rectified. On our couch in the suburbs, the world still feels whole.

Track 6

Every memory is turned over and over again.
—Marilynn Robinson, *Housekeeping*

Two sisters live with an eccentric aunt in an isolated house in an isolated town near the railroad tracks. Their mother has killed herself. Then one day they fight after finding some pressed flowers in a dictionary. The older sister knows they're important to their family's history, but the younger one, she is making a dress, and just wants to rid herself of everything from the past. She throws the flowers in the fire. The afternoon we bury my grandmother's ashes, flowers fall from the sky, and I am hungover. We are in a rented minivan heading toward the cemetery and we have just pulled off the highway, past the Hudson River and onto a road winding through green, when suddenly there are pollen tufts in the air everywhere that my brother says are cottonwood and my mom calls ragweed but I think look like flowers made of snow. Two days before this, my sister was so high she took her socks off in the airport and wove them around in circles. Her eyes were barely a slit. But today she is sober. Six days before this, my mom got drunk at a party and my dad told her this has to stop. My sister repeated what he said and I told her to focus on her own problems for once. At this point, I still think my mom's drinking is setting her free. But my sister knows better, just like both sisters think they know better when it comes to the pressed flowers. The younger one wants a normal life outside of their aunt's chaotic home; the older one is passive and more imaginative and, like her aunt, prefers seclusion. Eventually the courts threaten to break the family apart, to take both sisters and put them in a proper home, so the aunt and the older sister walk off together down the railroad tracks and jump a train toward nowhere, while the younger one stays behind with another family and the life she always wanted. At the close of the memorial service for my grandmother, we all throw yellow roses in the grave that holds her urn, but then the youngest among us, my cousin's son, gathers up the flowers *one by one* and tries to plant them again in the ground—as if to celebrate a beginning rather than mourn another end.

Track 7

How did this happen? —Mary Gaitskill, "The Other Place"

A father harbors a desire to capture young women and make them scared, maybe even hurt or kill them. Once, as a teenager, he almost fulfilled his wish, but the woman got the upper hand by refusing to show fear. Then the man grew up and became a real estate agent, and gave up drinking and drugs, and had a son, who, he slowly notices, seems to conceal a similar desire. Or at least his son is drawn to similar images of women: women bound, chased, mutilated, scared to death. The man worries for his son and begins retracing his boyhood: what made him this way? He remembers how he would wander the neighborhood alone, how he loved peering into other people's houses when they couldn't see him, how he left gifts sometimes or stole lawn gnomes from yards: a subterfuge form of interaction. I would take bananas from the fruit bowl on our kitchen table and leave them in a neighbor's mailbox. I would pick flowers and arrange them around the banana inside the box's darkness. I imagined the neighbors I didn't know finding the banana and flowers and thinking someone loved them. My gesture tied us together in a moment only I would understand. The man calls his desire to hurt or scare women "the other place" and decides that his son has "the other place" in him too. They never speak of it, but it will always be a secret they share. For a long time, I kept my mom's drinking a secret. I would confront her but not tell anyone else. My dad did the same. And, I suppose, my sister did too. Then one day we started to talk about it, bringing our secrets to the fore, and it felt for a moment like we were breaking free of some constraint. But soon after that the story slipped back behind the curtain of another tale, the one we wanted to tell ourselves: that she was better now, that we were all better, that everything was just fine. A family is a collection of secrets we all pretend we don't know.

Track 8

There's often an impressive similarity between two people sharing the same genes. —Ulric Collette, artist statement, *Genetic Portraits*

An artist named Ulric Collette combines photographs of two family members and makes them into one. Half of a mother's face is mashed with her daughter's. Two sides of two sisters come together to make one face. There are half-bearded brothers mixed with their bleached blond sisters. Young men whose faces slope and sag on the side where their fathers have been blended into them. Eyes bulge or appear withdrawn. Lips are misshapen. Nostrils slant slightly up on the right and then down on the left. And yet the portraits, for all their monstrosity, also make sense. In a picture I keep on my desk while I write, I am sitting on the floor with my mom, our backs together, her belly beginning to swell under her favorite red and black plaid shirt. She is six months pregnant with my sister and younger than I am now. In the photo I am almost two years old. Her hair is long and blonde and she looks so much like me, or I like her, that sometimes when people see this photo they think that it is me there, pregnant, a little girl smiling beside me. When my sister arrives three months later, she will look like none of us: curly red hair and freckles. Except for her eyes. Me, my mom, my sister: we share the same eyes—so dark blue they're almost black. In the photo you can no longer see the blue. Time has faded blue to brown. The photos in the Collette collection that look the most unnatural mashed up are the parent-child shots. Because in those what you notice is not genetics but time that wears at a face. It's as if the past and the present were contained in a moment. Or as if the present and the future had suddenly become one.

Track 9

I'd rather not consider any moment definitive.
—The author, in an email to her mother

A woman comes out of the bathroom with her purse over her shoulder. Now that she says she doesn't drink, she brings her purse with her wherever she goes and she always has a new bottle of water that she never shares. The woman is my mother. She is visiting after my first child is born. When she returns to her hotel that night, I go into the bathroom and find the water bottle she left in the trash. It smells like gin. I drank gin and tonics all night in New Orleans a few months before my wife gave birth to our daughter. I was at a bar with friends, and there was a brass band that marched in tooting their horns and beating their drums, and I knelt on a barstool with my hands flung above me in claps I was sure were in sync with the brass band song. When my mom drinks her gin and tonics at home, she says it is sparkling water, but she always goes to the closet or to another room with her glass before sitting down to drink it and read the *New York Times*. When I am home visiting, I sometimes watch her from the couch, where I pretend I am watching TV. Her head nods the more she drinks. She clears her throat. When she gets up for more, she walks like someone who believes she is alone in the room. When I drank gin and tonics that night in New Orleans I woke up the next morning with the smell of it licking me. I told everyone at the bar that I wanted to get all the fun out of my system before I became a mom myself, as if that were possible, as if we ever lose *the other place* inside. The woman who leaves the empty bottle in my bathroom goes back to her hotel that night and has at least one more before she goes to sleep. Most likely she waits until her husband is snoring to drink it. She mixes it with sleeping pills and dreams of nothing.

Bonus Track

You can see where it hit. —A woman next to the author in an Al-Anon meeting

The church where we meet has a vaulted ceiling and a great oval window that lights a quarter of our circle with noon sun. I find a spot in that sector and look up at the glass, noticing twin cracks, two circles overlapping like a Venn diagram. "A bird ran into the glass," a gray-haired woman to my left tells me. "You can see where it hit." I follow her pointing finger to the then-obvious, bird-shaped smudge among the rings. I am at the meeting to talk about my sister and how she got high and crashed her car into a tree, how she lost her job and called me crying, saying she was an idiot, and how I told her she wasn't but how I wanted to say that she was. Later I will return to the church to talk about my mom, and then again about my sister, though mostly I want to talk about myself. The twin cracks are always the same. Sometimes I sit under the shaft of light and sometimes I choose a seat in the shade. My mom gets better and then worse. My sister follows. Or maybe leads. She is in a homeless shelter. She has a baby. She loses custody of the baby. My mom has a new bruise. She has a gash in her forehead. She breaks her arm. Always accidents, she says. But they are always at night, and she rarely remembers a thing. She and my dad fight, and eventually he starts drinking again too. But at least he seems happy. Every story I have ever loved ends either ambiguous or sad.

Nevermore

KATIE MANNING

It wasn't until after your death that the combination of barking with my little boys and teaching poetry to college students opened a page of my memory to an old book of animal sounds. You read it to me so often, going through the standard noises—*bark*, *meow*, *moo*, *baa*—but then, beside a photo of a large black bird, the words: "And you know what the raven says."

But we didn't know. I was only a few years old and wouldn't read Poe until high school. You didn't go to school past eighth grade because you were working in the fields with your family. The book was making a joke we couldn't get. "*Caw?*" you'd say. "I think so. I wonder why they wrote it like that." And now here I am, crying out for my lost love, and I know what the raven says.

Classified

SUSANNA DONATO

a: a small advertisement grouped with others like it

My friend X and I tired of each other's company midway through a college summer, an ennui of classification—would we remain friends?—that eventually placed us in a café beneath a downtown viaduct, nursing a plastic carafe of cappuccino.

We waited for a stranger with whom we'd had one phone conversation. His voice was softly sibilant, his confidence assumed and effete. My pulse skittered in my throat. We'd listed our personal ad under "Friendship," but one could hope for more.

"How will I know you?" he'd asked. With a hand muffling the mouthpiece, we conferred and decided on the bowling pin that now wobbled on the varnished table, a gleaming odalisque with pale cracked skin, salvaged from a shuttered Brunswick Lanes.

He appeared amid the smoke, black garments swirling like ashes around a fireplace poker. Though he'd mentioned The Cure in his response to our personal ad, I hadn't anticipated his degree of commitment. He had bad teeth and an overbite. I considered whisking the bowling pin back into my bag, but his narrow right hand, weighed down with silver ankh rings, had already pulled out a chair.

Then something fragile in his eyes softened me.

b: arranged or assigned according to type, as in a caste system

X dubbed my new companion (for he became mine and not hers) Weird Brian. The name distinguished him from the normal Brians we knew, with his stringy black hair and the Dead Can Dance badge on his bag. We met him the summer X and I both planned to drop out but then didn't. For me, that first year, financial aid came through. The next year, I dropped out anyway when I realized I was middle class, Western, and crazy in a way that divided me irredeemably from my peers. Thus I classify myself as a dropout at two different points in time, both true and both imprecise.

When you're part of a group and then no longer part of it, the absence feels urgent, like waking from a dream of falling. You flail arms. I'd been a gothy teenager, then an Ivy League punk. Now I was a nineteen-year-old with an office job. I flailed when I looked at my receptionist costumes, not-black in my closet. Who had I been? Who was I now?

I took comfort in how others avoided eye contact or made way when Weird Brian and I walked down the street together. Each quirk I tolerated—his florid handwriting, his cigarette holder—restored me to what I considered my original self.

At one time, I'd rehearsed in the bathroom mirror so I could appear unimpressed when someone flourished their scars: puckered pink burns on translucent forearms, pills rattling in a purse, a ragged homemade piercing in a flared sunset of infection. I pretended I no longer believed that external scars equaled internal depth. After all, I'd left school when I realized that no careful shell could erase my internal mortification. I'd originally chosen goth culture because it gave me a classification, a place to be. Black clothes and black eyeliner, creepers and ankhs, permitted people to assess me and dismiss me at a glance, and empowered me to hate them for it. In this respect, Weird Brian reinstated a home I had lost.

c: sorted by the constituents of a substance (as ore)

He was several years older; maybe that was it. All of twenty-five, perhaps. He blurred our edges, masculine and feminine, into a kind of liberation. I can imagine how his body must have looked—white, wiry, a scar or two. But my memory can't arrange the components of his face. I can't remember if he was as tall as I was.

His affectations abashed me. Twice while I knew him, he changed his name from his mother's Anglo-Saxon commonplace to add the Greek for *life*, a flash of white in the darkness. First it was complicated; then he changed it to zzoe, easier to pronounce. *P. Revere's dad changed the family name for the same reason, from "Revoir,"* he wrote me. *". . . On account of the bumpkins."*

He made me feel loud, pushy, normal. He liked drugs as entryway to the subconscious; I considered them cheating. He had a GED; I'd quit Barnard. He read Kant on the bus to Boulder; I read Faulkner at cafés on my lunch break. Did psychedelics disarrange a brain or make you egalitarian?

I can't remember what caused him to ask, "Do you think you're an intellectual snob?" Accusation or clarification of similarity? I took a moment to consider his question. (If you have to think about it, the answer is yes.)

I said no.

d: withheld from general knowledge for reasons of security

Neither of us had a car. We stayed in touch via postal mail. He inked elaborately infrastructured, triangle-based cartoons. I returned philosophy and poems. For him, I exaggerated my surreal side, wanting to impress, to keep him close, or maybe curious if I could frighten him away.

We collaborated on a comic. I was words; he was images. We pretended we thought others would care about our pockmarked, fairy-tale world. We pretended not to know they might not care. We pretended not to care about their indifference.

From my other friends, I cloaked our relationship the way he cloaked his body. *Oh, we're working on art that day,* I'd say, or *I've got to get back to Weird Brian about our book.*

e: organized by degree

Once he came to my place in the afternoon. Buses were safer during the day. Also, I wanted to avoid any connotations that might arise between us if he were in my apartment after dark. Seeing him again, I was struck by how he matched his artwork: not tall, built like a paperclip, all black lines and condescending wit. Against his slightness, I was self-conscious of my height, my swells, the breadth of my shoulders.

We never went to his house. He lived with his mom.

One night we met at the coffeehouse to write. A pinched nerve made me squirm with pain. But Weird Brian had suffered back problems himself. Affecting clinical cool, he tucked a lank lock behind his ear.

"For me, the remedy—" his eyes swam behind granny glasses—"was sex."

I gaped at him.

"I'd be willing to help—if you wanted to give it a try," he said.

I smiled thinly. How badly I wanted to be wanted. At twenty, I'd never been propositioned. I'd been pawed and pressured by boys I didn't want, and not-kissed by those I did. Was my desire to be desired measurable in ounces, degrees, leagues? I slept naked in an empty bed, as if pretending to be desirable would attract desire, and here he was.

The failing winter sun backlit his silhouette. Luminous red rimmed his Fu Manchu mustache as he pawed through his medieval magician's carryall, pretending he would find what he needed in its depths.

What decrees attraction? Who is permitted to desire? How gently his eyes skirted mine. His obliqueness moved me. I scanned my body to detect any response to his offer, but there was none.

My decorum mimicked his own. "Thank you, but I think I'll pass for now."

"Certainly." His fingers scrabbled inside his bag. "Certainly. Just keep it in mind."

I told him I would, and it's true. I never forgot he had offered.

f: assigned to a category

Weird Brian began renting a room from a sturdy blond hippie. Upstairs: parrots in the kitchen, caged quail in the yard, two chickens—Lucy and Ethel—on the back patio. In the basement, Weird Brian, in a room. Not really a room: the closet beneath the stairs. (At that moment, in England, JK Rowling was writing *Harry Potter*.)

He penned an invitation in spidery script. *She's permitted me to invite you to dinner. I'd be honored if you would attend.* He had no money. He didn't work.

We ate on a blanket on the living room floor. I've forgotten the menu, except the delicate quail eggs he'd obtained at some cost from the room-mate.

I'd inveigled a friend into coming, not only because I had no car to reach the suburbs. Weird Brian wished I'd come alone, I could tell. He turned his body at a not-impolite angle, his slightly stooped, black-clad back to my friend. He was trying to show me something, show me his home, that he could have one, that he could be human. Was this love? I scanned my emotional taxonomy; I couldn't classify him. Friend, more than friend, less. All and none. I couldn't bear to picture him without his black garments. I used him like a priest for my absolution. I required that he curtain his desires.

He wrote, *I keep seeing a woman who looks like you at Ground Zero*—a dance club in Boulder. *I can't think of what to say, only stare. She probably thinks I'm a pervert. Maybe I am, by now. I guess it's been a while.*

His pleading, categorical loneliness. I wanted him but did not desire him. He was a control group, between past and present. I was learning to decide what I wanted. How.

g: characterized by variation or contrast

If he had collected me, we could have dressed like Renaissance Festival refugees and listened to Sisters of Mercy twenty-four hours a day. Our skin and teeth would turn gray. In his closet, the walls painted black, we could have whiled away evenings with his pet rat, whose fur glowed luminescent under the black light.

If I'd told him we called him Weird Brian, he would have taken some delight in the word's archaic implications: the fates, the otherworldly, the eerie—traits to which he aspired.

I liked knowing the weird, I realized, but I no longer wanted to become it.

After that, we lost touch.

Four years later, when I ran into Weird Brian at a bookstore, his hair was scragglier, and a silver septum ring grazed his mustache. A woman in green velvet with black-dyed hair brushed imaginary crumbs from his sleeve. She was making excuses to touch him, I saw.

What pang is as bittersweet as the happiness of someone who offered themselves to us? Even if we declined. Especially then. The woman smirked as if I'd lost something.

My boyfriend, soon to be fiancé, was upstairs somewhere. A few promotions into a PR career, I was taking up the yoke of standard adulthood. I hesitated to reveal anything that would let Weird Brian define me. That day, I might have been wearing Docs, but during the week, I wore Ann Taylor. I didn't want him to know that I was sliding into the bourgeoisie, indistinguishable from any other twenty-something yuppie.

Biological classification sorts organisms according to observed similarities. Brian and I had seen only our likenesses until our taxonomy stretched too thin to sustain us. How strange that I'd found him in the first place by advertising for him. I'd bought public space to call out my loneliness. *I can't find anyone like me*, I'd cried, and he answered—but meeting again, it was almost as if we'd never had anything in common at all.

That day, I felt only relief as we parted. But sometimes, still, I see a stark, witty, India-ink drawing in a gallery, and I hope it's his. It never is.

Prophecy

ERIC TRAN

A patient says his god is almighty and most of the staff agrees with salvation and devotion. He says his god will crush us underfoot and we have nothing to say in return.

The next day he focuses on his healing god powers: He passes me in the hall, his hands in prayer: "Be blessed, not stressed."

*

I admit I've been thinking a lot about comic book heroes, their movie and TV adaptations. A sentient android constructs a family of robots. A young gay couple—one alien, one wizard, both nearly omnipotent—break up again and again. A detective with super strength has PTSD from an abusive relationship. I describe them to my best friend Z, who says of them, "poorly veiled metaphors for suffering."

*

Almost no titular superheroes have powers to heal others. If they do, it's one tooth in a smile, alongside others like spellcasting, flight, prophecy.

*

To cut to the chase: Z dies unexpectedly a month before I start residency. One night he texts me that he's having intractable vomiting and he's not asking for advice but I suggest ginger tea and then he's in the hospital and then he's gone.

*

The patient is only in his mid-twenties, but he's been hospitalized more times than my geriatric patients. In some ways it's frustrating how rote the story seems. In other ways, it's like returning to book I haven't figured out yet, with notes bled through, a spine cracked under my fingers.

*

In one comic series, a powerful lawyer develops an incurable neuro-degenerative disease. Western medicine tells her she is doomed and in response she frees her lover's former lover from prison because he is an alleged healer. When the healer's hands hovers over her body, we don't see heavenly light or seizure, but still she trembles and sobs, her mouth broken open in bliss and surrender.

*

In some religions, the laying-on of hands is the act of bestowing divine favor or healing through physical touch.

*

Z suffered from depression and anxiety. I only ever gently pushed him to go to therapy, to stay on medication, because I thought all he needed was a little more time.

*

Because the patient won't take medication and threatens staff, we consider injections, euphemistically *non-emergent forced medication*. He wanders the halls proselytizing our doom; we hope for improvement, like we can will it into being.

*

In psychiatry we call restraining someone by physical touch a *therapeutic hold*.

*

The day after the lawyer is healed, we see her argue down—downright bully—superhumans. After a day of victories, she opens the door to her light-filled apartment and finds the drawers emptied out, jewelry boxes like corpses on the floor, and her would-be savior gone.

*

I only know of one contemporary comic hero whose main ability is to heal. The first time he heals his skin turns gold, like he's wrapped in tinsel; the first time he kills his skin becomes a metallic black. Even when he reverts there's a black spot that moves around his body, always staying a little out of sight.

*

I've ordered forced injections before. One patient was just hours out of a meth binge and screamed that we might as well kill her. I imagined, again and again, all the details—the needle, the security, the screaming that would live in her nightmares.

The morning after her injection the patient woke up and poured milk into her bran flakes and told me she didn't remember anything.

*

Sometimes patients say, "You can't help me," and I think they're right. Most doctors I know didn't go into medicine because of the field's miracles; more often it's for the loved ones who died of cancer, pneumonia, suicide, whom medicine failed.

*

One of Z's favorite comic book characters cast spells by speaking them backward. Once, her enemies shot a hole through her voice box and to save herself she wrote *leaH em* with the ink of her own hot blood.

*

We finally decide to give the patient an injection, and the patient doesn't ask us what's going on but sits calmly on the bed. He faces the window, which in the mornings shows a line of mountains holding up the sun. He asks us to pray for him and a nurse holds his hand. *Dear heavenly father, please help us get well.*

*

doG pleh em, I ssim uoy os hcum.

Scars, Silence, and Dian Fossey

ANGIE CHUANG

My scar is about four and a half inches wide, across my very lower abdomen. It was carved into my flesh in the summer of 2006 by the scalpel of a skilled surgeon, who had calculated it was the least invasive, but safest, way to remove a large ovarian tumor that turned out to be borderline cancerous. I was thirty-three at the time. I had been single, and obsessively career-focused, when I had the surgery. Suddenly, I had to consider concepts that felt foreign to me: fertility and the importance of having children, the meaning of family and partnership.

I had loved my work as a newspaper reporter, and never more than when I was traveling on assignment. I had gone to Afghanistan, Vietnam, the hurricane-ravaged cities and rural towns of Louisiana after Katrina. A couple months after the surgery, I felt relieved to escape hospitals and medical decision-making to take a trip to Taiwan to visit family, one I had planned before the diagnosis. But my usual delighted anticipation at boarding an international flight was interrupted—by the airplane seat belt. It chafed, and the buckle sat heavy, in just the wrong place, reminding me of the rawness of the healing incision site for sixteen hours across the Pacific. The "low and tight across your lap" of flight-attendant safety lectures never felt innocuous to me again. As I squirmed in my seat and attempted to find relief by loosening the seat belt and tucking a rolled airline blanket between the buckle and my body, I started thinking of long-haul flying, and what it represented, as a struggle against my human frailty. The scar was the site of that testing, where cells would be remade in the image of forward motion or of stasis. I had always feared stasis more than I had feared pain.

*

After the interruptions and changes in my life and career spurred by tumor and surgery, it would take seven years before I would take another flight close to that long and far. As I settled in my seat for that May 2014 trip, I recalled the old tenderness of my body underneath my lap belt. This flight was even longer than the one to Taiwan, due to the many stops between Washington DC and Kigali, Rwanda. The scar had toughened up by then.

My good friends Laura and Patrick, who were married to each other, had been living in Kigali for about a year and had encouraged me to visit. They talked about genocide memorials, gorilla preserves, and Dian Fossey, whose work in Rwanda was credited for saving the endangered mountain-gorilla population. The idea of a journey that required a nearly twenty-four hours of flying and layovers, as well as a yellow fever card, stirred up the old traveler in me. By then, I was a journalism professor in Washington DC, traveling to more domestic conference hotels to present academic papers than to places that tested and excited me.

Stepping into the non-air-conditioned terminal of the Kigali airport felt like coming home to an older self. Patrick and Laura enthusiastically greeted me at the airport, ushering me and my luggage to their battered secondhand SUV. The ironies of tourism in Rwanda were not lost on me, even as I fed them with my dollars and presence. We paid admission to the genocide memorial to view piles of skulls, femurs, and humeri with machete slashes and bullet holes; I felt both horrified and strangely numb as I peered into a window built into a one of several mass graves and saw the neat rows of skeletons.

"Gorilla tourism" was a significantly larger contributor to the Rwandan economy than genocide commemoration. The rare mountain gorillas of Rwanda's Volcanoes National Park had proven to be more valuable alive than dead. Foreign tourists flocked to the park, paying many times an average Rwandan's monthly salary to be taken by local guides into the habitat. With this income, a battalion of gorilla trackers, trained locals with two-way radios, essentially became the primates' full-time bodyguards against poachers and habitat encroachment.

As we pulled up to the Hotel Muhabara on the outskirts of the park, signs advertised that the no-frills boarding house was where primatologist Dian Fossey—known by many via Sigourney Weaver's portrayal in *Gorillas in the Mist*—encamped when she came down from the mountains. The hotel bar offered a signature Dian Fossey cocktail, and guests could pay double the nightly rate if they want to stay in the room she typically had, decorated with mementos.

I learned later that Fossey herself would have turned over in her grave—also available for visits on a paid "Dian Fossey and Digit Tomb Hike Tour"—to know of these promotions. During her life, she vehemently opposed any tourist access to the gorillas she lived among and protected; it was not until she died that activists who worked with her paved the way for gorilla tourism.

Digit was Fossey's favorite gorilla, a semi-exiled male with whom she bonded, and who was later killed by poachers. She had asked to be buried next to him.

To critics both African and Western, Fossey was a white, privileged interloper who prized gorillas over human beings, especially Africans. She was known to be fierce and cruel not only to poachers but also to locals whom she suspected to be colluding with poachers or who wanted the land for pyrethrum farming or other needs they saw as economically necessary.

"I have no friends," Fossey once said. "The more that you learn about the dignity of the gorilla, the more you want to avoid people."

*

I had arrived and traveled in the country as a privileged outsider, neither African nor white, and the very kind of tourist Fossey would have abhorred. Even my contemplation of Fossey's life and words meant I was viewing the country through the lens of an American white woman. The more I interacted with Rwandans on my trip, the more I wondered if Fossey's outsized profile was by design. The romanticized Sigourney Weaver version of her with a signature cocktail and quaint hotel room was a relatable tourist attraction, yes—but the complex, raw-edged Fossey, who spoke to me more than the former, also served a purpose.

The Rwandans I met were eager to talk about Fossey, about the boon of gorilla tourism, the best varieties of Rwandan coffee, and the progress the country has made since the nineties. "The nineties," of course, was code for the 1994 genocide, which followed years of civil war. Guidebooks and my hosts were all quick to remind me not to ask Rwandans directly about the war or their ethnic identity, and that such topics were rarely publicly spoken of. So many Rwandans in their twenties or early thirties were orphans or had no living family. "My mother and father are not here," many a young person told me—the same way I had responded on our house phone as a latchkey kid. For Rwandans, it was a crisp and formal way to signal that the subject of family was closed for conversation.

Fossey was a popular figure for Rwandans because her story stood in for theirs. It was public, it was outwardly romantic, and it gave outsiders a place to enter Rwanda's story while allowing Rwandans to circumvent scrutiny. Journalist Philip Gourevitch wrote that in modern-day Rwanda, no conversations were had about the genocide—and yet every conversation was about it. The telling and retelling of Fossey's story, the invitation to know its palatable surface, or to excavate its broken, deeper layers, *was* the conversation I was having with Rwandans.

*

A couple weeks after the mass on my right ovary was discovered, I learned I would be acquiring my first surgical scar.

"I had hoped to do the surgery laparoscopically," my ob/gyn had said, "but the mass is too large. We're going to have to do a Pfannenstiel incision. It's a horizontal . . ."

"A C-section incision," I said. I had done my research. I didn't share the next thought that popped into my head and lodged itself there: *Well, check "stripper" off the list of possible future careers.*

Why was I thinking of this? Shouldn't I be focused on my health, the possibility of having cancer, of dying, or losing my fertility while I was still single and childless? Abstractions, all. While I had been focused on my reporting career, I had dated men who were inherently unavailable— much older, much younger, married, fellow commitmentphobes—in a not-entirely-subconscious ploy to avoid getting professionally derailed. Having to explain such an intimate scar, to utter the words "ovarian tumor" upon getting naked with a man for the first time: that felt tangible.

I sheepishly Googled "stripper Pfannenstiel scar." As I studied women with scars covered by elaborate tattoos—for example, a single yellow rose laid across the pubis, the thorny stem twisting with the gnarly contours of the scar—I felt little comfort. They were covering their scars, attempting them to erase them with ink.

Until then, my scars had been souvenirs of experience, acquired suddenly and unexpectedly. The barely visible line of hypertrophic tissue on my lower lip from a dog bite at age nine. Childhood chickenpox scars. Bike accidents and kitchen mishaps. I had never had the arguable luxury of being told what a scar would look like before it happened. Friends advised various remedies: Vitamin E, emu oil, silicon creams and patches. When one suggested a strategically placed tattoo, my face grew hot, but I couldn't bring myself to admit to my surreptitious Googling.

I learned that my tumor, though large, had been classified borderline cancerous. I wrestled with treatment options and a gauntlet of tests and doctors and second opinions, third opinions. I ultimately decided not to pursue the chemo and further surgery that some doctors recommended. With my left ovary intact, I was still preserving my options for motherhood, maybe, someday.

*

I'm generally a suggestible person, especially if a good story and research are involved. It might be my journalist's instincts to pursue all leads, or it may have been my desire to accommodate Rwandans' attempts to point me toward Fossey—whichever the case, I found myself Googling her story any time I got online in Rwanda and embarking on more searching and reading after I returned. Much had been written about her interactions with gorillas, with Digit especially. Yet I kept finding myself drawn to her complicated relationships with humans, especially men. They felt uncomfortably familiar.

Despite being portrayed as an obsessive loner, one who preferred the company of animals to humans, Fossey had profoundly meaningful friendships and love affairs. She had been engaged early in her life. However, her biographers tend to focus on a later, years-long relationship that took place in Rwanda, with Robert Campbell, a married *National Geographic* photographer, who came to document her work. They had an affair—she had two abortions—and those who knew her reported she was devastated when he left. "The part of her that yearned for a mate and children was shattered," according to a *Vanity Fair* article written in the wake of her 1985 murder. The story posits that post-affair, her growing isolation, sealed by the 1977 killing and mutilation of Digit, led her into an alcohol-fueled psychosis. She antagonized locals, including but not limited to poachers, and took unnecessary risks. These actions might have stoked the tensions that led to her own brutal and unsolved murder by machete.

Fossey had been drawn to Digit in the late 1960s because he was an orphaned male who never quite found his place amid the social dynamics of his group. As a "peripheral male," Fossey noted, Digit was more open to approaching human observers like herself, for play and curiosity.

Digit himself was physically scarred in a distinctive way. Fossey had bestowed his name because of an old injury that distorted and discolored the third finger of his right hand, causing it to appear pink and stuck in an extended position. It had likely been the result of his hand being caught in a trap intended for a smaller animal. In the attention that Fossey gave to describing Digit's scar in her writing, she seems to be saying something about herself, about us all: our wounds heal, but they continue to define us.

Over the years, she noted with sadness his increasing alienation from the group, and how Digit's personality seemed to become less social and lively as a result. Later, Fossey backpedaled, explaining that her pity had been "maudlin"—she had been temporarily blinded to the practical function of Digit's outsider status in gorilla society. In late 1976, she recalled, Digit, set apart from his group, confronted one of her trackers by standing upright and screaming, exposing his gums and canines. She stepped into view, which caused Digit to drop to all fours and rejoin his group. "Here," she wrote, "was graphic reconfirmation of the value of the peripheral silverback and other maturing males to serve as 'watch dogs.'"

A year later, Digit would be killed while serving as his group's watchdog, slain by poachers who hacked off his head and hands to sell for ashtrays and souvenirs; they received a grand total of twenty dollars, a figure that haunted Fossey for its relative insignificance. It's hard not to see the parallels between Digit and Fossey as lonely sentries, even if such an analogy would have likely earned Fossey's label of maudlin. I paused over the accounts of her "yearning for a mate and children"—was this a *Vanity Fair* romanticization? Or maybe that yearning was real, deeply rooted in Fossey, just as real as her conviction that she had to end the pregnancies because her lover was married, and she could not raise a child alone and maintain her commitment to the gorillas.

Even seven years after the cancer diagnosis, I was single and childless at age forty-one, and not as unhappy about it as society, members of my extended family, and some doctors were telling me I should have been. I had become used to being an observer, comfortable remaining a bit on the outside, as a journalist and a woman. Yet both Fossey and Digit paid the price for remaining on the lonely periphery, for their watchfulness while standing apart from their groups.

*

On the day for which Laura, Patrick, and I had prepurchased passes for hundreds of U.S. dollars to enter the preserve with guides in northern Rwanda, about one hundred others were with us. We were mostly North Americans and Europeans, waiting at dawn in the monsoon rain to be split into smaller groups to hike into the mountains and contact various gorilla groups. We hiked in the mountains for several wet, muddy hours. I strained against the high altitude and slippery footing but was grateful my backpack's waist strap did not chafe at my scar, and that my body felt strong, not fragile, as it had in the years following the surgery.

Given Fossey's anxiety about the scourges of tourism, I had expected more evidence that this land had been tamed into commercial submission—perhaps some cleared trails, signs, or bridges over the creeks that became raging rivers as the rain came down in unrelenting sheets. As Benson, the Rwandan guide nearest me, cleared brush with a machete, and occasionally turned around to offer me a hand when I struggled with the steeper and muddier stretches, I saw this was not the case.

At first, I had hesitated to accept Benson's help. I was embarrassed that I, in two-hundred-dollar Gore-Tex boots, was far less surefooted than the guide in his rubber galoshes. Then, we forded a thigh-high creek-turned-cascading-river, and I grasped the hands of the guides, who waded in and formed a human chain in lieu of a bridge, for dear life, grateful in a way that felt novel, like a relief. Benson was the last link of the chain, machete tucked into his belt as he helped each of our group of about ten up the last, most precarious, step onto the opposite riverbank. I gripped his hand firmly enough to feel the roughness of his palm, the surprising strength of his wiry arms, and the unwavering stability of those galosh soles on submerged rocks that felt like polished glass. I guessed at his age—late thirties, possibly forties—and imagined the experiences, the generational trauma, he might have spoken of if, shy of intermittent small talk, this silent exchange were not the only conversation we were having.

When I stepped safely on the opposite riverbank and let go of Benson's hand, I felt regret and guilt more real than I had in the week prior in Rwanda. I had traveled across the country with Laura and Patrick, for that time. I had been moved by the beauty of the country, the brutal history of the genocide, and the friendliness of the people I met, even as they skirted around references to the past. I had shed tears at the unflinchingly brutal exhibits in the genocide memorial and felt rage as I learned how the insidious project of Belgian colonization paved the way to civil war and genocide. But in truth, I had trouble grasping the enormity of those events on a visceral level. They still felt unreal, even as I looked at the machete notches slashed into human bones and skulls. I felt ashamed that my attempts at imagining, as sickening as they were, had failed.

After a few more hours of hiking, Laura, Patrick, and I found ourselves staring, rapt, at a huge silverback gorilla strutting, leaning on his cantaloupe-sized fists, before a tableau of smaller females, one of them suckling a baby. The white hairs on the male's coat that signaled his age and dominance were sprinkled like moonlight across his lower back. The clan looked back at us with limpid eyes, their lush fur impossibly black, their leathery faces so human, yet not.

Our guides moved us on to a younger silverback, a peripheral male, like Digit, alone in his own clearing, sitting on his haunches and stripping a branch for food. Compared to the hubbub of activity in the family group, the grunts and vocalizations that seemed like background noise once we got used to them, the lone silverback's space was still and quiet, save the sound of tearing bark and his soft breathing. I thought of Fossey's sadness for Digit, of her envisioning the family he might have had, if things had played out differently for him. I imagined, maudlinness be damned, that Fossey had seen the loss of her own parallel life, with Campbell, with children, when she looked at Digit, alone.

I made eye contact with the peripheral male. He stared back in a way the others had not, at once guileless and searching. I felt kinship and loneliness so unexpected in that moment that, for the first time in the hours that had preceded it, I forgot how soaked and weary my feet and body were. My face had been cold and wet for so long, it was not until I tasted salt and felt warmth that I understood my tears were mixing with the rain.

*

Contrary to my presurgery fears about a marred body (the stripper fixation), I came to see in time that the scar itself wasn't the problem. I had learned to live with it, even appreciate that my surgeon had taken care to make the incision appear organic to my body. The incision arced, like a landscape painter's shorthand for a seagull in flight, below the swell of flesh on my lower abdomen, the one that countless exercises had never budged.

Once I found my way back to the dating pool after surgery and recovery, the scar became a Rorschach test in intimate situations. I always preempted its revelation with a brief explanation: borderline cancer, surgery, still have the other ovary, technically still fertile (in case you were wondering). One man said, "Sorry you had to go through that," and then avoided looking at, asking about, or touching it. His silence and averted eyes became a metaphor for the rest of our short-lived relationship. Another asked, "Did it hurt?" To which I wanted to answer, "*Of course it fucking hurt,*" but mumbled a quiet "yeah" instead. A married man I became involved with said, before he could censor himself, "My wife has the same scar." The statement took root as a reminder of his daughter's birth by C-section— and that I was party to betraying his wife *and* their child.

As these encounters played out, I missed the physical pain that created my scar, the searing sensation of split flesh held together only by sutures and Steri-Strips, dulled but not erased by narcotics. As that clarifying focus had become diffuse a couple months after surgery, other more complicated, ambiguous aches took its place. In the end, what disturbed me the most was my inability to articulate what I'd want them to say when they first saw my scar.

I couldn't shake this cynicism when I went on a second date a couple weeks after returning from Rwanda. It felt trivial to be dating, even, after the trip. I had first met this man, the one with arresting blue eyes and an easy smile, in a coffee shop, days before I left for my trip. As we had exchanged information before parting that day, I mentioned I was leaving the country for a month. In spite of my doubts that I would ever see him again, we had stayed in contact.

Near the start of our second date, sitting on his housemate's overstuffed leather sofa, beers sweating in our hands, I decided to bring up my surgery and my scar. Why wait for the moment of intimate revelation, as I had with other men?

". . . So I have this scar, on my lower abdomen," I concluded. "And a missing ovary."

I told him about my surgery and diagnosis, and then braced myself for the usual reactions and questions.

"Me too," he said, surprising me. "Well, not the ovary, obviously. But I have a scar. And I'm missing a kidney."

He had been born with a Wilms tumor, a type of kidney cancer that usually develops in very young children. The scars from multiple surgeries grew with him, he said, and they crossed the entire lower half of his torso. He was lean, with an athlete's body I could see under his T-shirt, though it was not tight. He instinctively reached for the hem of his shirt as he described the scars.

Then he paused, rethought, and said quietly, "Maybe you'll see them later."

His "later" was the most lovely, and sensual, single word I had heard in a long time.

Later, we were each surprised by how negligible our scars seemed in physical reality. His were worn into his ribcage and abdomen as if he were a weathered oak that incorporated a lightning strike from four decades ago. When he first saw mine, he said, "That looks like part of your body," and paused. "Well—it *is*." He wasn't afraid to touch it like any other part of my body. As we spooned, I would find his hand resting in the slight groove it made on my torso, the way one's thumb might naturally find the indentation in a hand-thrown Japanese teacup.

Even then, I knew better than to believe that finding a similarly wounded partner would answer all the questions surviving an ovarian tumor had stirred. Cancer teaches the inhabitant of a treacherous body to distrust concepts like clean margins and remission; the skepticism carries over into the blurry boundaries of our lives and intimacies. Rwanda, Fossey, and Digit had shown me that not every conversation or revelation occurred in the direct, confessional ways American culture favored. Sometimes, proxies and metaphors made offerings to the negative space of silence. Sometimes, they were all we could bear, for the time being.

Nausea

LAYLA BENITEZ-JAMES

I wake to hagfish twisting into a dead whale; was this my last dream or first thought?
Hagfish belong to the Myxini family: skull but no vertebral column. I see the *Osedax* boneworms, zombie worms, bone eating, burrowing; they often enter and eviscerate the bodies of dead and dying sea creatures much larger than themselves.
They are known to devour their prey from the inside.

Nausea is a nonspecific symptom, which means that it has many possible causes.

After a decadent weekend in Madrid—beef, just slightly and worryingly pink, and pear salad, pulpo, steak, tuna, jamón, anchoa and boquerón toast, razor clams in coconut milk, rich mozzarella with truffles, duck dumplings, and fried fish—there is Monday; car sickness begins; I have known for sixteen days.
All meat is out, except boiled chicken; pesto seems horrible; leaves are horrible.
My own morning breath.
The sound of German.

In brief praise, nausea keeps me in the present moment—
It reteaches me each moment is change—anicca—I remember the two ten-day sessions of Vipassana meditation, learning impermanence (Pāli: अनिच्चा anicca; literally meaning inconstant). I remember the slow fade of that learning once I was back inside my life.

An alien perched in my throat with its long fingers reaching over my ears now decides what I will eat and what I will want.
It does not care what I loved before.
It does not care what I like.
It possesses me.

It does no good to remember what was once pleasing.
5:50 a.m.—three cranberries
6:40 a.m.—sips of strawberry smoothie
9:00 a.m.—oatmeal with cranberries and dates
1:00 p.m.—two tacos: egg and kale and mushroom, sour cream with drops of Valentina
6:30 p.m.—four dates
7:30 p.m.—Texas caviar
8:00 p.m.—avocado and knockoff SunChips

I struggle through mint tea and a green apple.

Nausea must have been part of Eve's punishment. Craving and aversion. Not just painful childbirth but desire for that which will cause her the pain. Because you *ate* from the tree, *eating* will cease to bring you pleasure.

Pudeur (French noun): a sense of shame or embarrassment, especially with regard to matters of a sexual or personal nature.

A dream returns: I feel a tickle on my shoulder—looking down I see an ant crawling there and brush it away—it happens a few times before I notice a little hole—ants are crawling in and out, and I realize I have a whole colony inside me—I am in public; I am too embarrassed to call for help. What would people think of me? That I am so dirty and careless that I let an entire ant colony move into my body? That I live in filth and eat in my bed? I am going to die, and I don't know if they will start biting me inside if I try to plug the hole. I'm afraid any doctor would just tell me I'm going to die and kill me more quickly. I wonder if I can pour anything into the hole if I make it bigger with something . . . What could I pour inside that would kill them but spare me?

It is our friends' due date and I'm woken at 6:35 a.m. by nausea; by 7:34 I'm eating dates and drinking sparkling water. Nothing is happening, they say.

I find Sartre's *Nausea*, and the old book smell, which was a favorite, makes me nauseous.
La Nausée: First mention on page 22, *A sort of nausea in the hands—* later—*The Nausea hasn't left me and I don't believe it will leave me for quite a while; but I am no longer putting up with it, it is no longer an illness or a passing fit: it is me.*

After getting blood drawn, a cotton ball is pressed to the tiny hole in my arm. Walking out, I keep it pressed tight, holding it there for a while, not wanting to get any smudges of rust on my yellow sweater. Soon the blood stops, and I keep thinking of throwing the cotton ball away and realize I cannot. I remember the tenth week and hearing it was now the size of a prune; the woman said, *if you cannot imagine a prune, imagine a cotton ball*—and the thought of throwing this little cotton ball with my own blood being held within it seems impossible—I keep it cradled in the crook of my arm until we are home.

Manual

AMY BOWERS

Fine lime dust hangs in the air and settles in my hair, nostrils, and mouth. The ceilings of our century-old house are dismantled room by room. We use crowbars, laughing and screaming as the chunks rain down on us, occasionally hitting our heads a little too hard. In a photo from that time, I smile: flushed and sweaty. Rocky, my Boston terrier, is held, curled into my waist. My stomach is perfectly round and hard.

We fill plastic grocery bags and bring them down two flights of stairs, out the tiny backyard and sneak them into the alley dumpster of the converted house apartments.

We are making a new room for a new person. This is the moment before. A tick in time that remains unadulterated, sealed up, like a shoebox diorama. I find myself returning there to look around

even now.

The work of memory collapses time. —W. Benjamin

1.

3 a.m. Rocky's nails click on the wooden floors disrupting my already fretful sleep. He moves from window to window, breathy and whining.

Hoisting myself out of bed, belly in hand, I peer outside into the darkness and sense agitated energy but cannot see clearly. I stumble down the hall into the solarium, and my eyes quickly cast down as the alley behind my house comes into focus.

Creeping dark figures are everywhere. Police cars line the streets; their lights are off. More arrive, so slowly. Officers walk, hands on holsters, so slowly.

The light from a Goya painting dresses the alley. *The Third of May, 1808*. In it, executioners are lined up anonymously, bodies angled at their victims, who, aglow, react emotively to the horror of the night.

Tonight's shadows contain officiated power.

Surrounded and backlit with pulsating, halogenation, I see a young man's figure silhouetted in a door frame. Light pours out and over from the tight space between his shoulder blades. I run my eyes down his arms, hanging, surprisingly relaxed, at his sides. My sight settles on his left hand, which looks like it could float up if not weighed down; its anchor is a gun.

2.

An eon is compressed into a few seconds; all I do is look. I look with every cell, twisted nerve, and sinew of myself until the doors close in on me.

3.
I breathe out, N O .

The letters of the word are tangible, they escape my mouth and settle in the torpid southern air.

A premonition unfolds the map of the next few moments, and I know. Damnit, I know. Time fast-forwards and then nauseatingly stops.

"Kill me," he commands to no one in particular.

"I see you," I telepathize. My mind narrows to only him; a communicative diode flows between us.

"I see you. I see what is happening."

He does not know how he is surrounded in the humid night, but I do. Like dermestid beetles, they scurry and click, self-assured but twitchy, convinced they are on the right side, convinced they have a skeleton to clean of its tissue.

Last week, I ran into him in the alley and complimented his puppy. He held its wiggle in his hands as I pushed my way to pet it. His smile was kind, and his eyes awkwardly avoided mine. I embarrassed (or annoyed) (or bored) him by talking to him.

Now he is gone. I wonder what happened to the dog.

4.

Some things around here just don't last.

The oak pollen rains for a solid week, staining everything ochre. Eyes and noses water and then a real downpour comes, and it is all over.

Azaleas and tabebuia color the neighborhood in magenta, the palest pink, and bright yellow. For a fortnight we think we are the luckiest people in the world to live amid such vibrancy.

Occasionally a house burns down or is ruined when a live oak falls on it in a storm. People like to blame the Spanish moss, saying it made the tree too heavy. But the truth is, the moss thrives on trees that are already weakened. And live oaks topple easily; despite their strong limbs, they have such shallow roots.

My Dualit toaster needs to be discarded. The timer stopped activating the heating coils. Now I have to plug it in to get it to heat up. After the bread is toasted, I have to unplug the machine before it burns. The coils just get hotter and hotter. A persistent threat of self-immolation exists on the toaster's part. All our cabinets wear dark half-moons of burned wood from when it sat underneath.

A dent in the stainless steel charms and shows that we like expensive things but treat them with an elegant insouciance.

When we first got the toaster, we polished it like a car. It sat on our counter as a sign of our imagined wealth.

I read the Amazon reviews to justify my purchase:

"Toast just tastes so much better in it, you know."

"It's really basic, no frills, just well-made machinery. Its manual operation allows you to check on the toast while you are making it."

"You can adjust the controls to whatever level of brown-ness you want."

It cost three hundred dollars.

5.
alley
back alley
right up your alley
don't get caught in a dark alley

Alleys are liminal.
A stasis between moments.
A speculative scrim onto which we project our fears, memories, and wishes.

As the World Trade Center towers fell, my university evacuated. Dazed students left, some running across the quad to the parking lot. Frantically calling on their cell phones or exchanging news, theories, concerns with each other. A wave of fast, blistering chatter carried me to my car.

I came home and walked my alley, numb and confused until my dog pulled me stomach-first onto the ground. I came home yowling, throwing myself on my back steps, knowing I must have hurt my baby.

Later, the alley became a safe and sheltered space, different than the "Good evening, Miss Pam!" front porch. My children learned to ride bikes on the uneven asphalt bordered by trash cans, dog poop, and power lines.

Our alleys were secret arteries that took us to the library, swim class, and friends' houses. And they offered up treasures as we scanned the refuse, bringing home golf clubs, a papasan chair, bowling balls, bad art, and even the minutes to the local lawn bowling club.

Once, we wrote poetry on vellum, cut it into leaf shapes, and hung it from our favorite trees.

6.

A tick bore itself into my eleven-year-old's thigh. Before I remove it, I pace around the house in a hyperventilating panic gathering supplies: pointy tweezers, cotton balls, antibiotic cream.

The tick is half burrowed into his long, skinny leg. It ate its way in. Its back legs look like it's furiously trying to swim right into him.

Stripped to his underwear, his knees are like tree knots that make my stomach twist each time I see them. Vulnerable and depending on me to navigate us out of this minor trauma, I never feel captain enough. And I am bitterly nostalgic for this moment already. Like the last time I held his hand.

My son has goosebumps and keeps twitching his thigh and butt muscle. He alternately laughs at the spectacle and yelps at the pain.

The tick and I fight for his skin, his blood.

7.

A chorus of bullets spray-pop into the air. The electric lines that stitch the neighborhood together start buzzing as if suddenly charged. Cicadas pause and then resume their incessant song.

Scrambling on my hands and knees up the stairs, I gasp and reach for words. Weird half-words slip from my mouth.

(This, the part that no one ever knew: the extreme fear and awkward, pregnant, desperation to stay safe. For the briefest moment, I thought a bullet would hit me as I stood in that window watching).

I gasp to my husband, "Nonotheyshothimfuckno."

Pulled from his doorway and rearranged, he loses blood in a dark stain spreading out from underneath. His melting life is lapped up by his cat, who emerged from his apartment.

Even after the cleanup, that stain remained for months. Subsequent tenants sat in plastic chairs over it until it faded.

8.

A tick is just an instant, a moment. Time passes in a series of ticks.

Tick,
tick,
tick, tick . . .

I want to crawl inside the ticks to feel the time with my hands and body. Maybe ticks are rooms with images rushing through like traffic. Or scents filling one's nose before dissipating.

I want to see how to stretch and condense and reorganize the ticks. They must be building blocks with their instruction manual written as they are handled.

9.

After a night of shaky hands holding hot cups of tea until they grew cold and nibbling toast, the police call me for an early morning interrogation.

They are three. I am not allowed to bring anyone in with me.

Words are put in my mouth over and over and over. They are flaccid and dry and choke me. I refuse and spit them out, over and over and over. Juttering in a subterranean room with the guilty, I am being consumed. Hinged mandibles bruise and tear and wear me down.

My ears still echo. From a faraway corner in my mind, I can hear the mother and brother as they arrive on the scene. The brother, spitting vitriol so incendiary I fear they would shoot him next. The mother bovinely yell-moaning makes me vomit. This is a sound I have never heard from a human.

This is what it means to be a mother.

I hold my stomach again and steady my breathing. Every second I am damaging my fetus, electrified bile is running through my veins, directly into her pumping heart.

She saw, too, the extermination of a young life. A few months later, she is born; she stares directly at me in a cogent and unsettling way. She saw. She knows the flash of what vibrates just below the skin, the ever-present possibility. Her innocence was lost while she still breathed water.

10.

Earlier in the year, in the apartment above the shooting, a schizophrenic named David paints swastikas all over the detached wooden garages that line the alley. He waves a gun around in the searing afternoon sunlight. He won't look you in the eye and refuses to respond to casual greetings. The police do not kill him. They know him and, more importantly, his father, who bought the apartment building and relocated him into our neighborhood.

"He's harmless," they say.

He kills himself a few years later.

11.

Within the week, two officers wide with weapons knock on my door. I refuse to let them inside and instead invite them to sit on my porch. They pull down "bless your heart" masks and explain they are victim advocates.

Apparently, I am the victim.

One hand rests on my stomach. The other, palm facing out, lobs their words like unending tennis balls.

I'm fine. I'm fine. No, thank you. I'm fine. It's okay. I'm fine. Goodbye.

I take their limp business card, "in case I need anything," walk back inside, lock the door and toss it in the trash.

12.

A round, black, and clunky knob manually lowers the bread into my toaster. The action is so direct, my heart sinks a little along with the bread. Like the quick catch of breath at the top of a roller coaster. The timer stops and I raise the toast quickly, trying to make it pop out of the slot in a little jump.

It is the anthesis of every digital tool in my life.

My toaster is pale yellow, almost too pale. It reminds me of Wordsworth's daffodils—a favorite of my children. On the coldest morning, it cheers and warms the room.

The lack of hot-buttered toast for breakfast is anomic, I am sure. So, in that way, this toaster might save us. Being sent into battle after a plate of warm toast steadies the warrior. Some mornings when I look at it, I really feel that way.

I am conditioned to perform my good intentions through savvy consumer purchases and skilled domesticity. I can transition my shopping into powerful social work: minimal engagement and maximum self-satisfaction.

I dream I am making toast for the world, buttering one slice at a time. And I always go to the crust's edge, offering full coverage. The salty melted butter pools, soaks in, and is so good. Like Jesus, I pass out toast to the crowds. People put down their guns and caustic language and eat toast together.

When I look up, smugly benevolent, I notice people's mouths are stained crimson. They keep talking and eating and holding out their hands for more. I stretch my arms to give out more toast only to notice I have buttered them all with blood. The bread soaked it up beautifully.

It's stupid, I know.

13.

I am shocked at how hard I have to pull. His skin stretches, and I am worried that the arachnid will break in two. It is far in; I think it must have been there in for a day or two. Stationed there, eating in a few millimeters at a time.

The horror stories I hear surrounding Lyme are severe. I tune them out.

Ixodid (hard) ticks take three hosts in their year-long lifecycle. What number is my son? Has the tick already taken blood from a chipmunk or deer?

I look and continue checking for the ring-shaped rash. A halo of red under his long striped underwear will mean doctor visits, tests, courses of drugs, and the hope that this fucker did not leave a pathogen deep and sleeping in my boy's body. I imagine it settling into his joints, still knobby and growing.

Secretly, there is something about this I love. I am called into action. I am relevant. I can solve the problem, organize solutions, carry the burden in ways that I feel slipping away daily. I hold on tight to the connection, even checking his thigh for longer than I need to. To extend my usefulness, my role.

But sleep is rattled. My guilt makes a bitter cocktail. Why did I let him wear the same clothes two days in a row? Why did I not insist he take a shower? Where is the cold weather to freeze these tiny transgressors to death?

"The problem," a friend casually tells me, "is not even the Lyme."

"It's the parasites that come in with the Lyme. They lie dormant for a while, in your blood, and then start reproducing and causing all sorts of havoc. They are just there, lying in wait. Can you imagine?"

No, I can't.

14.

On the fifth anniversary of the shooting, I am once again startle-woken. My eyes focus on a figure at the end of my bed, a shadowed man. I am immobilized; terror courses cold through me as I struggle to shake the weight from my body.

Then I recognize the hand, the way it rests at his side like Michelangelo's David. Familiarity calms me.

"I saw you," audibly beats out of his holy body. His hole-y body. He grows faint and is gone.

Finally.

Elementary Primer

MICHAEL DOWDY

A, dear daughter, when later this month you begin first grade, remember your letters and numbers, a delight or two, the words of others, the pain of mothers and brothers, all seared onto the pallbearer's atlas of your country like 10,000 crossroads.

Blacksburg, where I was born and lived for 24 years, where your beloved grandparents remain, where a college student—he'd been a hostile presence in the poetry workshop with Nikki Giovanni, the poet who penned a ferocious poem after the assassination of MLK 39 years earlier, the poet who knew rage when she saw it—murdered 32, including your Aunt R's best friend, a dancer, this 5 years before you were born, on a September 11, in New York City.

Columbine, where when I was living in Blacksburg, at the turn of one brutal century into another, working at the university whose name would be reduced 8 years later to the worst mass shooting on our atlas of infamy, 2 students gunned down 13 at their high school.
    Or,
Charleston, just down I-26 from where we live, in Columbia, where a white supremacist who was born in our city killed 9 Black parishioners—you've never been inside a church but I think you get me on the gravity—where the poet Nikky Finney wrote years before the shooting that the slaying of Black people was "regular just like summer come / and winter go."

Dayton, where the night before we dropped you off in the mountains for your first overnight camp, another white man took 9 lives, including his sister's, where his former classmates testified in the days after that he hated girls, like you, and women, like you may become.

El Paso, where two days before we left you at the sort of sleepaway camp I never dreamed of going to as a child a white supremacist drove 9 hours from Dallas and at a Walmart ended the lives of 22 Latinxs and Mexican nationals.

"**Fragment**: the little by little suddenly," wrote the French philosopher Maurice Blanchot in *The Writing of the Disaster*, Blanchot, who survived the Nazi concentration camps, who your father intones today as he considers how time can collapse, expand, and burst.

"**Gather** the fragments left over, so that nothing will be wasted," so says the Gospel of John, so says the book I haven't picked up in decades and won't now that I'm being urged to offer my prayers for the 22 in El Paso and the 9 in Dayton, the 3 murdered a week earlier at the Gilroy Garlic Festival by another white supremacist already, apparently, prayed into their graves. Gather the fragments, A, gather them and let them groan.

"**Home. Home. Hell**," wrote the poet Adrian C. Louis of Pine Ridge Reservation, his history-haunted home. Yuri Herrera ends his novel *Signs Preceding the End of the World* inside the final level of the Mexica (Aztec) underworld, if not hell exactly, then its kissing cousin. As you enter first grade, is there a better description of our country, your home, than "The Obsidian Place with No Windows or Holes for the Smoke"?

"**In** this rhythm, I am caught," Prometheus lamented, without thought of dead ends or exit ramps.

Juan Felipe Herrera, who in his memorial poem for the 9 Black men and women lost in Charleston admonished us, "when the blood comes down / do not ask if / it is your blood."

Key for your journey, no. 574. "Travels in North America," the poem Weldon Kees wrote in 1952, its "ragged map" of what would become your country, 60 years later, showing you:

Journeys are ways of marking out a distance,
Or dealing with the past, however ineffectually,
Or ways of searching for some new enclosure in this space
Between the oceans.

Know this, A: my journey will not be yours, nor will my oceans, which
are coming for you.

Las Vegas, where at a concert 58 died under a white man's reign of terror,
where when you were 5 the topography of the map of infamy gained in
altitude. "Look into the dark heart," the poet C. D. Wright implored us,
"and you will see what the dark eats other than your heart."

Muriel Rukeyser, whose words I return to more than any other's, whose
sentence "These roads will take you into your own country" resounds more
than 80 years after she typed them, Rukeyser, who wrote the phrase "a
landscape mirrored in these men." A, *your landscape mirrored in these men*.

"Never Again," like all action-worthy slogans, must be redeemed from
its dissembling speakers.

Orlando, where in the city you know only for Disney World, where your
mother and I refuse to go, where your grandparents took you for your
5th birthday, in the city the poet Sandra Simonds in her book *Orlando*
calls the city of "dented sun, dented hotels, shiny and sad, remote / as
money," where at a club called Pulse—you've never been inside a club
but I think in your dancing bones you get me on the gravity—49, most
of them LGBTQ+, were murdered by a man who'd learned to despise the
beautiful bodies inhaling and exhaling all around him.

Pittsburgh, where in a synagogue an anti-Semite white supremacist killed
12 at prayer, where my friend, the poet Mauricio Kilwein Guevara, who
grew up there, once wrote, "I say Captain / look at your river old Monon-
gahela / Even John the Baptist would not wade in that water." But wade
we must, without wetsuits or saviors.

Questions, A, dear daughter?

Ross Gay, who proclaims in *The Book of Delights*, "The laughing snort: among the most emphatic evidences of delight," because at the apex of your raucous jibe, play, and prance, your snort carries me for a moment one toe-tap into the world I want.

Sutherland Springs, Texas, in a church, 26.
   Or,
Stoneman Douglas, a school, 17.
   Or,
Santa Fe, Texas, in a school, 10.
   Or,
Sandy Hook, where in an elementary school 27 were slaughtered, 20 of them kindergarteners, by a young white man. The night after the shooting, at 2:00 a.m., our live-in super, another young white man, broke into our Brooklyn apartment, in a frenzy, presumably "triggered" by the massacre, demanding to touch your sleeping 3-month old body. Unarmed, in this country, what choice did we have?

Tremors and terrors you've gathered from your 6 years on this earth: Anne Frank, bruises, cages, dog bites, extinction, flags, global warming, Hansel and Gretel, iPhones, Jesus, karst caves, Lyme disease, moving trucks, Nazis, ovens, princesses and queens, race, scars, truffula trees, undertows, vomit, the Wall, exile, yourself, zzzs.

Underwear, of which The Coup's Boots Riley raps in "Wear Clean Draws," telling his daughter:

> Wear clean draws
> Every day
> 'Cause things may fall
> The wrong way
> You'll be lying there
> Waiting for the ambulance
> And your underwear
> Got holes and shit.

Know this, A: my wrong ways will not be yours, nor will my ambulance. Soon, the sirens may churn endlessly, like this summer's cicadas. The sirens, like summer, may come and never go.

Virginia Beach, where near your grandmother's childhood home 12 were killed by their coworker, another white man.

"**With** my harvesting stick I will stir the clouds," so declares the Tohono O'odham poet Ofelia Zepeda. *Tohono O'odham* means "Desert People," of the Sonora, near Tucson, where the Congresswoman Gabby Giffords survived a white gunman's bullets, on lands stolen by men like these murderer-men, men who look like your father. Desert poet, let the clouds burst, let them wash us away. Let them cleanse the wounded, whom I haven't counted here. Their caregivers, the mourners and undertakers, the dying planet's pallbearers, those bearers of gloom.

X, the unknown variable, the next crossroads to be branded on the map, the target I hallucinate on your back.

YETI coolers, which in our state of hunt clubs are all the rage among white men of shooting age. When I lop the *i* from the *Yeti*'s stinging tail, you're left with *yet*, a delightful word. *Yet* signals a turn, a clawing back, claiming ground from those who'd kill. You and I and your mother, on our only child island, joining an archipelago of *yet*, the word that portends the end of the sentence.

Z, the letter, doesn't appear once on the Wikipedia page "Mass shootings in the United States." Not a single word includes a Z. No place name. No given name, surname, or nickname. No endnote source. Z, the first letter of the country you and your comrades, the young, the zealous, the restless, the fed-up and relentless, must build on the ruins of the one you've been given. Dearest A, you must begin at the end.

The Punch

CHRISTOPHER LINFORTH

My run takes me from Hemingway's grave down to a bagel café and around the back of Ketchum's YMCA. The thin air in the Idaho valley slows my jog, renders the six-mile route a painful affair. On the path, the other side of the bridge, I come to a broad expanse of sandstone slabs, the jagged outcrop extending all the way down to the Big Wood River. Garter snakes sit coiled on the flat rocks in the late afternoon sun. A white-haired man looms over the gray snakes, whipping his winter-gloved hands at ghostly hisses. His fists jolt out erratically: combinations of off-kilter straights and wild uppercuts. By chance, he catches one snake flush on the side of its head. The serpent jerks against the rock then disappears into a shadowed crevice. As I dodge past the man, unable to process his motivation, I recall a time with my father back in England. At eight years old, I owned a pair of boxing gloves and felt the mystic power of the raw crimson synthetic leather. On that afternoon, I punched the exterior wall of my house, enjoying the thuds reverberating off the brick. When I raised my arms in the air, a meaty fist cracked my soft cheek. My father towered over my felled child-body. *I thought you were a fighter,* he said. He egged me to stand, to come at him, try my luck. I stayed down, watched my father sneer, light a cigarette, and swagger back into the house. Now, all these years later, I see this white-haired man, a wiry shard, a vessel of thin bone and worn muscle. I shout at him to stop. He continues to flail, his arms pinwheeling. I get up close and tap him on the shoulder. *Enough,* I say. The man swipes at a snake stuck on a chest-height ledge. I edge in front of him, feeling my fists bunch. His gray eyes avert mine; he spits in my face while cursing something incomprehensible. Then he backs off. I watch his retreat for a moment, make sure he is done. I wipe the spit from my face and start my run again, and I loop back to the cemetery. I kneel once more in front of Hemingway's grave, and I clear from the flat expanse of granite a few empty beer bottles and foreign coins, a love letter to Papa. I press my knuckles against the cold stone and think of how hard I would have to punch to break a man.

Intersectional Landscapes

KRISTINA GADDY

1.

Everything should mimic the horizon, follow the lines parallel to the earth, Frank Lloyd Wright thought. These horizontal lines "do the most to make the buildings belong to the ground," he says in *The Natural House*. These lines would evoke nature, would evoke beauty, would be pleasing to the eye.

Everything then, in his Usonian homes—affordable homes designed for the everyday man—would be horizontal. Or designed to make the eye see only the horizontal. The cypress-board siding: horizontal. The roof: flat and cantilevered. Windows and doors: placed together so they created a horizontal block. The windows just below the ceiling: long, creating a strip of light. Even the bricks could be manipulated to look like one strip of burned red. He wanted the horizontal mortar between the bricks deeply dug out, while the vertical mortar would remain flush with the brick and be colored red. The eyes see only the horizontal line, although the vertical remains.

2.

Erasure (a noun) and *erase* (a verb) come from the Latin *erasus*, the past participle of *eradere*, from *e-* + *radere*, "to scratch, scrape." To arrive at the brick pattern as Wright wanted it, a mason scraped away the sand, lime, and water mixture from between the bricks.

With a building, an act of erasure doesn't have to be so intentional. Simply stop taking care of a structure and the world will erase it. Wind will rip off siding. Rodents will gnaw on wood and insulation and wires. Rain will wash away the mortar between bricks. Nature leaves only a trace of the building's past life.

More dramatically, humans can scrape a building from a landscape. We can tear it down and make room for something new. The Virginia Department of Highways wanted to insert a highway through one Usonian home Frank Lloyd Wright designed. In the early 1960s, the house was only twenty years old, not historic, not worth saving.

3.

The owner of this Usonian home, Marjorie Leighey, felt differently. She saw a house that would become historic, that should remain. She negotiated with the National Trust for Historic Preservation to have the house dismantled from the Fairfax landscape and reconstructed in a small patch of woods on a former plantation near Mount Vernon.

Nearby stands the 1805 Woodlawn Mansion. The architect of this home was also famous: William Thornton, who designed the United States Capitol. But just as Wright didn't build the Usonian home, Thornton didn't build Woodlawn.

With history, an act of erasure can happen by removing people. Language provides an easy way to erase people. Today a tour guide at Woodlawn can say, "When the crops were harvested," and in 1817 a visitor to the estate could write, "The table was spread with double tablecloths. . . . The first cloth was removed. . . . Clean glasses were brought on. . . . Coffee and tea were sent around at eight." The passive voice denies the existence of the actors making the actions happen.

Active denial can also eliminate these lives. After a tour of a plantation in South Carolina, one woman left a bad review, stating, "We didn't come to hear a lecture on how the white people treated slaves, we came to get this history of a southern plantation and get a tour of the house and grounds." She wanted to scratch out the stories of the enslaved on these forced labor camps, leaving only what she thought was a pleasant story.

4.

And yet, even if we obscure and deny, the lives of the enslaved inhabit all parts of the Woodlawn property even if the places they lived in do not remain. Outside, enslaved people once cleared the land for the house and the farm. They harvested the crops and grew them and nurtured them. In the smokehouse, they built sweltering fires to cure meat on humid

Virginia days. Inside the house, they spread the table with tablecloths, removed dishes between courses and brought new ones, brewed the coffee and tea and served it, and cleaned up when everyone was done. What the reviewer of the South Carolina tour failed to realize is that the history of a southern plantation is a history of enslavement, a tour of the house and grounds cannot exist without a tour of forced labor.

Woodlawn functioned because of the enslaved men, women, and children who had to work, who could not leave this place. Even the physical structure of the house itself reveals the enslaved, if we look closely enough.

The bricks on this house are mortared in Flemish bond, a decorative brick pattern popular in early America. Enslaved men, and maybe boys, made these bricks by hand at Woodlawn. Sometimes, you can see a trace of the maker in the form of a fingerprint on the surface. They laid two bricks long ways, then one brick across, two bricks long ways, then one brick across, until they completed the entire structure. They wiped away the mortar between rows and between bricks, creating a pattern where vertical lines and horizontal lines intersect.

Frank Lloyd Wright's elimination of vertical lines was part of his philosophy on simplicity. But he didn't believe in simplicity for simplicity's sake. He looks to language as a reference point: "to eliminate expressive words in speaking or writing—words that intensity or vivify meaning—is not simplicity. Nor is similar elimination in architecture simplicity." Instead, that elimination "may be, and usually is, stupidity."

The root of *erase, eradere*, comes from Latin *rōdere*, "to gnaw, nibble, eat away." To scrape away the physical landscape of enslavement is to gnaw and eat away the truth of American history. The bricks, the lines, the fingerprints on pre-1865 buildings from Williamsburg to Baltimore to Albany to Virginia to Charleston to New Orleans can show how enslavement and forced labor were the economic system of the United States.

Rōdere may go back to Sanskrit *rádati*, "[someone] bites, gnaws, cuts, opens." What if we cut open the landscapes instead of nibbling away at them? What if we rip apart buildings to see what they really hold? What will we find? Will we be able to ignore it? What if in each building we enter, in each landscape we walk, we fully examine, accept, and reconcile the history behind it?

In a Flemish bond, we have horizontal and vertical lines and lives. We have the lives of the white enslavers and all the white people who benefited socially and economically from enslavement and white supremacy. We have the lives of the enslaved and free people of color, Black and Native, whose land and hands built the United States. In Flemish bond, we have intersections where mortar meets, and a fuller understanding of American history. When we erase the intersections, a dangerous optical illusion appears.

My Mother's Mother

DAVON LOEB

But when I imagine my mother's mother, all I can see is her tying an apron around her waist, and there is a dark smudge in the middle, like how some old White crowds stood watching the swinging knot around someone's neck that my mother's mother knew. And yet still, she soaked her hands—wrinkled and wet—the brined black leather in the blinking soapsuds, washing china and other plates from other places she would never go. And so what if she lumbered, and she stretched, and she cleaned, and wiped her tired brow because her shackled wrists could earn only enough change for the backseat ride on the bus back home?

And while cleaning those houses, polishing wood and dusting corners, she and the many other Black women she knew reminisced about some old promises. Someone long ago said that they'd all get a mule and forty acres. And the promise lingered—the notion that one day things would be better—that they'd finally have a leg up—start fresh, start new—endless possibilities. And this even motivated some of those women to scrub harder—dig deep into their souls, but my mother's mother would say— *you're promised nothing but your first name.* Maybe she was a pessimist—or maybe she just really considered things, like lineage. She considered how they used to be slaves, all of them, with no saving accounts, no trust funds, no land, no family money; rather, they were unshackled in 1865, and kicked in the ass—*get*, their masters said. And they got going, with some scraps of skin still on their backs.

Then again, that's just one chapter in the story, one narrative that belongs to a part of her, but not all of her. And it's important for me to tell you that her life is not to be defined by all that struggle. That there was beauty in her body and skin before it was bent and broken and blackened—that her skin was just skin before. And maybe there's irony in all of this, thinking back on her childhood, the whole southern home, her living life normal: breakfast at seven, lemonade, Sunday school, and the way love smelled like butter and bread around a dinner table. And I'm so ashamed by how surprised that makes me feel. How hard it is to imagine my mother's mother first and her color second. How it's so much quicker to assume what it meant to be her was what it meant to be Black, and nothing else—with no separation. Maybe it's instinctual to take on her narrative and tell you those prerequisite hardships: about inequality, discrimination, and what it might have meant to be Black back then. But to be honest, I don't know; she never told me. I just know her name, and her face, and the way she could tell me the past as if it were yesterday.

*

She was born in 1932. One of eight children—five brothers and three sisters. From a big family, but from a—*bigger family, God's family*, my mother's mother would say. So, when one of those sisters died as a baby, they knew it wasn't the end; they knew God had just brought her home sooner rather than later. And they buried that little baby somewhere out on their farm, and on the third day, the sun said *rise*—and flowers grew from out that grave—lilies and mayapples. It was a miracle, some proclaimed, and everyone believed it. Because back then, on any given Sunday, you could see optimism alive on those mornings—alive in the sun, alive in their eyes, how it was all the same. And they hummed the old hymns together, hands held, like a ladder—strong and bound and candid while walking to church. Nothing could stop them—not rains, nor winds, or any weather, because Sunday, family, and God was rightfully theirs—if nothing else was in America.

Even though they barely owned their own name, they did own a house, somewhere in rural Coy, Alabama. And no matter how bad things were for Black people in America, my mother's mother would say—*we still had our pride*. She'd say—*no matter if they told us we could drink from this, but couldn't drink from that—if we could sit there but not here—go to that school and not this one—we still had that house*. She said this with pride because ownership is undefined by race—because blood and sweat, no matter if one were Black or White—it would always be the same color. And that house that her family owned, her daddy built from the ground up. It was beautiful, by any standard. For he built it with callus and hammer—with muscle and brawn—and as she said—*with God in his belly, pushing his body, strengthening his heart—board by board, stretching from floor to wall to roof—an altar to his family.* My mother's mother would say that maybe some things were built better back then, things like family.

They owned that house outright but did not own the 160 acres of farmland. It was leased land. And the real owners said my mother's mother and her family could stay there as long as they wanted—forever and a day, but the land would never be theirs—for their skin would never change. They could build there, start their lives, marry, give birth, and die—but never, in any deed would it say—*this land is your land.* And in Coy, her family was one of the only Black families to actually own a home—to actually say *this is ours.*

Some people they knew, other lots from church, side-eyed, whispered about her family going back home, to *The Big House—where them White people let them stay.* And even White families across the street, coming out of their church, looked with envy in their eyes, knowing they were trotting back to a little shack. But my mother's mother and her family walked out of the church service with their heads high, in their Sunday best: elaborate prim pillbox hats, skinny ties, two-toned Oxfords, dresses like giant flowers, and their Bibles at their sides—shielding them from whatever wasn't God's will. And somebody, White or Black, probably said that they looked so much different than how they first arrived in the South.

*

The land surrounding the house was covered by hundreds of trees— thick, swollen, sturdy trees—trees that never warped under the hulking Alabama sun—trees whose boughs never broke—trees whose roots never loosened—trees that, for however many years, lived in testament to never change. They were imposing, and often frightened my mother's mother. As a child, she swore they watched her. She said there were crows in some; crows that crowded the branches and cawed viciously. And in other trees, when the wind blew, she thought she heard the willows lean in and whisper to each other, maybe saying—*we're finin' get ya*. And how some of the biggest trees, the ones that reached the far ends of the property, stood heavy and lopsided—as if still holding the weight of something—and that those were the trees that her daddy told her about—told my mother's mother what those trees were really for.

Apocalypse Logic

ELISSA WASHUTA

My great-great-great grandfather Tumalth, headman of the Cascades, was hanged by the U.S. Army in 1856, a year after signing the Kalapuya Treaty. He was accused of treason, but he was innocent. I feel like I should say I'm tired of writing this again. I am always writing that Tumalth was hanged a year after signing the Kalapuya Treaty. I am always writing that his daughters were taken to Fort Vancouver when the Cascade leaders were hanged. I am always writing about the resistance of the women who hung tough along the Columbia River for generations, even after the disruption of the systems of hunting, fishing, and gathering our family maintained for thousands of years. Actually, I'm not tired of writing about this, and I may never be, but sometimes when I say once more that *my great-great-great-grandfather was hanged by the U.S. government* I can feel someone thinking, *God, she's back on that.*

X

The last time I watched television, a man kept touching a screen with a red-and-blue map on it. After a while, I was nauseous and my whole body felt held up by metal rods. *Stop putting your hands on that map*, I wanted to tell him. I was in a huge room full of people who were booing, crying, and drinking heavily. *Termination*, I thought. *They are going to terminate my tribe. They are going to finish what they started.* I am certain that I was the only person in the whole venue—a concert space—thinking about tribal termination. I am always in this room and I am always lonely.

X

From 1953 to 1968, the U.S. government tried to wipe out some tribes by ending their relationships—withdrawing federal recognition of these tribes as sovereigns, ending the federal trust responsibility to those tribes, allowing land to be lost to non-Natives. The tribes terminated, for the most part, were those the U.S. government considered to be successful because of the wealth within their tribal lands: timber, oil, water, and so on. Terminating a tribe meant fully forsaking all treaty responsibilities to them.

X

In 1993 Donald Trump testified in front of the House Native American Affairs Subcommittee:

If you look, if you look at some of the reservations that you've approved, that you, sir, in your great wisdom have approved, I will tell you right now—they don't look like Indians to me. And they don't look like the Indians. . . . Now, maybe we say politically correct or not politically correct, they don't look like Indians to me, and they don't look like Indians to Indians.

Earlier that year, Trump had made efforts to partner with the Agua Caliente Band of the Cahuilla Indians as manager of their proposed casino near Palm Springs. The tribe declined.

In 2000 Donald Trump sent a gold-monogrammed letter to the Cowlitz Indian Tribe, of which I am an enrolled member. Hoping to partner with us, he toured our proposed casino site, which he said was the most incredible site he'd ever seen. In 2002 Trump submitted a proposal to partner with the tribe in developing the casino. The tribe declined.

In the letter he sent us in 2000, he wrote, "I want to assure you and all of the members of the Tribe that I do now, and always have, supported the sovereignty of Native Americans and their right to pursue all lawful opportunities."

Our casino will open in April. By then, Donald Trump will have a hand in determining what's lawful.

X

While I watched television and listened to the pundits talk about the man who loves revenge, I began having a panic attack that, as I write this, is eight days deep, the longest I can remember in my decade of PTSD, which I developed and cultivated as a response to multiple rapes, sexual assaults, threats of violence, and acts of stalking that accumulated over the years. For me, a panic attack is dread made physical, an embodied trauma response: nausea, insomnia, a pounding heart, headaches. My psychiatrist said my triggers are many because I went years without PTSD treatment.

In *The Beginning and End of Rape*, Sarah Deer writes, "Colonization and colonizing institutions use tactics that are no different from those of sexual perpetrators, including deceit, manipulation, humiliation, and physical force."

I watched the man touch his hand to the map and knew what my body was trying to tell me: the sexual violence against my body has been carried out in response the settler state's instructions to its white men, and now the instructions would be delivered clearly, from behind no screen. Maybe my triggers are many because to live in the United States of America is to wake up every day inside an abuser.

X

Boston is the Chinuk Wawa word for "white" (adj.) or "white person" (n.).
Boston-tilixam also means "white person" or "white people."
Siwash is the white-people word for "savage Indian" (n.).
I saw the word *siwash* attached to a photo embedded in a wall in a park in the Seattle suburbs.
I know only a few words in Chinuk Wawa:
Mahsie is "thank you."
Klahowya is "hello."

Some people say Chinuk Wawa, also known as Chinook jargon, isn't a real language. This, I think, is because, before the boston-tilixam had us speak English, the jargon was the assemblage of words we used to talk to each other, all up and down the coast.

X

A few days after the last time I watched television, I went to a community response forum in my neighborhood. A line of people hugged the side of the building, waiting to enter. Two boston-tilixam asked the people in line behind me, "Is this the line to get in?" When they heard that it was, they went to the front of the line. Inside, a volunteer said that people who live north of the ship canal would meet in a gallery down the block; people south of the ship canal would stay here and would split into groups by neighborhood. A group of boston-tilixam didn't want to be split up. The volunteer assured them that it wasn't *mandatory* that they separate. The boston-tilixam, relieved, chose a group they could all agree upon.

X

Chief Tumalth's daughter Virginia Miller (my great-great-grandmother's sister) was photographed by Edward Curtis, a boston best known for his sepia-toned portraits of unsmiling Indians posed in their ceremonial dress. Curtis interviewed Virginia, who spoke through an interpreter about traditional Cascade life and her father's hanging. And she told Curtis this, presented here in his words:

An old man dreamed and announced that new people were coming, with new ways, and the Indians would die. He made them put coyote-skins over their shoulders and two by two, men in front and women behind, march in a circle, while he sang his song of prophecy. The old woman who told [Virginia] about this said it happened when she was a little girl. She took part in the dance, and laughed at the flapping tail of the skin on the girl in front of her, and the old man seized her by the wrist, flung her aside and said, "You will be the first to die." As it happened, she outlived all the others.

X

The United States has been a party to many treaties.

Some bind the United States to its allies: an armed attack on one member of the alliance is considered a threat to the other members, who agree to "act to meet the common danger."

Some are with other international sovereigns, settling all sorts of agreements.

Some are with tribes; all of these have been broken.

One is with my great-great-great-grandfather and a bunch of other men, some of whom were hanged for treason.

The United States did not enter into treaties with tribes in order to create alliances.

This feels like a logic game that I am too tired to play.

X

Now I see I'm inclined to write, again, about how my great-grandma gave birth to my grandmother with no help but from scissors and string because she didn't want any boston woman messing with her. Like I do in all my essays, I try to explain that she did this at a time when boston-tilixam were stealing Indian babies because it was the quickest and easiest way to turn Native people into boston-tilixam: turn their tongues before they take on an Indigenous language they'll have to unlearn, keep them sheared so there will be no braids to cut. I am alive because of the scissors and the string, because of the everyday resistance that led my great-grandmother to turn away the boston ladies who wanted to help her learn to do white-lady things like crochet.

I am most thoroughly colonized by the desire to have the boston-tilixam like me. I look like them, and I try to use this to say things that wouldn't be tolerated from someone who doesn't look like them. But sometimes my desire silences me. Sometimes it speaks so loudly that I can hardly hear the ancestors' instructions for surviving genocide.

X

I sleep less than before. I wake up before sunrise and research things I don't understand. The river where Edward Curtis photographed Virginia Miller with her canoe, the river that is home to salmon and smelt and steelhead, the river where my family lived for ten thousand years—I am forced to imagine it covered in oil. I learned about Environmental Impact Statements and tribal consultation ten years ago, when I was in an entry-level position with the USDA Natural Resources Conservation Service, making best practices flowcharts and compiling resource manuals, but I abandoned that to become a writer.

Boston-tilixam keep asking me, "What can we do?" and I explain that the Lower Columbia River Estuary—our tribal homeland—is threatened by a proposed oil terminal, methanol plant, and coal terminal that could bring major environmental disaster and undermine ongoing habitat restoration efforts. The Army Corps of Engineers is ignoring tribes' concerns despite active tribal involvement in the consultation process. The coal terminal's environmental impact statement says, "As it currently stands, the tribes exercise their treaty fishing rights in Zone 6, which is outside of the NEPA scope of analysis for this EIS." The focus here is narrow and fails to respond to concerns about coal train dust. This would be the largest coal export terminal in North America.

I tell my Facebook friends that the public comment period is still open. I wonder whether there will be a point at which direct action like the water protection at Standing Rock would be needed, but it's too early to know.

I am wedged inside a small window in the boston people's attention, and I am screaming.

X

In James Welch's novel *Winter in the Blood*, white men gather in a bar alongside the Native American narrator. "But you're mistaken—there aren't any goldeyes in this river. I've never even heard of goldeyes," one of the white men tells the (unnamed) narrator. Another one says, "There are pike in the reservoir south of town. Just the other day I caught a nice bunch." They continue to disagree. The narrator asks, "In the reservoir?"

I want to know whether he thinks there are fish in the river, or in the reservoir, or anywhere, but instead he studies the white men in suits and listens to them talk about the sunfish and the goldeyes and the "clarity of the water" until the subject changes.

X

In 1957 Celilo Falls, part of the Columbia River, near where my family is from, was the oldest continuously inhabited community in North America, with archaeological records dating Celilo village sites to eleven thousand years ago. This was once an important site for trade and fisheries, but the opening of the Dalles Dam created a reservoir that flooded Celilo Falls and Celilo Village to make Lake Celilo. Last year, the Army Corps of Engineers thought it might be neat to lower the water for a couple of weeks to reveal Celilo Falls again. Susan Guerin (Warm Springs) wrote of the idea, "My people can't return to Celilo Falls to fish. It won't mend the broken hearts of my family from whom the Celilo Falls were taken. The study will tear off wounds long scabbed-over, and for what; the benefit of spectators?"

X

I used to like to keep safety pins attached to my messenger bag because I used them to clean pepper out of my teeth when I was out of the house.
I used to drink water straight from the tap.
I used to have no idea what my blood quantum was because nobody had ever thought to tell me something like that.

I began to carry floss.
I began to drink from cups.
I began to tell people my blood quantum when they asked, even when I didn't want to.

Somewhere, someone wearing a safety pin on her jacket is saying to someone else, *I'm so sorry for what your ancestors went through. May I ask, are you full Native?*

X

Boston man: white man.
Boston klootchman: white woman.
Many white fur traders, the first to whites to occupy the Lower Columbia River Plateau, were from the city of Boston.
Boston Illahee: The United States of America.

I am the descendant of Chief Tumalth of the Cascade people. The United States in which I live is the descendant of the Boston Illahee in which Tumalth was hanged under orders of Philip Sheridan—"The only good Indians I ever saw were dead"—and his daughters were taken by the military to Fort Vancouver.

Why I have used *boston* in this essay when I am talking about *white people*: for the white people who have already made up their minds about their own whiteness; for the white people who have forgotten that their whiteness is new here, that whiteness is not a phenotype but a way of relating; for the white people who don't believe me when I say that the most thorough answer to the question, "What can we do?" is, "Remove your settler state from this land and restore all governance to its forever stewards."

X

At the end of *Dances with Wolves*, Wind In His Hair shouts down to Lieutenant Dunbar from a cliff. The English subtitles read, "Do you see that you are my friend? Can you see that you will always be my friend?"

Because I don't want boston-tilixam to think I am a *nasty woman*—there is already a word for this when applied to Native women, a word we don't use, which is *squaw*—I want to explain that I love many boston-tilixam. Some are relatives; some I love so much that they are family to me; this has nothing to do with anything and I'm embarrassed that I even feel the need to say it. There are some boston-tilixam I don't like, but it's not because of their whiteness. Sometimes, it is about the things their whiteness motivates them to say and do, but none of that is really my business. The boston-tilixam are responsible for their own whiteness.

When the boston-tilixam came here, we traded at the river.

When they wanted our land, representatives of Boston Ilahee killed and relocated us.

I am descended from many boston-tilixam and I hold them inside my Indigenous body. I look like them. I have never said that I "walk in two worlds." I walk in the world in which Native nations welcomed visitors who responded by creating a government on our forever land whose mistreatment benefits them.

I don't know of a Chinuk Wawa word that translates exactly to *whiteness*, maybe because we experience it not as an abstract noun but as an action verb. None of us can choose the legacy we are born within, but all of us choose our alliances. We make and reinforce our commitments with every action.

The problem: that Indigeneity is viewed by the boston-tilixam as a burden while whiteness is not.
The result: some boston-tilixam pour energy into defending the wearing of safety pins.
The weather forecast for Standing Rock: blizzards.

X

"You're an old-timer," the narrator of *Winter in the Blood* says to a man he meets in a café. "Have you ever known this river to have fish in it?" The old man only says "Heh, heh," before he drops dead face-down into his oatmeal.

My students, at times, used to struggle with the fish motif. Maybe that happened because I couldn't guide them through seeing the river as symbol. How can we speak in metaphor when we need the river to be seen as literal?

X

For a while, I thought that because my work had me at energetic, physical, and emotional capacity, I was doing enough. I was writing, teaching, and informally educating. I changed my mind last week. I found more energy; it had been tucked into night hours I used to use for sleeping. I want to rest, to comfort myself, to meditate, to relax, to practice self-care, but I have a sick belly and a sunken face now. I would like to take a break from the work, but my nausea is telling me that I don't really have a choice. I can't let myself stop with small steps—a Facebook post, a retweet—when Native people are being teargassed, shot with rubber bullets, and threatened with live ammunition for doing the thing the ancestors are still, from within my body, from the other side of genocide, doing: committing to the river.

I want to hold the scissors. I want to tie tight, constricting knots with the string. I want to inhabit my body so fully that I know how to use it to protect the people and the land I love. Because I, too, am asking, *How can I help? What can I do?* And my ancestors tell me clearly, *Find us in your body and we will show you.*

X

When the Cascade leaders were hanged, some of the people went onto reservations and some remained in the homelands by the river. These people, like my family, were called renegades. To be a renegade is to have betrayed an alliance. Who is betrayed by the act of staying alive in the place where one has lived for ten thousand years?

Tumalth signed that treaty with his X that meant he and his fellows would *acknowledge their dependence on the government of the United States, and promise to be friendly with all the citizens thereof, and pledge themselves to commit no depredations on the property of such citizens.*

If my survival is a betrayal, make no mistake: I'll betray.

X

Tyee is "chief." *Tumtum* is "heart." *Klushkakwa* is not a word I can translate for you but you might hear me say it instead of *goodbye*, which is not what it means. Instead of *goodbye*, my mom says *toodle-oo* because saying *goodbye* isn't done, just like stirring batter counterclockwise, just like walking on the parts of the cemetery where there are graves that could cave in. If this doesn't make sense, don't think about it. Don't try to find explanations consistent with what might be called *logic*. Know that, if you are not from a postapocalyptic people, you may not be familiar with these strategies we use to survive.

If you are a boston, and when you hear me mention that my tribe's casino will open in April, your first impulse is to say it's a shame that we're doing that, try this instead: trust that we are doing what we believe will help us survive your nation. Instead, say it's a shame that we are still forced to react to the settler state built upon intentional efforts to kill us all.

X

During the summer of 1829, four-fifths of the Cascade people were killed by a white disease. The year before Tumalth signed the treaty, there were only eighty Cascade people left.

Apocalypse comes from an ancient Greek word that's supposed to mean "through the concealed."

Apocalypse has very little to do with the end of the world and everything to do with vision that sees the hidden, that dismantles the screen.

We have known for a long time that they intend to kill us. I have spent almost every moment of my life in an America that will not rest until I am either dead or turned boston klootchman. I make my way in an America that wants to assign me whiteness because that will mean they've exterminated the siwash they see in me.

It doesn't work that way and it never has.

Boston-tilixam ask me, *What can I do?* And I talk about the river.

Klushkakwa.

The Sound of Things Breaking

RU FREEMAN

In the towns that resemble nothing found in China we bought nothing that mattered except hope, a wish for daughters three, whole, coral-colored fish swimming among the blue bloated two in the us we once were: young and counting thirty-five dollars for a plate made in Taiwan in a factory brimmed in disregard and horror (Such poor taste! Such vapid renderings! *O Americans*), and then perhaps, those three periods, three dots, three beat pauses for effect, shaken heads.

Though we weren't, not then, for me, not now; I am not never was never will be as I have tried to seem—American—all these years of our lives stitched together in clumsy denial and occasional soliloquy, a cry we might have offered to each other but did not, choosing places to live, instead; this plant, not that, these friends, not those, as we moved from table to couch to bed and back again.

But then, O then, we treasured that one, that bowl-shaped hope, something that could hold, barely, fragile things, that curve of which we asked nothing except this: to depict what could be, what came to be, prized above the pottery hand-signed by its maker, not that, *this* one, *this* design, but one in an assembly of thousands shipped across seas for others like we wanted to be, thought we could be, simple, content, without price or artifice, no navels but those of our children to mind, knots tied, cords cut, little treasures, until now we reach this end, this precipice from which vantage I look at the broken blue shards falling from our firstborn daughter's hands, and begin to weep.

Self-Portrait in Apologies

SARAH EINSTEIN

Apology to an Ethically Inconsistent Friend

I'm sorry for picking the chicken out of the soup and telling you it was vegetarian. I was broke, and there wasn't anything else in the house to offer you. Besides, the last time I saw you, you were eating a cheeseburger and smoking a Marlboro.

Apology to Three Lovers from My Youth

I'm sorry for telling you I was a virgin that night in the back of your car. In your parents' basement. In my dorm room. As you may have guessed years ago, I wasn't.

Apology to the Boy Who Wasn't Quite Right

Even in the comparatively egalitarian world of first grade, it was social suicide to be seen with you on the playground. Until third grade, you were The Boy Our Parents Made Us Be Nice To, the one who was invited to birthday parties and sat in a corner alone, except when our mothers dragged you out of your chair to play some game they rigged so you could win.

It wasn't until we were almost ready for junior high that we realized you'd started to disappear. Your skin became translucent, like the skin of the dead goldfish floating at the top of a tank. You stopped talking and it seemed your parents kept you home more days than they allowed you to come to school. If we hadn't stopped noticing you years before, maybe it would have occurred to us that something was wrong, but I doubt it. We were safe children whose understanding of danger didn't extend beyond the laughing, swinging-too-high, running-too-fast sort.

At some point, you disappeared altogether. I vaguely remember thinking you were away at a boarding school for frighteningly smart children, but that may have been someone else. It wasn't until years later that we learned your scoutmaster had raped you almost daily. You weren't the only boy, of course, but for almost a decade you were his favorite. I like to believe that, had we known, we'd have rallied behind you and launched some sort of children's crusade to protect you. But, really, I'm certain we would have seen it as just one more reason to avoid you. I'm sorry.

Apology to a Friend with a Difficult Love Life

There wasn't someone at the door; it's just that you were going on and on about what a jerk your new boyfriend had turned out to be and I had better things to do. Had I listened to you for one more minute, I would have said, "Look, you're only dating him. If he's such a jerk, move on. You do this every time." Instead, I rang my own doorbell. I'm sorry.

The First Ghost Who Lingers, Waiting for an Apology

An old woman I didn't know—the grandmother of a friend—reached up toward the sound of my cough and muttered *who are you* and *where am I* as I witnessed the spectacle of her death. I'm sorry for intruding on a moment I had no right to attend.

Apology to a Man I No Longer Love

I'm sorry for hiding your favorite Leonard Cohen CD in the bottom of a box of tampons when we were dividing up our stuff after the breakup. I still have it, all these years later, and sometimes forget it wasn't a gift from you.

Apology to a Well-Meaning History Teacher

We were as cruel as thirteen-year-olds always are and didn't care that you'd escaped a world war by hiding in the dank basement of a strange family's house. We laughed at your accent but didn't listen to your stories about surviving on rotting apples and hard brown bread. We hid your glasses when you stepped out of the classroom, as you often did, to hike up the pants of your ill-fitting suits that shone at elbow, knee, and seat. We rearranged ourselves with utter disregard for your seating chart, knowing you could not tell if we had moved or if you had simply grown confused.

We laughed at everything except your small jokes meant to show that you, too, knew you'd grown a little pathetic and befuddled. Instead, we whispered "creepy old man" to one another behind our pink, uncalloused hands on which we'd inscribed the names of Renaissance artists, just in case there was a quiz.

Apology to Everyone in the Dress Row at the Metropolitan Opera, Seats 114–120, on October 13, 1995

When I woke up with a hacking cough and runny nose, I thought only, "These tickets cost a fortune" and "I'll never get another chance to see Placido Domingo sing Otello." I didn't think of how my constant sniffling and wheezing would ruin your evening. And, to the lady in seat 118, my particular apology for sneezing so emphatically that I caused you to drop your opera glasses onto a gentleman in the grand tier. I hope no one was hurt, and that you were able to retrieve them after the curtain fell. They looked expensive and heavy enough to raise a good-sized lump.

Apology to the Man I Hit with My "Peace in the Middle East" Protest Sign at the Antiwar Rally in DC on March 26, 1991

I didn't see you until after I felt your hand on my arm, pulling me out of the phalanx of marchers armed with placards and chanting our way down Pennsylvania Avenue. The people, united, will never be defeated and What do we want? Peace! When do we want it? Now! I was hopped up on adrenaline, a sense of moral certainty, and the bourbon Paula and I were passing between us to fight off the cold. I was marching, and then out of nowhere you were pulling me out of the ranks and shouting at me that I was to blame for every one of our soldiers who died because I was a goddamned bleeding-heart liberal. It scared me, and before I knew what I was doing I felt the thud of your skull against the two-by-four to which I'd stapled my peace sign. I am sorry for the bloody gash across your forehead, and for making you think you'd been proven right.

In This Story, Christmas Past Is the Second Ghost

The Peters boy died on Christmas Eve in 1977, his head in our yard, his body still in his brand new convertible, the top down in spite of the snow.

The drunk who hit him was yelling "You cut me off, you little shit" at the dead boy. I watched for a while from my bedroom, the scene strobing off and on with the blinking Christmas lights that framed my window, and then went back to bed.

What I remember most about that Christmas is the Major League Baseball pinball machine from my father, with real bumpers and a slot for the quarters it no longer needed. My brothers and I loved that pinball machine, and all the younger kids in the neighborhood spent Christmas Day at our house, trying for the high score and looking out the window at the torn up patch of lawn and the blood in the snow.

I'm sorry for being part of the crowd that stood away from your younger brother at the bus stop when school started again, shuffling my feet and looking down whenever he glanced at me from his lonely post by the stop sign.

Apology to a Great-Aunt, Who Got Just What She Expected From Me
I didn't really want the shoes; I had a little trunk full of Barbie shoes at home in my bedroom. I wouldn't have thought to steal them if you hadn't said to me, "You can play with these, but only as long as I am in the room. They belong to my daughter, and I wouldn't want anything to go missing." What else could I do, really, but pocket a pair of pink rubber mules and then insist I was too old for Barbie dolls, anyway?

Apology to the Armless Guy Who Used to Steal Panties
from the Laundromat in Tuscaloosa
After the second time, Putt and I started washing our panties and bras in the sinks of the dorm bathroom. We should have told you, when you rushed for our dryers, that all you'd find were T-shirts and socks, but we were afraid that if we spoke to you, you'd speak back to us, and then we would have to know you. And we were too young and too skittish to know an armless man who stole panties from the laundromat. I don't regret foiling your theft, but for thinking of you as less than a person, I'm sorry.

Apology to the Man Whose Woods We Burned Down

We were fourteen years old and brave in that stupid teenage way, learning to smoke and flicking lit matches into a wet pile of leaves in the woods behind your house. Fifteen minutes later, we were back in Donna's room, pretending to only then be getting up for the day, and heard sirens wailing closer and closer until they Dopplered past her house. The street was a dead end; they could only be going to the woods. We yawned in our little-girl pajamas and asked her mother what was going on. "Oh, some vagrants caught the woods on fire," she said. We asked for pancakes and plopped down in front of the television, laughing in that stoned teenage way as we watched *Scooby-Doo*, worried about getting caught but not about whether or not we had done something wrong.

Both you and Donna are dead, so maybe there isn't any point in apologizing. Still, I wish you could see the hillside now. With the pine all burned away, it has become a Georgia O'Keeffe explosion of pastel mountain laurel; in the spring, it stands out among the scraggly evergreens like a swath of virgin-pink lipstick.

The Third Ghost, Because in Literature There Are Always Three Ghosts

I met Great-Aunt Bethel, with her shriveled hands and sunken cheeks, in a nursing home when I was ten. She held my arm with surprising strength and begged, over and over again, "Please get me out of here." Finally, a nurse pried Bethel's fingers from around my wrist and took me outside to the horse they had stabled in the backyard. When Bethel died, a year later, my father said, "Well, it's not like anyone is going to cry over her grave," and we laughed. I'm sorry for not understanding that it wasn't a joke, and for laughing as if it were.

Apology to the Spider I Killed in the Bathtub,
Even Though I Tell People I Don't Kill Spiders

I was already naked, and you were bigger and more menacing than the simple brown house spiders that usually crawl down from the attic. I should have cupped you into a water glass and carried you safely to the garden, but you looked poisonous and I needed to get into the shower. You died because I overslept.

Apology to an Accidental Cannibal

We were docked for every sandwich we wasted, and it was only a minimum-wage job. So when I noticed that I had sliced off a thin layer of skin along the back edge of my right hand, and that the flesh and fatty tissue had fallen into your roast beef sandwich, I just slapped some American cheese over it and served it to you anyway. I am sorry for not telling you, and also for telling the other girls at the counter once you were safely seated and chomping away and I had a rag tied around my hand. You must have wondered why we kept looking at you, laughing, and then doing the stiff-legged zombie walk up and down the service area. "Brains," we said, "must eat brains. Or hand sandwiches."

Apology to the Birds We No Longer Feed

After you ate the sweet inside of the nuts and seeds, the rats gathered for the bitter husks.

Apology to My Martyred Forebears

When Christmas time rolls around, someone always says to me, "You know, you had family that died in the holocaust because of their faith. How do you think they'd feel if they saw you in this Mennonite church of yours? Don't you ever think of them?"

And I say, "Which holocaust was that? There are so many."

But, in truth, I think of you all the time. I picture you miserable in some version of the Hereafter that fits neither my old nor my new religion but looks something like a bus station in Poland in the late 1930s. You are dressed in drab damp coats and eating greasy food from rolled-up newspapers. Your eyes are tired, your bodies lumpen and dirty. You are the miserable dead, and I am your misery. I am sorry for my thousand betrayals. Forgive me.

Fragment

Strength

CASANDRA LÓPEZ

ʔahašìš kìpɨ kasiyexpeč kìpɨ kasiyexpeč hikasʰeqenus
hihusifɨminwaš kʼesʰuʔuškal /
Spirit they sing and sing they sing and sing it took
away her fear and made her strong.
—Sarah Biscarra Dilley

I thought myself too small for this world, a classroom, a field of green trees. Feet dangling from chair, stretching to the floor, reaching for some ground to land. I thought myself too big for a white wicker chair, a seatbelt, a mirror. What right to have to gaze upon myself, to let my fat spill out without boundaries, parts of myself always trying to escape? When my lover desires me I think there must be something wrong, some affliction connected to this desire.

I never thought myself unloved, only unloveable, desirable only despite my own excess. I thought myself unworthy of abandoned pleasure.

The first time I dominate a man I abandon myself into another self. My lover and I stumble into these other personas. He wants to bend to my will, a tree branch angled in my direction, willing to break at my command. I bloom fierce. My voice a quiet rise of heat. There is so much play here in this power, in this give and take. I think myself a beauty, and for a moment I catch a glimpse of myself in my lover's eyes and do not turn away.

I order my lover to his knees and I grow so tall the roof can't contain me. Most days I'm a *please and thank you* girl, an *I'm so sorry for my mere presence* type of girl, but right here I'm rooted strong.

Once upon a time I was a little girl with a lisp, an owner of a slippery and unwilling tongue. I kept my mouth closed to hide each word struggling in a pool of saliva. Once upon a time I was older and police were raiding my family home. They wanted to open so much. Permission is granted elsewhere. There was yellow crime scene tape, a white van, rushed in doors and cabinets open with their contents spilling out. DO NOT ENTER.

Once I abandoned Brother running into the night to survive Bullet. By which I mean, once there were two men, and six bullets that stole Brother's life. By which I mean, once I was a woman dry on the inside and a river on the outside.

Once upon a time I was not born, but my ancestors believed I would live. They held that belief in their breath even when the Spanish came and took and took and then the Americans came and took and took and then the Mormons. Words were written, then broken, names taken. Land is broken up, maps drawn cutting and cutting into what was once whole. How are these borders not scars? How can one not fracture in this America?

My lover wants me to break him, and I want to never again be broken.

Body Wash

Instructions on Surviving Homelessness

DOROTHY BENDEL

Directions

Shake well on a bus station floor your first night without a home.

Pour all your belongings into the backpack you once used for school and place it under your head.

Work yourself into a lather when the locked door rattles, when a deep voice curses at you from the other side, when he tells you what he will do to you when he gets inside.

Rinse with cold water from the bus station's bathroom sink before you move onto the next concrete floor.

Use all your strength to keep from falling apart daily.

Warning

Avoid direct contact with the man who offers you a ride to the downtown shelter. Even though you are not alone. Even though the ones you travel with have more weeks, months, years of this life under their belts than you do. Even though they carry themselves like they are stronger than concrete. You've been there when the sun sets, when the darkness stretches wide and you huddle together to make yourselves bigger than the night, big enough to fend off the other animals, and you see that these creatures are just kids who wish they had clean beds and open arms to go home to. You know that this man, bigger than your father, could grab you and take you somewhere even worse than these streets.

If contact occurs, rinse thoroughly with water so hot it sheds all the layers of who you once were and reveals someone new, someone you never thought you would be.

Ingredients

Too much alcohol; not enough time; violence; silence; the next paycheck; history; secrets; blind rage; and blind love.

Does not contain empathy.

Not suitable for sensitive skin.

Made with 100 percent organically grown fear.

Tested on children.

♻ Recycle after Use

Recycle the images of men cornering you at night, men asking if you need a date, men asking if you need a place to sleep for the night, men asking you just how old you are—*oh, wait, maybe don't tell me, I'd rather not know.* Recycle one day into the next, even decades later when you leave the shelter and you are invited to dinner parties and you remember you will never see those recycled kids again in the flesh but you still feel them like suds slinking over your body into the shower drain.

Informed Consent

ELIZABETH K. BROWN

FOR IRB USE ONLY

IRB ID #: ▇▇▇▇

APPROVAL DATE: 01/31/2000

INFORMED CONSENT DOCUMENT

Project Title: ▇▇▇▇▇▇▇▇▇▇▇▇▇▇▇▇▇

Research Team: ▇▇▇▇▇▇▇▇   ▇▇▇▇▇▇▇▇

▇▇▇▇▇▇▇▇   ▇▇▇▇▇▇▇▇▇

▇▇▇▇▇▇

> If you are the **parent or guardian** of a child under 18 years old who has been invited to be in this study, the word "you" in this document refers to your child. If you are a **teenager** reading this document because you have been invited to be in this study, the word "you" in this document refers to you. If you are **over 18 years old**, your parents will not have access to information regarding your willingness to participate in this study.[1]

This consent form provides important information about **what you will be asked to do** during this research study, about the **risks and benefits** of the study, and about **your rights** as a research subject.

---

1 It's the year 2000, and you are now thirteen years old. You will continue to participate in this study, roughly every other year, up through your thirtieth birthday, at which point you will request a copy of the materials used to administer this study. Some of these materials may give insight into your experience as a research subject.

- If you have any questions about or do not understand something in this document, you should ask the research team for more information.[2]
- You may discuss your participation with anyone you choose, such as family or friends.[3]
- Finally, do not agree to participate in this study unless the research team has answered your questions and you decide that you want to be part of the study.[4]

What Is the Purpose of This Study?

This is a research study. The purpose of this research study is to identify genes associated with drinking. Iowa is one of seven medical centers that the National Institute of Alcohol Abuse and Alcoholism (NIAAA) is funding to study families in which some family members have had "drinking problems."[5]

---

2   Though we will not be able to tell you why, specifically, you have been selected to participate in this research study, we will be able to help with directions to the site location—a small, brown, one-story building that looks identical to your dentist's office—over the phone. We will also be able to suggest a nearby restaurant where you can get a meal for less than the allotted five-dollar meal reimbursement for which you qualify as a result of your participation in this study. McDonald's is right up the street.

3   However, you may want to avoid bringing it up with your father. We understand he is suspicious of doctors, lawyers, bankers, insurance agents, telemarketers, professors, pharmacists, credit card companies, the government, etc. We are not certain how he feels about researchers, but it is likely he will feel threatened by our questions. Is it true that, in general, your father does not like questions?

4   You are desperate to be a part of things—at thirteen, this is normal—and so we're confident that you'll sign your name on the dotted line. You are practicing a new signature and you are eager to use it. We are aware you may not yet know the type of questions to ask here. Please note that the questions you will have later in life may be questions we will not be able to answer.

5   A note on "drinking problems": We understand that the Drug Abuse Resistance Education program (D.A.R.E.), adopted by millions of elementary and junior high schools across the country in the 1990s, actually worked for you. You even still remember some of the songs:

People can tell me what they've done / Maybe some things, maybe none / But people can't tell me what to do / I will choose a way that's true—for me // Don't want to fall into the trap / Don't want to be somebody's sap / I'm better than that! / I'll go to the mat! / To prove I can be . . . DRUG FREE! // Yeah, yeah. (Chorus, in a round) // D—I won't do Drugs / A—I won't have an Attitude / R—I will Respect myself / E—I will Educate me now.

How Long Will I Be in This Study?

If you agree to take part in this study, the interview, questionnaires, and brain wave tests will take between 4 and 6 hours. We plan to continue following study participants for at least 5 years.

Will I Be Paid for Participating?

You will be compensated for time and inconvenience involved in participating in this research in the amount of $75 for the interview, $75 for the brainwave test, and $50 for the blood or saliva sample.[6]

How Many People Will Participate in This Research Study?

Approximately 4,000 people will take part in this study at the University of Iowa. The total number of people who participate at all sites nationwide will be approximately 14,000.[7]

Not only have you chosen not to drink, but you are against all "drugs," including tobacco. In fifth grade, you were shown photos of a former professional baseball player dubbed "The Man without a Face." He had to have part of his tongue and jaw removed as a result of his snuff habit. You hadn't known that the pouch of Red Man your dad kept in his front shirt pocket was tobacco. ("You kids want some raisins?" he'd ask you and your sisters, a wad of "raisins" protruding from his lower lip, the bulge somewhat concealed by his thick beard.) For a while, you gave your dad the silent treatment. And then you began to look for patterns in the adults around you. You assumed the police officers and teachers leading the D.A.R.E. training didn't dip or smoke cigarettes or drink alcohol, and you decided right then that you'd rather end up more like them than your father. They were all so nice.

6   We know that your babysitting and lawn-mowing money doesn't add up very fast. You will likely save most of the two hundred dollars earned for participation in this study for your future, which is something you already spend a great deal of time thinking about.

7   By 2016 you will be one of more than 17,702 members of more than 2,255 families from around the United States who have agreed to be research subjects for this study. Thank you!

What Will Happen during This Study? *(Please initial on the line provided.)*

_____ Interview: We will conduct a 1- to 2-hour interview with you which will contain questions about drinking and experiences that can affect "drinking behavior."[8,9]

If necessary, we will conduct this interview over the phone, direct from your "early home environment."[10]

---

8   What is "drinking behavior"? We spent a lot of time trying to agree on a neutral term that would encompass the myriad expressions of individual drunken mistakes, spanning from despair (e.g., suicidal thoughts and/or attempts) to rage (e.g., physical abuse of loved ones) to pleasure (e.g., engaging in unprotected sex), etc. In the end, "drinking behavior" was chosen. Other terms considered included: "drinking conduct," "drinking performance," "drinking phenotypes," "drinking practices," "drinking habits," and "drinking customs."

9   While you are vaguely aware of the actual effects alcohol could, hypothetically, have on your life were you to partake, you are concretely aware of the effects alcohol has had on your mother's life. You—the fact that you exist—are proof of her "drinking behavior." You've done the math. Your maternal grandmother died young, after a brief battle with leukemia, in *July*. You were born the following *April*. When you're older, your mother will tell you she didn't realize she was pregnant for the first couple of months. You will wonder then how her "drinking habits" might have affected you, specifically, the development of your brain. Your mother's "coping mechanism" for all that grief was an impressive "drinking performance." She got married in *November* and gave you her mother's name. In about fifteen years, you will begin to feel guilty for being alive, for ruining her life. Try not to dwell on these feelings for long.

10   Because you are too young to make the trip to Iowa City on your own and your mother has her hands full with your younger brother and all his health problems, we will conduct the interview over the phone.

     Here's a scene: You sit in the corner opposite the basement door with the phone pressed to the side of your face. The phone has a long curly cord and is located in the center of your house, in a small cubby just off the hallway that connects the kitchen to the living room. This hallway is filled with tools and building materials: a circular saw and sawhorses and power drills, stacks of sheetrock and buckets of mud, and boxes of nails and screws in all shapes and sizes. Strewn about the tools are small piles of clothing and coats, dirty dishes, construction-paper craft projects, and letters from your teachers that are supposed to be signed and returned, but which will inevitably be lost. Your younger sisters and brother run circles around you, screaming and laughing and arguing over the remote control. The television is blasting *Roseanne*. Your mother is in the kitchen placing a tray of fish sticks in the oven. Your father is asleep, lying face-down in the middle of the floor in the hallway, still in his work clothes: grease-stained Wrangler jeans and a solid navy blue Hanes T-shirt with a front pocket, Redwing steel-toed boots still attached to his feet, his toes splayed out on the kitchen linoleum.

Many of these questions about drinking and experiences that can affect "drinking behavior" may not be applicable to you.[11] Next to these questions you may write N/A.[12] Other questions in the interview are concerned with your *moods* and *feelings*.[13]

_____ Questionnaires: We would like you to complete some or all of the several questionnaires, which measure (a) your early home environment; (b) levels of stress; (c) social support system; (d) how you might react in particular situations; (e) your attitudes about drinking; (f) relationship with your parents and family rules;[14] (g) coping skills;[15] and (h) important people in your life.

---

11 Abstaining from alcohol is only part of the equation, but we want to applaud you for your efforts, both now and in the future. However, we recognize that you are currently at work constructing the scaffolding for a lifelong practice of extreme self-control. Please note that this type of vigilance will serve you well in academic and athletic endeavors but not necessarily in social situations. As an adult, you may attempt to impose on others the self-restraint on which you will come to pride yourself. This will likely be especially true for the men in your life. A few of these men will have a "drinking practice" of their own.

12 While N/A may be the appropriate answer now, we anticipate that this will change as you grow.

13 Later in life, you will recognize that your participation in this research study was the closest thing to therapy you'd ever experienced, and for this you will be grateful.

14 While completing the over-the-phone interview from your "early home environment," you may experience a "level of stress" due to your "social support system." Just try to focus on the questions, on the sound of the researcher's voice coming through the hard, white plastic telephone receiver. While it is not our job to determine how you are "reacting in *this* particular situation," we might be taking notes. By now we've covered your "attitudes about drinking," and we understand that your "relationship with your parents" is somewhat reversed from what is typical. We have also observed that there isn't much in the way of "family rules." We're fairly certain you will create rules of your own to establish a sense of order for yourself. For example, strict rules around food and exercise may prove highly effective in providing relief from the feeling you have that nothing is within your control. We will be asking about this when you're a little older.

15 During the section about your "coping skills," the term <<suicide>> might come up. You have never talked about this word with anyone; it isn't talked about. This research study may prompt you to begin thinking about things you have not previously thought about. Merely thinking about the word <<suicide>> may cause you to feel as though you have done something wrong. (You have been trained to feel this way. This is not your fault. We have been notified of your father's oft-repeated rhetorical question: *What the hell is wrong with you?*) In response to the question, "Do you ever have thoughts of harming yourself or others?" it's okay to say, "No." We will not question you, or the question we hear in your voice.

NOTE: You may skip any questions in the interview or personality questionnaires that you do not want to answer.[16]

_____ Brainwave Tests: These tests (electroencephalograms, known as EEGS) involve no radiation or pain. You will sit in a comfortable chair in a private room for 2 to 3 hours and wear a cap to which wires are attached.[17] To improve the recording quality, a special paste will be applied to the scalp. This paste will wash out easily.[18]

During this portion of the study, you will be asked to respond to computer-generated stimuli by pressing a button.[19]

16 However, keep in mind that you cannot skip any parts of your life. We are sorry, but this is simply the hand you have been dealt. You do not get much of a choice when it comes to the "important people in your life." That will come later.

17 Here's another scene: You are sitting in a closet-like structure large enough for the chair, about three feet of legroom, and a small TV on a desk. The chair will be brown and hold the bodily odors of other "research subjects." You are young and so you do not yet have body odor like that—like stale bread and coffee breath and twice-worn slacks; your stink is that of a little girl who sweats when she is nervous, who picks her nose, who does not wash her hands often enough. In addition to the cap and wires, you are wearing a headset that covers your ears entirely. The room is completely dark except for the glow of the television. Even with a shrill beeping noise penetrating the fuzzy silence, you fall asleep within minutes. "Try to stay awake," we say to you through a speaker, startling you awake. For a few minutes, your heart pounds and you feel as if you've let us down, but soon your eyelids grow heavy again.

You are chronically sleep deprived, and this will go on for years, a decade, even longer. This has something to do with all the nighttime bedwetting and the device you are supposed to sleep on that buzzes whenever you have an accident. (We hear an echo: *What the hell is wrong with you?*) It may also have to do with nerves, and possibly the lack of "family rules." You and your siblings do not have a bedtime, for example. An additional complicating factor is that you and your siblings all sleep in the same bed with your mother, and who can sleep with limbs on top of limbs, a sweat-sticky mess of unwashed feet and tangled sheets?

18 You may wash your hair in the bathroom sink in the front waiting area. Towels will be provided, as well as Suave shampoo, the Vanilla Bean kind, which we know is your favorite.

19 For first portion of the test, you will hear a beep in the right or left ear of the headset and will be asked to click the button on the corresponding side of the Nintendo-like controller. The next portion of the test will involve rapid flashes of words on the screen. The word RED will flash in *red* letters, GREEN in *blue* letters, YELLOW in *red* letters, BLUE in *blue* letters, and so on. For each of these fraction-of-a-second flashes of words, you are to indicate whether the color and word matched (left button) or did not match (right button.) There are many, many tests of this sort, but after two hours you probably won't be able to remember much past the colors and the beeps.

_____ Neuropsychological Tests: You will be given 2 computerized tests that measure your ability to remember patterns, to plan ahead, and to respond accurately.[20] These tests will take about 20 minutes to complete.[21]

_____ Relatives: We may ask your immediate relatives (sisters, brothers, parents, spouse and children) to participate in this research study.[22]

_____ Return Visits: We may invite you to participate in an additional phase of this study. In this phase, we would invite participants to return every 2 years for the interview and brainwave test described above. To help us contact you in the future, we would like the names of 2 or 3 people who are likely to know where you are in 2 or 3 years.

    _____ I allow you to contact others for the purpose outlined above.

    _____ I do NOT allow you to contact others for the purpose outlined above.

Name	Phone Number
Name	Phone Number
Name	Phone Number

---

20 You will still be working on these skills by the time you are thirty. You will have certainly proven your ability to "plan ahead" at that point—and you will do this with gusto, even when it is not necessary. But as for your ability to "remember patterns" and "respond accurately," you will continue to show room for improvement. Take, for instance, all those older men you will date, or spend time with, whatever it is you will ultimately decide to call it. They will comprise a pattern in shades of gray. Will you be able to say that you "responded accurately" to their advances? We understand that it will be easy to keep on believing that these father-figure types are only trying to help. You may need the help, but not from them.

21 One of the tests is just like Tetris but with exploding jewels. Another consists of a bouncing ball and a platform you must move to strategically knock out bricks. The ball bounces back faster and faster until you are unable to keep up and it zooms past your tiny platform. While you complete these tests, we will sit in the office with you sipping pop from a Styrofoam cup and paging through loose files. Because we remain in the room, you might believe that we will be impressed if you score high, and so you do your very best. You have learned by now that high scores and good grades tend to get you the attention you crave from grown-ups. Please remember: your performance is not being graded, only recorded.

22 Your sisters and brothers have been invited to participate in this study as well. Your mother has not been invited. Your father has most likely declined.

What Are the Risks of This Study?

You may experience one or more of the risks indicated below from being in this study. In addition to these, there may be other unknown risks, or risks that we did not anticipate, associated with being in this study.

- *Inconvenience of the interviews and brainwave tests.*[23]

- *Loss of confidentiality of the information you give us.*[24]

- *Some of the questions are personal and could make you uncomfortable, but you do not have to answer any questions you do not want to answer.*[25]

- *Discomfort of the blood draw and possibility of bruising around the site of a blood draw.*[26]

---

23 Because you are young, you do not think of things in terms of being convenient or inconvenient. As for your mother, participating in this study may prove to be an inconvenience. After all, she will have to shuttle you, and possibly your siblings, to our offices in the family van and wait for you in the waiting area for hours.

24 Confidentiality is akin to keeping secrets or having privacy. We know you're good at keeping secrets. However, you are quite unfamiliar with the experience of privacy. A few examples:

Secrets: You don't mention it to your father when your mother buys you a new pair of basketball shoes or a new curling iron because you know it will make him yell at your mother. You aren't yet aware of how credit cards work but will later learn that your mother is responsible for paying the bills, and so your father never knows exactly where his money goes; he won't know this until it's all gone.

Privacy: You are used to your sisters and brother and mother and father walking into the bathroom to look for Vaseline, a Scrunchie, or ibuprofen while you are on the toilet; brushing your teeth while someone else is taking a shower; or streaking through the house nude after showering, searching for something to wear in the pile of laundry on the scratchy green recliner.

In fact, respecting the privacy of others is another area in which you will continue to demonstrate room for improvement for years to come. As an adult, your boyfriend will have to ask you to please stop entering the bathroom while he is on the toilet enjoying his morning bowel movement. You will leave the bathroom door open at all times. "But I just need to grab my tweezers," you'll protest, and he'll tell you that you have to wait. This may hurt your feelings; you may feel left out. Doesn't he love you? Doesn't he feel comfortable with you? Your therapist will be able to help you with this, as will the many self-help books that have been recommended to you by well-meaning friends.

25 Refraining from answering any such questions in your real life, outside of this study, might be defined as having boundaries. Setting healthy boundaries will likely prove to be a difficult practice for you. However, you may want to answer all of the questions we ask you. You will most likely not have another opportunity to talk about these things with anyone else for a very long time.

26 We understand that you've never been squeamish about needles. In fact, it's been reported that you never cry at all.

What Are the Benefits of This Study?

You will not benefit from being in this study. However, we hope that, in the future, other people might benefit from the data collected in this study.[27]

Your signature indicates that this research study has been explained to you, that your questions have been answered, and that you agree to take part in this study. Please retain a copy of this document for your records.[28]

_____   _____

(Signature)   (Date)

---

27 While we will not be contacting you to share the results of this study with you, you will be able to find information about it online. You may have ideas about how to improve the study: Why don't they ask about what sort of benefits you've found through psychotherapy or meditation? Why aren't there questions about sexual abuse? Please understand that there are limitations to the work that we do.

28 Every couple of years, you'll receive an email from one of us, with whom you will eventually be on a first-name basis. We will ask you about your life. What are you studying in graduate school? How are your sisters? How do you like Saint Louis? We will ask if you are interested in participating again. Most likely, you will be interested. You could still use the extra cash.

Thanks, but No

EMILY BRISSE

More cranberries, puréed pumpkins, French-style green beans with cream of mushroom soup, yams cut up, yams, yams, yams, and those small white mallows falling from some other heaven all landing right on top of the dinner table. So much unrest and unsaid and unheard conversation—tabled. So much *but I wanted to be this* and *you never let me do that*—tabled. All of our feet moving underneath the high-gloss teak, some tapping, some scrunched, some stretched out in the quiet hope that they might touch someone else's toe, that there might be two-way laughter moving the candle's flame back and forth. There is so much food here. So much that was made, stirred, poured, filled, baked, laid out like so many bits of bodies. We will eat and eat and eat—mashed potatoes, rolls slicked with butter, turkey breast, turkey wing, turkey leg—and we will sit back with our hands on our stomachs. We will claim we are—like the bird was—stuffed. We will groan and moan and drop down on wide couches as if we'd been shot. As if we were the used-up lead. How hot was it inside the shotgun barrel, we think. How hot was the chamber as the bullet went flying, as the boom was born, as the finger clicked *go*. But we don't talk about it. It would be too much to ask for.

Frida's Circle

DINTY W. MOORE

The women sit on stools for eight to ten hours a day scraping the sharp spines away with small knives. Many of them seem elderly. One is sound asleep, hunched on her stool, knife still clutched in her hand.

Mestizo women tend to be darker, more round-faced than other Mexicans here in San Miguel de Allende, and selling cactus fruit is often their main or only source of income. During my month-long stay, I have seen the cacti everywhere along the road from Guanajuato to San Miguel. This is painstaking work, or painful: the spines can stick in the soft flesh of your hand, break off, and take weeks to work themselves free.

*

One afternoon I stumble upon an exhibit in a local gallery, *The Heart of Frida*. Frida Kahlo's mother, Matilde Calderón y Gonzalez, was of primarily indigenous descent, and Frida knew more than her share about painful spines. The exhibit is filled with small notes tucked away into boxes, poems and doodles on odd slips of paper with titles like "Frida, the Crippled Eagle," and "Diego, the Fat Amphibian." The notes and pictures are overwhelmingly hopeless. In a poem titled "Wasting Away," she compares her crippled body to the ash of a cigarette, waiting for Diego to flick her off, into eternity.

*

During my time in Mexico, I am surrounded by images of Diego Rivera, a circular man I am coming to resemble in my middle age. Rivera consumed human flesh at least three times, he claimed, out of curiosity, feasting on cadavers purchased from the city morgue.

So the least I could do, I thought, was to consume the flesh of the cactus. This wasn't so hard in the end, when I learned that the little green slices in my morning eggs were in fact *nopales*, or prickly pear. I had been eating them all along, without knowing. Still, I wanted more, and earned odd looks from the women in the market when I asked for a bag of round *nopales* with the spines not yet removed.

*

Frida's crooked spine grew worse over the years, as did her love for Diego, as did Diego's legendary infidelities. Frida progressed from unsent letters ending with "Diego, my great love, I am here, I await you," to poems declaring that Diego the useless toad was good only for eating, "in tomato sauce." She had gone full circle. Looking in a mirror for years, painting her own picture, she found beauty in her stern face and dark eyes, until Diego's endless appetites made her hate what she saw.

*

In one of her late-life paintings, *The Circle*, Frida Kahlo depicts her own body, with missing limbs, and no head—a woman disintegrating. Not unbroken.

A few days before she died, she wrote in her diary: "I hope the exit is joyful—and I hope never to return."

A Catalog of Faith

KELSEY INOUYE

When I was seven years old and three thousand miles from home, my cousins cornered me in our hotel room and pleaded that I come to God. *We don't want to see you and the rest of the family in Hell.* I sat on my hands and pressed my thighs together, feet dangling from the edge of the bed, unable to speak.

You just need to have faith, they said.

*

For years, I tried to disappear. I worshiped measuring tapes and bathroom scales, memorized nutrition facts like scripture. I've read that fasting has long been linked to purity and protest—suffering for the sake of a larger, more ascetic goal. Just picture the waif: regal, detached, un-needing. Translucent skin and ripe, bruised bone. The body has a way of articulating the things we cannot say.

Even now, these are things that I fear: Creamy pasta sauces. The marbling in beef. Milkshakes and whipped cream. Salad dressings. Soft drinks and sugared teas. Full-size bags of potato chips, their glossy packaging and the salt on my tongue. Also: Loneliness. Hunger. Want.

*

Six weeks into my first semester of graduate school, a girl asked me to stay after class. In the empty corridor she told me a story about how she learned to love God after attempting suicide in Korea years before. *Will you let me pray for you?* she asked. *You don't have to believe.* She took my hand and closed her eyes. *Repeat after me*, she said.

Recently my therapist noted: *You're always on the borders, aren't you? Even the lips are boundaries. Keeping in. Keeping out.*

*

Once, I saw a documentary on Japanese chrysanthemums. The autumn flowers represent longevity, and women used to drape cotton over the blooms overnight and in the morning rubbed the dew on their skin. Today, chrysanthemums are grown with great care. The perfect flowers are unified clusters. *The petals should curl upwards from every direction, toward the center.* One gardener stroked each petal upward with a metal pin. Another sang to his blossoms in the afternoon. Others grafted hundreds of flowers onto a single stem. I read in a *New York Times* article: *It enjoys pain. . . . The more you manipulate them, the more they give.* In a different piece, a Japanese floriculturist observes: *Chrysanthemums reflect your very soul.*

I wonder what happens when the season is over, when the competitions and shows have come to an end. I imagine cascading blooms perched in autumn gardens, once twisted and lovingly sculpted, now wilting and brown-edged. In the wind, petals scatter like prayers.

Practical Magic

A Beginner's Grimoire

ROWAN McCANDLESS

In the Beginning

I was raised Catholic, in accordance with my mother's faith. My father came from a Baptist background, but I have no idea what, if anything, he believed in terms of religion. A spiritual child, I thought of following a religious vocation when I became an adult.

But I had many questions that I was not encouraged to ask. I prayed for piety, and for my early-formed cynicism to be forgiven.

Forgive me, Father, for I have sinned.

By the age of ten, the Catholic church had lost me. As much as I loved the ritual, I couldn't find a way to reconcile my sense of spirituality and justice with the elements of patriarchy, misogyny, and colonialism that permeated the religion. I couldn't accept a faith that had initially refused to marry my Black father and White mother.

Q.

Q. Why do women and girls have to cover their hair in church, but my brothers, father, and grandfather, all men—amen—don't have to?

Q. If the priests thought Mom and Dad's marriage was wrong, then doesn't that mean that I'm a mistake as well?

Q. How come I could become a nun, but I can't be a priest or the pope?

Q. How come there's a God but not a Goddess?

Q. Why does Eve carry all the blame for getting kicked out of Eden?

Q. Why should women be made to suffer in childbirth?

A. Good Lord, stop asking so many questions. Don't you know children should be seen and not heard?

Magic[k]

I had magical powers as a child—not like Hermione Granger or Samantha Stevens on *Bewitched*. I couldn't wave a magic wand, say a few magic words, or twitch my nose and POOF, there was a unicorn, juggling dishes, in the kitchen. No, mine was a practical magic, lacking in high jinks and general hilarity.

Magic: a sleight of hand, a performance trick, a source of entertainment, an illusion.
Magick: a belief system often othered and considered less than by Euro-colonial religious systems; the ability to effect change by working with the elements of nature, in concert with personal energy and focused desire.

I thought I could prevent catastrophes from happening—if I believed hard enough. It was a skill that came in handy because monsters lurked in the musty basement of my childhood home. They roamed the cobwebbed attic while vampires hovered at the threshold to my tiny bedroom, waiting to drain me dry. Perhaps the belief that I could prevent bad things from happening was my way of dealing with the lack of security and safety I experienced at home. A home in which my parents constantly screamed at one another and made me their confidante and scapegoat. A home in which my father had affairs, and one foot, always, in or out the door. A home in which my mother had regrets, and rage, and RX bottles.

Magical thinking:

- The belief that your thoughts, wishes, and desires directly influence the world around you.

- According to Jean Piaget, in the preoperational stage of cognitive development, children—ages two to seven—make use of magical thinking to understand and exercise control over their environment.

- A mental illness in adults.

- Culturally agreed-upon beliefs lacking scientific basis.

Perhaps it was my way of dealing with the lack of safety I felt, in a world in which four little African American girls, preparing for Sunday school in Birmingham, Alabama, could be murdered in a bomb blast at a Baptist church. Perhaps it was my way of dealing with the nightly news as I witnessed children—captured on camera—being beaten with firehoses, bitten by police attack dogs, cudgeled with police batons, called *nigger* and told, *go back to where you came from* and that civil rights were civil wrongs, as they marched for freedom, for segregation to end, and for Black lives to matter.

Surviving in this white, colonial, cis-heteropatriarchal society is a form of BLACK GIRL MAGICK:

god bless the child.

it was 10:22 a.m. when the blast occurred in that church basement down in birmingham, alabama. 10:22 a.m. when twelve sticks of dynamite planted by hate beneath an outside staircase of the sixteenth street baptist church exploded with an intensity that shook the ground and could be heard three blocks away. the blast scattered hopes and dreams and body parts. pages from song books and the bible floated in the air like autumn leaves and fell to the ground, to be covered in blood, chunks of concrete, shards of broken glass. all of the stained-glass windows were destroyed except for one. jesus with a group of children, his face shattered. suffer the little children to come unto me.

After my brothers and I survived church with Mom, we'd pile into the car with Dad—time for a leisurely Sunday drive followed by dinner at his parents'. To journey to their home we'd have to cross the Redwood Bridge.

We lived in a city crisscrossed by rivers and creeks, which meant bridges, which meant holes appearing in the middle of them (cue disaster movie sequence; cue terrifying, crumbling abyss; cue family car teetering on the edge, plummeting over the precipice, careening into the murky depths, a family trapped inside and drowning).

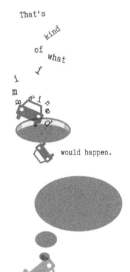

That's kind of what I imagine would happen.

And so, for my second magick trick, I learned to conjure an invisible protective bubble that would envelop our car, transporting us safe to the other side. My parents and brothers were oblivious to the danger. Was it because Mom and Dad were too busy fighting and my brothers too busy hiding that they had no cause for concern? Or was it because they were secure in the knowledge that I would do all that I could to save them?

I once dreamed of four baby rabbits hiding among the perennials in my cottage garden. The next morning, as I watered my garden, four baby rabbits sprung from the exact spot in my dream.

It's considered good luck for *rabbit, rabbit* to be your first words spoken on the first day of the month. It's been reported that the comedian Gilda Radner would say *bunny, bunny* instead of *rabbit, rabbit* to bring peace, love, and joy to the world.

Childhood Favorites

As a child, my favorite television show was *Bewitched*. Part of the attraction was that *Bewitched* was the only depiction of a "mixed-race" marriage on television. Granted, the union was between a witch and a mortal—but still. The television show resonated with me as the outlier offspring of a Black father and a White mother.

I never understood why Samantha tried so hard to conform to Darrin's narrow-minded, patriarchal definition of "respectable" womanhood, the role of "traditional house-wife," catering to her husband's every whim and desire. I never understood why she chose to deny her true self, her magick, just to please some man. Every week, I kept watching, hoping Samantha would come to her senses, twitch her nose, and blow that pop joint.

Favorite TV show:
   Bewitched

Favorite movie:
   The Wizard of Oz

Favorite Disney movie:
   *The Three Lives
   of Thomasina*

Favorite holiday:
   Halloween

Favorite book:
   Grimms' Fairy Tales

Favorite place(s) to be:
   as a child, hidden
   among the peonies,
   irises and bleeding
   hearts that bloomed in
   my mother's garden;
   walking next to the
   creek, among the
   towering oak and elm
   trees, along the path
   to the witch's hut in
   Kildonan Park.

"No matter the century, unruly
women are always witches."
—Roxane Gay

Mom always said that I was a
stubborn and willful child.
#MagicResistance

Rootwork

Rootwork: a form of African American Folk Magic. Also known as Conjure or Hoodoo in the southern United States. *Hoodoo* derived from the word *Juju*, meaning magic(k). A practice based on herbs, rocks, and stones, working with the elements of Nature and the ancestral spirits, to promote healing, spellcasting, and problem-solving. In order to pass on traditional teachings, Christianity was used as a way to mask rituals and spiritual beliefs from the motherland.

At one time, Webster's dictionary defined *Hoodoo* as:

n. 1. One who causes bad luck.

2. Same as voodoo.

3. Bad luck.

v. t. 1. To be a hoodoo to; to bring bad luck by occult influence; to bewitch

Ancestral grandmothers, across an ocean of tears, of blood, in chains, you brought your strength, your courage, your wisdom.

"For its part, Conjure spoke directly to the [en]slave[d]s' perceptions of powerlessness and danger by providing alternative—but largely symbolic—means for addressing suffering. The Conjuring tradition allowed practitioners to defend themselves from harm, to cure their ailments, and to achieve some conceptual measure of control over personal adversity."
—Yvonne Chireau, *Conjure and Christianity in the Nineteenth Century: Religious Elements in African American Magic*

La Madama is traditionally known as a spirit guide, providing assistance and advice in times of need and with daily affairs. She is the matriarch of home and hearth, knowledgeable in the ways of herbs and herbal medicine. Of those she cares for, La Madama is fiercely protective. She is the embodiment of the spirits of female slaves, the old Root workers and Conjure Women, healers and midwives and carries their wisdom. Treat her with respect and love.

I've collected Black Americana for years. When I find a vintage piece, I purchase the item and bring it home. I feel like I am offering the object as well as my ancestors, respite, solace and sanctuary.

Instructions for erecting a shrine to La Madama:

On a suitable surface, set down a white, orange, or red cloth. On top of this cloth place a doll or statue of La Madama. Offer a glass of fresh water, a vigil candle, and an offering. Suitable offerings include:

- A deck of playing cards
- Tobacco
- Cooked rice
- Brown sugar
- Liquor
- Molasses
- Home-cooked meals
- Black coffee
- Healing herbs
- Flowers

Catholic Folk Magic

The women in my mother's family were a superstitious lot. If a bird flew into the house, it was a harbinger of death. If a mirror broke, count on seven years' bad luck. Our futures, or lack thereof, were divined in the slew of tea leaves, swirling on the bottom of delicate teacups. The shapes formed by melting candle wax were a tool for divination. A key suspended from a cord, held over a pregnant woman's belly, could reveal the baby's gender based on the pendulum's direction of swing. Saints were called on and petitioned for all manner of things: to provide safety while driving, heal sickness, help sell property, encourage weight loss, improve Grandma's odds at the casino. None of this was incongruent with their Polish Catholic faith.

Petitioning Saint Joseph to Help with the Sale of Your Home:

Supplies needed:

- A statue of Saint Joseph
- A hand trowel
- Prayer to petition Saint Joseph

Directions:
Bury the statue of Saint Joseph upside down in your front garden, facing toward your home, and recite the following prayer. If you're not able to do this yourself, ask your realtor to oblige.

O, Saint Joseph, you who taught our Lord the carpenter's trade, and saw to it that he was always properly housed, hear my earnest plea. I want you to help me now as you helped your foster child Jesus, and as you have helped many others in the matter of housing. I wish to sell this [house/property] quickly, easily, and profitably, and I implore you to grant my wish by bringing me a good buyer, one who is eager, compliant, and honest, and by letting nothing impede the rapid conclusion of the sale. Dear Saint Joseph, I know you would do this for me out of the goodness of your heart and in your own good time, but my need is very great now and so I must make you hurry on my behalf. Saint Joseph, I am going to place you in a difficult position with your head in darkness and you will suffer as our Lord suffered, until this [house/property] is sold. Then, Saint Joseph, I swear before the cross and God Almighty, that I will redeem you and you will receive my gratitude and a place of honor in my home. Amen.

Divination with Tea Leaves

A thin wall divided the living room from the kitchen, where my aunt and grandmother, who were visiting from California, sat around a Formica-topped table with my mother. Through the open doorway, a globe light hung from the kitchen ceiling, casting a full moon eerie glow against the screen of our black and white television, from which cartoons and the Civil Rights Movement broadcasted daily in black and white.

I pretended to be asleep on the pullout sofa in our living room—attuned to their conversation—the mysteries of womanhood and marriage bandied about mostly in English and at times in Polish.

My father was out of town, on a run as a train engineer with the railroad. Living a block from the railroad tracks, there came the sound of the train whistle, comforting as a lullaby. I caught and released snippets of their kitchen conversation that held no meaning for me. At ten, the only thing I hoped to find out is when we would be going to the States to visit my grandparents, and more importantly Disneyland.

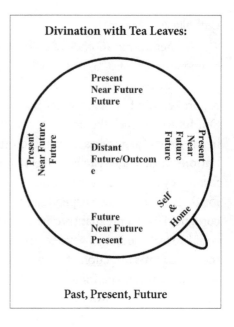

Divination with Tea Leaves:

Present
Near Future
Future

Present
Near Future
Future

Present
Near
Future
Future

Distant
Future/Outcome

Self
&
Home

Future
Near Future
Present

Past, Present, Future

"You're welcome to come with the kids," my grandmother eventually said. "But if you come to visit, *he* [meaning my father] can't come with you and you'll have to pretend that the kids are Spanish."

My body tensed as I waited for my mother to respond, to say something, anything in protest against my grandmother's demands. There was the push back of a chair against the linoleum floor. And then silence.

My mother's figure was captured on the TV screen as she stood over the kitchen sink and washed tea leaves from the bottom of delicate cups made from bone china. No need for further divination. At the age of ten, I understood we would never visit my mother's relatives in the States.

On Ritual

A ritual can be that first cup of coffee in the morning, the one you swear your survival depends upon. It can be a prayer, a blessing, a sacrament; the brushstroke of fingertips, the sign of a cross made forehead to heart, left shoulder to right. A ritual can be the flesh of defrosted cod, coated in cornmeal, fried in a pan, and served with canned green beans, mashed potatoes, and plenty of Our Fathers at Friday dinners. It can be the waft of frankincense and myrrh from the censor. Words spoken by men in a dead language, words imbued with the power to transform wine into blood, bread into flesh. It can be a wafer balanced on the tip of your tongue, a wafer swallowed whole, filling a spiritual emptiness with purity and goodness.

Protection Rituals during Sleep:

Freshen nightly:

Water: Fill a small glass with water and leave next to your bedside table at night. The water will trap negative energy. Never drink this water. Come morning discard it outside.

Freshen weekly:

Salt: Lightly sprinkle black or rock salt on your mattress, as well as beneath where your pillow will rest.

Rosemary: Place a sprig of rosemary in each corner of your bedroom to deter unwelcome spirits.

Ritual can be the casting of circles and spells, Rootwork and Conjure, the celebration of Sabbats and Esbats, goddesses and nature, the nurturance of all living things, respect for field and forest, mountain and stream, river and ocean, the air you breathe. Ritual can be the remembrance of ancestors, of who you are and have always been.

"Matthew, Mark, Luke, and John, bless the bed that I lay on. If I should die before I wake, I pray the Lord my soul to take."

I had a nightly bedtime ritual during my childhood. I would leap onto the mattress, in hopes of avoiding whatever monsters lurked beneath the bed waiting to grab hold of an ankle. I crafted a protective fort made from scratchy wool blankets. Touched my fingertips to eyelids, prayed and conjured guardian angels, tiny as Tinkerbell to circle overhead as I slept. And to hedge my bets, I always said my nightly prayers.

Premonition

I sat across from Sarah, the hospital chaplain, in a private room assigned for family. Halfway down the hall was the neonatal intensive care unit, where my granddaughter was receiving care. A floor above was the maternal intensive care unit, where my eldest daughter, Beth, spent her first nights after the delivery that had almost claimed her life. "How did you manage?" Sarah said. "Given what was happening in Calgary, how did you do that drive all the way from Winnipeg?"

I didn't tell Sarah about my premonition—the one I had a couple of weeks before leaving for Calgary; the image that flashed like a still from a waking nightmare of a crimson operating room, my daughter lying beneath carmine sheets, on a carnelian red table, blood everywhere. I didn't mention that I left, despite family and friends saying, "Relax. Beth's not due for weeks. You've got plenty of time."

Talisman

I told Sarah about the talisman I brought with me; a photograph, that I'd removed from my refrigerator and tucked on the dash, the morning I'd loaded my luggage and ninety-five-pound dog into the car and headed west out of Winnipeg. My daughters were posed in my garden, beside the front porch covered in clematis. They were surrounded by stocks of lamb's ear, delicate sprays of pink astilbe, variegated dogwoods, a Crimson Frost birch with fairy bells from last winter's solstice hanging from its branches. Over her summer outfit, Beth wears a black choir robe and skinny tie. Annabella, the youngest, is dressed in a black cape, over a blue T-shirt and skinny jeans with Harry-Potter-style glasses resting on the bridge of her nose. Raven sports similar eyewear and a black and white striped scarf wrapped around her neck. Next to Raven is Jesse, the husky mix she rescued as a puppy. Jesse flaunts a purple cape and a black witch's hat. My adult daughters carry smiles on their faces and broomsticks in their hands.

"It's my favorite photograph, of my favorite people, in one of my favorite places," I said to Sarah. I drew strength from that photograph, when, parked at a gas station in Brandon, my son-in-law's texts started coming.

Map data © Google 2019.

11:58 a.m.
Jason: Please pray, rushing to hospital from ultrasound. Baby's heartbeat has been low then high. We could be delivering today. Will update once we get to hospital.
Rowan: Please take care. I'm sending prayers!!!!!!!! I thought I'd be there on time. Send Beth my love and tell her Mama's on her way.

Drew courage as I drove the Trans-Canada Highway.

Map data © Google 2019.

Jason: Baby is coming and Beth is in the operating room now. Please pray.
Rowan: I just saw your texts. I was on the highway. Please send her my love and blessings for Beth and baby. I hate that I'm not there!!!

Jason: Baby's here . . . Baby's great. Such a cutie.
Rowan: How's baby? When will Beth be out of surgery?
Jason: She's still in the operating room. Lost lots of blood . . . but they're taking care of her.

Jason: Beth's finally stabilized and is going to be moved to ICU shortly. Still not out of the woods but this is appreciated news.
Rowan: You tell her mama's on the way. I absolutely hate not being there. I feel sick. All I want is for my baby to be okay. Driving into Regina.

Talisman:

A magical object providing protection against ill will or the supernatural, or bestowing aid such as good luck, good health, or power(s).

Drew determination as I focused on Beth, seven hours on the operating table, and the highway in front of me.

2:46 p.m.
Jason: Just got an update. She's losing too much blood. They're trying to stop the bleeding and are giving her transfusions. She's fighting but they say it's touch and go. So we need prayers for the bleeding to stop.
Rowan: Tell her mama's on her way. I hate not being there. I feel sick. All I want is for my baby to be okay. I'll text from Swift Current. Tell her I love her, and she's strong. So strong.

6:59 p.m.
Jason: Doctor came to see us and said she's slowly getting better. Thanks for your support and prayers throughout the day.

Fifteen hours I drove straight through to Calgary's Foothills Medical Centre; my fingertips touching that photograph like a talisman as I sent a litany of silent prayers into the universe, reminding my daughter that she comes from strong stock, and Mama's on her way. I channeled that love, that practical magic, until I was holding Beth's hand in the maternal intensive care unit, letting her know that I was there, and everything would be okay.

"She a wolf now, She say I ate the moon whole,
She say she full of brooms and weapons now."

—Falita Hicks, "Wolf"

Baby Gracie was discharged from the hospital long before her mother. Once Beth was home, after weeks in the hospital, the slow process of healing began. Female friends and family members gathered one evening to celebrate and honor Beth's entry into motherhood. We broke bread, drank wine, offered talismans that would be woven with yarn into a wall hanging to be placed in Gracie's bedroom. My gifts were birch and dogwood twig bundles, and dried flowers from my garden. To further symbolize our commitment, we sat in a circle and passed a ball of yarn from one person to another. Everyone was given the opportunity to share what Beth and Gracie meant to them, and how they would be there as part of a village of women, to guide, support, nurture and offer reassurance. A length of yarn was wrapped and tied around our wrists; bracelets to remind us of our solemn promise. They were to be worn until the yarn became worn and frayed and fell off on its own. As we celebrated Gracie's first birthday and Beth's first rebirth day, the bracelet around my wrist fell away to the floor.

How to Dry Herbs:

1. Harvest early in the morning to preserve essential oils.

2. Snip/pinch stalks.

3. Tie stems in bundles of twelve.

4. Hang upside down in a cool, dry place until dry.

Note: do not dry herbs in direct sunlight.

If saving seeds or flower heads, place the bundle in a paper bag before hanging upside down.

Depends on Who You Ask

SANDRA BEASLEY

I'd promised myself to be on I-35 South by noon, but my head kept nodding toward the steering wheel. The car rumbled along a strip marking the edge of the lane. I pulled into the parking lot of a small-town market. I tried to make it a practical stop—a chance to stock the fridge that awaited me—before realizing I had another six unrefrigerated hours to Wichita. Still, I'd been wandering Sunfresh for so long that I had to buy something. "A Kansas City souvenir," I said to the cashier. By the time I got to the car, a cup of coffee had sluiced through my system. I doubled back to the restrooms in the hardware half attached to the market. The other cashier asked, "How can I help you?" Embarrassed to admit why I'd walked back in, I reached for what cash I had in pocket. Not enough for a can of de-icer. That's when I remembered fussing at my husband, before leaving DC, for failing to keep our mat knife sharp. Perfect excuse.

She walked into our market and paced the aisles for an hour. She filled a basket with groceries, then returned them all to the shelves. Instead she bought a bottle of gin, came back for a pack of razor blades, and drove away. We never saw her again.

Against Fidelity

LESLIE JILL PATTERSON

Because, three years after our vows, I learned from a magazine that a woman can demonstrate her sexual zeal by penning a list of five sizzling moments she has shared with her husband—the list a gift to tuck in his briefcase or lunchbox—and I wasn't interested in lighting that match. Because I couldn't recall *five* fiery moments. Because later in the evening, while we washed dishes, I settled for reminding him about our first kiss: Did he remember his jaw popping? Me, straddling his lap? Us, lying on the floor? Because he replied, "You were stiff as a two-by-four. I thought, *This girl feels nothing.* I thought, *She's dead.*" Because as I swabbed the last pan dry then hung it on its rack, the red dishtowel done and thrown over my shoulder, he stared as if I owed him yet another apology. Because he added, as if his first comment wasn't definitive enough: "Honestly, I almost didn't ask you out again." Because I understood at that moment what people meant when they said, *Two sides to every story.* Because I understood at that moment that he and I didn't share a story at all.

Because flames begin with drought. Because they come with advanced warning—red flags issued by the National Weather Service when an upper-level low-pressure system kettles the wilderness beneath it, bringing dry storms to a boil, slinging lightning to the ground but evaporating rain before it can land. Because that summer, when I hid from our marriage in Colorado—a little R&R from *till death do us part* (though my husband would have used the letters AWOL instead)—high-alert flags gave notice everywhere. Because conditions didn't improve. Because, on top of a shallow winter snowpack, it rained only 1.31 inches, which failed to penetrate the canopy or seduce the forest floor. Because, by late June, the Animas River dropped to 172 cubic feet per second—600 cubic feet below "low." Because humidity levels plunged to 5 percent. Because temperatures seethed, record highs in the nineties, the sun wringing the trees dry. Because *alive* and *dead* were flip sides of the same song—the pines as desiccated as finished lumber at Home Depot. Because sometimes *dry* means "willing to burn."

Because Dr. Callahan, the celebrated oncological surgeon my ob-gyn recommended after finding the lump in my breast, couldn't see me for months. Because after sixty-one days squandered, I waited another two hours in her frigid office, wearing a bib, thin as a sheet of Bounty, for a shirt. Because when she finally made her entrance, this queen flattened me on the examination table, cranked my left arm above my head, patted my breast as if coating chicken with breadcrumbs, and said, "That's a lump, all right." Because, even then, she couldn't schedule the mammogram and ultrasound for two more weeks. Because after the radiologist finally took the films and told me, "Free and clear," after my father planted me a garden because I would live to see the harvest, after my husband hated him for doing it, and after I spent the weekend in Dallas to celebrate with my sister since my husband saw no reason to make merry just because an X-ray claimed his wife wasn't dead, I returned home to find our answering machine's red light blinking. Because the oncologist's assistant huffed into the recorder: "Where are you? Dr. Callahan needs you to call. ASAP." Because the sound of her voice, both urgent and chiding, at 4 p.m. on a Sunday gave me sixteen more hours to fritter away before their office opened Monday morning. Because when I called first thing, the assistant said, "I can't believe you left town when waiting on news this important." Because she sounded as if I owed her an apology. Because apparently she'd forgotten that I asked for medical attention three months ago, had given their office my number in Dallas, and, anyway, the radiologist said, "Free and clear." Because even though it was a matter of urgency—*news this important*—Dr. Callahan hadn't read the films the day they were taken. Because when I asked, "So I do have cancer?" the assistant said, "The doctor will speak to you in person. Tomorrow." Because I dropped another twenty-nine hours. Because, like a corrupt spouse, Dr. Callahan wanted me to confuse fear with reality. Because in her office the next day, she swore nothing on my film alarmed her, but she wanted to "put me under the knife" anyway and retrieve that stubborn lump. Because when I asked, "When?" she said, "I'm booked for weeks." Because she smiled as if proud of her popularity. Because right when I didn't think I could eke out one more tear, I started crying. Because she asked, "Do you know how hard it is to get an appointment with me?" as if I didn't. Because my mother, through the nurse at the middle school where she taught, scheduled an appointment with a different surgeon the next morning. Because he slated the biopsy four days, not weeks, later. Because he stared at me, hard, when I told him I'd found the lump three months ago. Because in three months, the blink of summer, I could have packed a little duffel and run for the mountains and kindled an entirely new life. Because three months can nail down IN CONCLUSION, SAYONARA, THE END, or it can kick off ONCE UPON A TIME.

Because, once upon a time in Colorado, a spark, the origins of which would never be determined, cartwheeled around a switchback on lower Missionary Road, north of Durango, and triggered an inferno. Because when a crew of fifty firefighters arrived minutes later, the blaze had already jumped the road, and she was gone. Because she was a queen, crowned, racing through the canopy at fifty miles per hour instead of cowing to the ground. Because she pinwheeled on herself, basculed across creekbeds, willy-nillied downhill as well as up, and, when cornered, she bucked smoke and ash and embers forty thousand feet into the air. Because no one could break her.

Because in 1981, Gay Talese—the Father of New Journalism—penned a book called *Thy Neighbor's Wife*, which explored the pre-AIDS sexual revolution, including profiles of Hugh Hefner, communes, swingers, and ordinary couples transformed by liberated mores. Because Talese pilfered intercourse with his neighbor's wife for months, a little immersion research, to prepare for writing. Because despite all of the book's breathing room and carte blanche and acreage to burn, its title still relegated women to a cameo—the possessed—instead of the unfettered starring role of flame. Because twenty-five years later, in 2006, Talese published another book in which he was still campaigning for penises, particularly married ones: *Did a married man's penis enjoy any legal leeway or sexual concessions that might be denied rightfully to the penis of a young bachelor or an older divorced individual who had not remarried? If one's marital situation was not relevant to this question, then from the perspective of a penis, it might be fair to ask, "Why get hitched in the first place?"* Because even a quarter-century after *Thy Neighbor's Wife,* not once does Talese acknowledge the sexual privileges denied the vagina. Because in the previous sentence, when I wrote "privileges," what I meant, even today, was "security." Because while the married penis is free, the married vagina is owned, but not by the wife.

Because my husband had chronic hyperhidrosis. Because of a little ruffle in his family's DNA, the same way nearsightedness, lactose intolerance, or cavity-prone teeth ribbon through other bloodlines. Because this little ember became yet another warning sign to heed. Because when his sister recommended a prescription antiperspirant that worked miracles for her and her oldest son, my husband received her suggestion as if she had slandered him, then vectored his anger in my direction. Because he was embarrassed. Because anyone could see the dark udders of sweat ballooning under his arms, staining his shirts. Because he refused to buy the prescription antiperspirant. Because, he said, antiperspirants weren't healthy. Because—look at me: using one instead of plain deodorant might cause tumors. Because my husband was a gushing fountain, but I was never wet. Because no husband, no matter how ashamed, should accuse his wife of bedding cancer simply because she gets dressed every morning.

Because for forty days that summer, the Missionary Ridge Fire scorched 70,000 acres in the Weminuche Wilderness. Because analysts thought they knew her, but they didn't. Because 32 National Guard troops and nearly 2,300 firefighters, as well as Durango Fire and Rescue Authority, U.S. Forest Service special agents, federal fire behavior experts, the Northern Rockies National Incident Management Team, 99 engines, 8 helicopters, and 5 slurry bombers couldn't satisfy her. Because every tanker hauled 8,000 gallons of retardant. Because every crewman, trekking 3 to 5 miles daily, humped 45 pounds of equipment—shovels, axes, bladder bags, drip torches, pulaskis, flappers. Because each fighter consumed 4,000 to 6,000 calories a day and drank two to three gallons of liquid. Because if my husband had been there, battling beside them, he would have drowned her with his sweat. Because that's a metaphor based on fear, not reality. Because, sort of.

Because in Colorado, a grove of aspen, a stand of women, is joined at the roots and shares synchronous habits. Because the entire grove comes into leaf during the spring and blushes together in the fall. Because if one starves, they all go hungry; if one is distressed, they all grow ill. Because when I called my husband, who was attending grad school in another state, and said my first biopsy was Monday, he said, "My schedule is booked." Because he added, "Besides, I drive the clunker. The trip wouldn't be safe." Because at the precise moment when my days might be numbered, he labeled himself the endangered one. Because before we married, he let the oil drain from his car, totaled the engine, claimed afterward he couldn't afford to replace it since he couldn't afford the car he wanted. Because by *the car he wanted*, he meant a convertible sexy enough for a dude like him. Because by *the car he wanted*, he specifically meant the del Sol I drove, the one I bought years before we met. Because he decided we'd do without a second car altogether unless I purchased the new one we needed and ceded to him my paid-for convertible. Because, he said, that's how partnerships worked. Because, back then, contrary to his opinion, I was a wet sack. Because, years later, he referred to the car I gave him as "the clunker." Because when I told my husband, "Use your savings this time, buy an airline ticket, you need to be here," he said those ten thousand dollars were for emergencies only. And because I said *need*, not *want*. Because neither of us *wanted* him there.

Because aspens do not readily burn. Because their hands are tender green leaves, not needles and cones, their limbs voluptuous, not twiggy bones. Because a queen swinging through the canopy bows to the ground when she encounters an aspen stand and may even extinguish herself in their presence. Because if the stand is wrapped inside coniferous trees, she may bypass them altogether. Because the flashpoint for wood is 572 degrees Fahrenheit, but the Missionary Ridge Fire hit a thousand degrees. Because she burned so ferocious, so apoplectic, that she took the aspens too.

Because my husband and I married in the most elegant chapel—designed by E. Fay Jones and built of glass and air and oak beams polished to shine like stones born in the river. Because one of my husband's nieces was so enchanted by the place and the possibility of the man she would marry someday that she peed her pants. Because even as she crouched behind her mother, embarrassed and damp, her cheeks were chubby with hope, her eyes the blue that beguiles cranes to mount the sky. Because at the reception, this little one approached me walking backward, as if the glory of a wedding gown strikes blind those who look. Because she kept her head tilted away, her eyes shut against the majesty, and whispered, "You're beautiful." Because when I walked down the aisle and said, *I do*, I believed in those two gold rings laced together by ribbon and embossed on the napkins as much as she did. Because, someday, that little girl will be the bride too. Because what fire will consume her if the analysis we leave behind is nothing but bullshit fairy tales?

Because when megafires billow columns of flame taller than twenty thousand feet, they modify local weather conditions. Because the Missionary Ridge blaze reared on her hind legs, forty thousand feet tall and indignant. Because as fire consumes fuel and oxygen, and spews the resulting heat upward, more oxygen and fresh air rush to fill the void. Because the cycle—more heat, more wind, more fire, more heat, etc.—spins faster, faster, higher, higher. Because, in mid-June, the Missionary Ridge Fire blew into the bowl-shaped valley beneath the Vallecito Reservoir, and the wind followed her, the whoosh of it like air sucked into an opened damper on a woodstove. Because, almost immediately, a pyrocumulonimbus cap A-bombed overhead. Because the anvil of it forged lightning and then a tornado. Because hundred-year-old trees were uprooted and snapped in half before they even caught fire. Because cars flipped. Because a small boat vanished. Because dead birds plunged from the sky.

Because every time my husband and I made love and he was on top, which was almost always, he huffed and puffed like a firefighter humping equipment uphill. Because sweat leaked from his underarms, a steady dribble on my face—on my forehead, my cheek, in my mouth if I didn't lock it, in my eyes if I didn't fasten them shut. Because sometimes I swore he aimed. Because drizzling sweat on a woman's face, or ejaculating on it, turns some men on. Because pinning a woman down so she can't turn her head or deny entrance to her mouth, and then shoving a penis into the reservoir of her throat so deep she gags, turns some men on. Because my husband swore our first kiss foreshadowed my sealed mouth and eyes, a woman lying in bed as if in her tomb. Because to solve our differing proclivities, he propped me in front of the TV so I could learn from his porn collection, in which women shoved conch shells and trumpets into their vaginas and called it gratifying. Because by *gratifying*, he meant "grateful."

Because one afternoon in Colorado, I packed a picnic and drove to Ridgway State Park and, confronting the view, knew that if my husband were there, the panorama would curl like a sketch caught fire and disintegrate to ash. Because as soon as I rounded the visitor's center and hit Lookout Point, the lake spread below me like a mirror, and the sky's face, wavering on the water's glass, was a young girl's—clear skin, nary a wrinkle—and he wouldn't have seen her. Because in the distance, a sandhill crane opened its wings and drifted north, on the lam from the smokestacks near Durango. Because meanwhile, I couldn't use the word *flight* in a sentence and mean it. Because even then—as clouds, strangers, lapped over Dallas Divide, foamy as ocean waves, and thunder tumbled about the valley—I was pondering the possibility of running home, my willingness to hold my breath, lie beneath him, stretched like an acre, parched and dying, that he could own. Because minutes later, hail the size of bullets hammered the ground, riddled the trees. Because the storm caught on the lip of Cimarron Ridge and slurred, like a whirlpool, back into the valley. Because she circled again and again, drunk on her own eddy. Because all those firefighters and engines and slurry bombers waging war, all those summer days in battle, failed to bring the wildfire to her knees, but Mother Nature disappeared her in four hours. Because that afternoon, first the smoke and the hard-boiled sun that tinged the air, and then the raw rain and wind—it lingered in my hair like a lover's aroma when he goes in the morning. Because whether or not I explored the body of another man, not my husband's, I'd already committed adultery with these mountains; I already loved the wilderness more than him.

Because one night in Colorado, when I came home late after my closing shift at the V&S Mercantile, where I was raising cash for my solo run, there was a vase of red roses on my porch, a note on the door that read, *So glad to be near you. Until tomorrow.* Because I spun around and scanned the trees, the darkness, my head tipped uphill, then down. Because I listened for footsteps, breaking twigs, a match struck, a pocketknife jacked open.

Because my friend, a nurse, said patients who want to live never stay with physicians who seem bored with healing. Because she said I could have left my marriage already except I was wedded to the story and needed the experience to keep writing. Because she said every sentence devoted to the woman with a disease was ten seconds denied the one trying to get healthy. Because she asked, "What kind of doctor are you?" Because she asked, "What kind of patient?" Because it hadn't occurred to me until that moment that I was both the protagonist and the antagonist, the surgeon and the breast, the fire and the trees, of this story.

Because, throughout that summer, the *Durango Herald* published before and after photos of the Missionary Ridge Fire. Because, in the early pictures, taken years before trouble sparked, when no one would have predicted this outcome, the trees are green, the meadows emerald, the homes pastels, the Animas River cerulean. Because, in the later shots, it looks like the photographers used black and white film, but they didn't. Because even the soil turned to ash during the cremation. Because trees like stick-figure carcasses were scattered across the hillside, some standing dead on their feet and others tangled in heaps on the ground. Because one camera focused on a doe, a furless berm, the color of gunmetal and hard as coal, her legs crooked at the knees as if still running.

But mostly because there are two sides to every story: drought and saturation, fire and hate. Because looked at head-on, the story runs one direction; held askance, it scuttles another. Because there is no unity of perspective, no fidelity to avow. Because fairy tales are both grim and snow-white merry. Because my husband brought me doughnuts in bed every Saturday, washed my car once a week, planted valentines in our house throughout the entire month of February. But because my husband also said I couldn't cook or wash laundry without his tutorials, that I didn't know how to drive or kiss, that I couldn't possibly be a good mother, that I likely caused my own tumors. Because one side of his story intended to prove his love for me, so I would swallow the other side. And because—if there's any truth to swear allegiance to, it's this—part of my story intended to prove my devotion to him, so I could start running before he realized I was gone.

Loss Collection

LIA PURPURA

Sparrow

Who cleared the bird from the stony path, the bird I was watching become something else, its wet feathers matting then drying and parting back to skin? In a few more months, the ribs would've been a house framed out, barrel staves, then once the spine showed, the keel of a skiff. Already wind was passing through the very body it used to lift.

Such strange reversals the end brings.

The bird was one of my private measures of time bent to its work, paring, reducing, and recomposing—those colonies below digging in and fattening on the body. I was tracking increments, how the bird wore its days. Or days wore a bird. I kept it as evidence of one of the ways the world goes on without me. That the world goes on without me is an old and familiar shiver. Lying in bed on a summer night and hearing the older kids still at their games, would join with a flash of kids in Japan at just that moment on the far side of the globe, rising and eating their morning soup. I was not moved to slip out to play then, or pinch an arm and confirm myself. I wanted only to be and not be simultaneously, for as long as the displacement lasted.

With the bird gone now, what's missing is a way to reset the day. I keep checking the path for the cycle ongoing: a being turned toward becoming again. Recently, in that spot, one rock balanced just so on another became a dark breast, feathered with dampness. A bent tab from a coffee cup was a beak. There was some solace in imagining, but without the body, time's renegade—it can't be illustrated by a diminishing wing. Its increments are not en route to anything.

Open Space

Spots that look bare at first—stretch of back, upper arm—are, if you slow your looking way down, sites of endless micro-scenes: angles thrown by sudden flexing, shadows cast by turning and bending, folds lit by sweat, outcrops catching wind. Once, the eye could rest on these. Sip from. Take in. Those spots on the body so full of suggestion, that inclined toward or beckoned seem now occupied with Tweety Birds, cuffs of barbed wire, anchors, planets, names of beloveds. All those images staking claims. A rise of muscle, like a hill once learned by climbing and roaming, is real estate. A place settled and named, with monuments, plaques, and private museums. It's always been the habit of conquering imaginations to call a place *empty*, and build there.

For a taste of what used to be, you can visit tall grass prairie preserves in Kansas and Oklahoma, spaces much like the unmarked body—efforts of conservation, and rare.

Fire

Of one form of lost intimacy, Thoreau wrote: "I sometimes left a good fire when I went to take a walk on a winter afternoon; and when I returned three or four hours afterward, it would still be alive and glowing. My house was not empty though I was gone. . . . It was I and Fire that lived there." Then things changed at Walden Pond. "The next winter I used a small cooking-stove . . . but it did not keep fire as well as the open fireplace. Cooking was then, for the most part, no longer a poetic, but merely a chemic process. It will soon be forgotten, in these days of stoves, that we used to roast potatoes in the ashes, after the Indian fashion. . . . The stove not only took up room . . . but it concealed the fire, and I felt as if I had lost a companion."

Such are small reveries improved away.

And what of other losses sustained? At the moment plumbing moved inside, I imagine I'd have felt very keenly the absence of wells—the thrice daily ("thrice" itself gone!) chore of fetching, the load awkward and heavy, but on the way there and back, a quiet all to myself; the scrape of the empty bucket descending; the plunge-and-fill sounds; the crank tense and rope spooling; my face in ripples surfacing; the overfull splashing on legs in summer, so sweet.

What's the word for an elegy that mourns a thing it never knew?
My tallow candle, its buttery crackle.
My jeweled preserves on a pantry shelf in winter light.

Trees

Once that sound, wind-through-trees, was *a forest breathing*. A body moving through woods understood it. Breathing meant many things: signs of rain or evening coming, early notice of seasons turning, a density of pines giving way to meadow. But now, even if you stand very still—in deep winter, high summer, it hardly matters—what you're hearing is likely distant traffic, planes above clouds, or generators. Not a deep sigh. Not a thought humming. To think that a forest might breathe now is a *fancy*—a state "modified by that empirical phenomena of will," as Coleridge said. Whereas it used to take *imagination*, that "higher form," the "living power and prime agent of all human perception." So went the Romantic notion that by overcoming intellection and knowing the world to be animate, we might regain for brief spots of time all that's been worn so thoroughly away.

The force that renders land, water, and trees *quaint* ("charming in an old fashioned way") settles in. Settling controls and legislates. To suspect that a thought might be called "quaint" cinches in imagining. Dams the changeable truths of a stream. Shrivels a phrase like *the wings of trees*. "Quaint" won't let a body see green in flight or suggest the song of budding pears is in any way pinkly audible.

Dodo

Once men with their dogs, cats, rats, and pigs overtook the quiet island of Mauritius, the dodo disappeared. In one 1622 account, a whole flock of dodos, hearing the squawking of a single bird, rushed to the scene and all were captured, snatched easily by hungry Dutch sailors. With no natural predators, safe and content on their wooded island, dodos nested on the ground and spent their days eating and sleeping. Though capable of running, there was no need. And their beaks, though hooked and powerful, found no occasion for self-defense. Imagine a flightless, three-foot-tall bird, heavy and round, with a tufty tail and afterthought wings coming easily up to you, tipping its curious, bald head to one side, fixing you in its bright yellow eye. Imagine it eating from your hand, or working beside you plucking crabs at low tide. Or that by watching and tagging along, you'd be led to all the fruit you'd need.

Speculation about the dodo's name confirms a very different stance: perhaps derived from the Portuguese *doudo* or *doido* meaning "fool" or "crazy." Or from the Dutch *dodoor* (sluggard) or *dodaars* (fat ass). As late as 1766, Linnaeus coined *Didus ineptus*—"inept dodo." And still, today, *dodo* means "addled, laughable, dumb."

And what might be the Linnaen for "one who blames a thing for its own demise"?

Once there lived an animal whose proportions were perfect, precisely suited for a quiet life, for roaming grassy spots near shore, gathering abundant fruits, seeds, roots, and nuts, who moved through its simple day in no hurry with no fear at all, in a place acknowledged as paradise. To find a name for such a creature, by which we might recognize others like it, to specialize innocence, classify unguardedness—we lost that chance long ago.

I'm No Sidney Poitier

CURTIS SMITH

I wake to a knock at my backdoor. An afternoon nap, my apartment a converted garage on the edge of a farmer's field. The rattle of window fans, a white noise that mimics the blur of interrupted dreams. The air moves on sticky currents scented with dirt and corn and the skunks that poke around my landlady's burn pile. I'm twenty-three. Behind me, my first year of teaching special education in a small-town Pennsylvania high school. My students a mix of surly and sweet. Motorheads and window-gazers. The angry ones itching to start a fight. The quiet ones wishing only to survive the day unnoticed. I feign interest in meandering stories about hunting and four-wheeling and pro wrestling. I teach language arts, lessons often punctuated by the necessity of soothing bruised egos or handing out Kleenex to dry the latest rounds of tears.

Another knock, and I navigate my apartment's cramped spaces. My trash-picked sofa. A coffee table littered with last night's beer bottles and an ashtray gritty with my girlfriend's cigarettes and more than a few roaches. "Hold on," I say, my voice lost in the fans' drone. I imagine my visitor is my landlady's handyman, a warning to close my windows before he sprays again for yellow jackets, or perhaps the Mormons or Jehovah's Witnesses I've politely shooed away before, but I'm wrong, and my sleepy heart skips a beat when I open the door.

*

I'm eight years old. LBJ is president. Tet and Ho Chi Minh. My father ex-army with the crew cut to prove it. My mother kind and steady and uncomplaining. My parents believe in hard work and good manners. They'd grown up knowing war and economic hardships, but these times are different. The hippies and their drugs. The questioning of institutions. The long hair and loud music. And perhaps they're especially concerned about their youngest, a boy fond of sitting close to the TV and asking questions.

My aunt from Cleveland comes to visit. She's young, her hairstyle and clothes my closest incarnation of the hip scene plastered on LIFE's glossy pages. She's recently widowed, the mother of a one-year-old girl. I'm not mature enough to understand this in terms beyond the surface facts. I can't comprehend her fears, her uncertainties and grief. All I know is she's fun and brings a new light to my ordinariness. And I know her life, like so much around me, is in flux.

On a rainy Saturday, she takes me to a local movie theater. Just the two of us. Those old days. The theater's cavernous space, four sloping aisles and a wide screen. Ushers with flashlights and red vests. The early matinee and there are plenty of seats. Later tonight, the theater will fill. Men and women in clothes they may very well wear to church the next morning, while above, the projector's light cuts through the cigarette haze. My aunt buys me a coke. The cup waxy and sweating and cold as we settle in.

*

If one can divine a common thread from the work of Freud and Erikson and Piaget, it's that the notion of self is an evolution, a process that forges us from a hundred different fires. We model ourselves after—and against—our parents. We witness the actions of others, in person and through the media, then pose before mirrors, imagining ourselves in new lights. Adherents of cultural relativism claim self-worth is based less upon personal beliefs than on the fulfillment of values deemed important by others in their culture. These influences bombard us, and from them, we pick and choose, constructing the ideals we either live up to or fall short of.

A child, incapable of comprehending the moment's subterranean churnings, simply *is*, their hearts still waiting for the words that will fill them. Their eyes wide as they sit in darkened theaters and try to comprehend how the disparate pieces they've been given fit together.

*

Denny stands on my porch. My backdoor a frame, me blinking back the cobwebs in my dim kitchen, him standing in the harsh sun. Our clashing expressions. His victory and relief. My shock. July's midday heat and the boy in jeans and hiking boots. Laying in the yard, a low-slung stingray, and I imagine him pedaling the miles separating our towns. The asphalt's radiating heat and the shoulder's broken glass. The noxious gusts stirred on a route made busy with trucks and tourist traffic.

"Denny, what're you doing?"

He beams. "I came to see you."

When I shopped for apartments, I had one stipulation—the desire not to live in the town where I taught. I needed a barrier. The luxury to let down my guard. To be anonymous. Yet I can't simply send the boy away. The Internet waits more than fifteen years in the future. He's obviously thumbed through a phone book and mapped out his route. His presence implies forethought and resilience and persistence, all commendable, but it's also a crossing of boundaries and, as such, a habit I don't want to feed. The trip must have taken more than an hour, perhaps two, and I picture the bike's mechanics, its design suited for parking lot stunts, not traveling long distances. Along the way, he must have questioned himself, both physically and the rightness of his mission. I see all of this—the day's history and the deeper, less stable history I glimpsed in the classroom written in a smile that refuses to wilt.

I don't invite him in—enough borders have already been breached. Instead, we walk to the local Dairy Queen, crossing the two-lane highway that connects a hundred-mile stretch of small towns like ours. I buy him a root beer float, and when he's finished, a chocolate sundae. We talk about the boys from his class he sees around town. We talk about fishing and the summer's coolest music videos and the truck he dreams of buying. I feel the need radiating from him, feel his sense of accomplishment. We sit in our booth long after we've finished. We talk, but I'm careful to keep us and our conversation on a neutral plane. A discussion of the personal that skirts the intimate.

We return to my place. I offer to throw his bike in the back of my car and drive him home, but he declines. He pedals off, waving as he wobbles up the gravel lane.

*

To Sir, With Love was released in 1967. Directed by James Clavell, it was adapted from E. R. Braithwaite's 1959 autobiographical novel of his time teaching high school in London's rough East End. Sidney Poitier, who in the same year also starred in *Guess Who's Coming to Dinner* and *In the*

Heat of the Night, plays the role of Mr. Thackeray, an engineer who views his time at the school as a stopgap in his larger plans. He encounters prejudice, poverty, the clash of generations. Thackeray, pushed and tormented, ditches the curriculum and reaches his students with a combination of tough love and common sense. In the end, he wins over even the hardest cases and discovers the heart that's changed the most is his own.

Lulu, who also acted in the film, sings the title track, a song that spent five weeks atop the charts and ended up as the year's number 1 single.

*

Nearly 90 percent of all silent films are gone. The nitrate stock disintegrates, and when the old tins are pried open, one is left with fragments and dust. And sometimes, with fire, spontaneous flames, the films' chemical attributes similar to gunpowder. For my last nonfiction book, I explored theories of time and the reality—or unreality—of memory. I look back, yet I understand my vision lacks the truth of film. Within those old tins, amid the dust, there often remain frames faded and blotched yet intact. So too do moments, some random, some telling, survive in my memory.

Yet these frames don't exist in isolation, and each, upon reflection, stirs into a murky tide. Memory awakens. A nickelodeon's viewer, the turn of a crank, the mesh of rusty gears. I hear music, a wheezing calliope, an appropriate tune, for my life has been, in the strictest sense, a comedy, my days spared all but the most expected tragedies. I peer into the viewer. The salvaged frames unite, a jerky dance, a movie I alone understand.

Truth isn't a photograph or a stenographer's verbatim report. Truth, at least the personal, flawed truth of understanding this life's echoes, must wait in the recognition of a frame that makes as much sense now as it did in the past. And so I see myself in a theater once grand but now gutted. The lights go down. The stage's thick curtains part. The movie's first flicker plays in a young boy's eyes.

I'm not proud of the fact that an act of artifice with a profit-seeking bottom line helped steer my life's trajectory, but the truth is Poitier's Mr. Thackeray played a central role in my journey. The screen's images cloaked my inclinations with a tangible narrative, my budding fascinations with injustice and poverty and race. I was drawn to the movie's flow. Its collision of interests and lives. Its discreet championing of compassion and empathy, weapons that seemed more real than the guns of gangsters and cops. Or perhaps I sensed a deeper tide that day, a trigger rooted in genetics and amino acids. I don't believe in fate, yet I can't deny predisposition. Can't deny that the connection I felt that gray afternoon still cups my heart.

*

Denny returns two more times, uninvited and unannounced. Perhaps he's looking for nothing more than an hour of my time, a sharing of ice cream, but I doubt his needs are that simple. By our third meeting, school is only a few weeks away, and I tell him I'll see him then. He says maybe he'll call. I haven't given him my number, but I assume he has it. I tell him that's not a good idea. I worry about the situation's optics. Worry about his safety on the ride. Worry about a future visit where I'll have to turn him away, beer on my breath or my girlfriend waiting inside. I worry how his perception of our relationship will spill over into the classroom.

He mounts his bike. "Well, I guess I'll see you at school."

"I'll look forward to it."

He pedals off, this time not turning back to wave.

*

I'd long known I wasn't cut out to be Mr. Thackeray. I lacked Poitier's charisma, my connections made less in classroom lectures than in small gestures and kind words. I haven't told many about the movie's place in my career. The images we craft for ourselves are private constructions, secrets we rarely voice because once confessed, we're forced to admit how short we've fallen of our ideal. Unlike Mr. Thackeray, my first year saw no lives turned around, no final scenes of tearful goodbyes. At best, I maintained order. At best, I imparted a few skills. At best, I offered an understanding face for the institution I represented. At best, my students left my room smiling, if only for a few minutes until their day's next crisis.

*

Denny and I will be together for four more years. I'll help him with his schoolwork, and at graduation, he'll thank me and shake my hand. But along the way, a quiet trouble brews. He becomes moody, distant, and at other times giddy and impulsive. I recommend him for counseling, but I know there's little hope for follow-through. There's an incident that involves the police, threats, underage drinking, and in the years to come,

I'll spot his name in the local police report. Trespassing. Restraining orders. Public drunkenness. In our last years together, I can't deny his sense of disappointment beneath our mannered exchanges. I have too little to offer, and he has too much hurt. I can never be the person he needs me to be.

*

Nearly fifty years later, I record *To Sir, With Love* on our DVR, a technology that would have struck the eight-year-old me as absolutely Jetsonian. A warm summer night, and above me, creaking floorboards and the sink's splash, my family settling in for bed. On my skin, the scent of chlorine, an evening swim and a pleasant fatigue in my shoulders. I've caught snippets of the movie over the years, but I haven't seen it in its entirety since that first matinee afternoon. I recall a few details. The boys' leather jackets. A boxing match. Lulu's mod boots and the title song.

I stay up later than I'd planned, amazed again by the pull of memory. Yes, there is sentimentality. There are convenient plot twists and victories too easily won, but tonight finds me in a forgiving mood. The scenes play out. Some have been consumed by the sea, but with a little help, I remember so much. I'm surprised by the movie's color—in my thoughts it had faded to black and white. But other parts rise to me. The class's trip to the museum. The faculty room's tea drinking and skepticism. The pretty girl who falls for her teacher. I saw all this a half-century before. A boy in the dark. A seed in his thoughts.

And here's what I remember most—not a scene or a line but an unspoken tide. The fact that Mr. Thackeray's journey took time. That his path, despite the plot's formulas, was sometimes rough. That he often doubted himself. That he saw himself as temporary, different than the lifers, the weary survivors, the ones who'd let their hearts harden and the others who hadn't. I remember some students hated him just for who he was. That he couldn't shield his class from poverty and death, but he could walk beside them when their paths grew rough. I remember he understood gestures and tones and how a thoughtless word could destroy what had taken months to build. I witnessed it all so long ago. A movie theater that no longer stands. A boy who's been consumed by the past yet who still exists, an essence. A foundation. The possessor of a truth beyond my understanding of truth.

The movie ends with a twist, one all but Thackeray saw coming from the second reel. His dream job comes through, an offer to pursue the life he'd so long envisioned, but in the final shot, Thackeray, after a moment's pause, tears up the letter. He has taught his students how to be adults, and in return, they have shed a light deep into his heart. I, too, started with other dreams. I, too, stayed put, the world not seen from the highway or an airplane's window as I'd imagined but from a tiny room, a welcoming port for the ones not cut out for high school's easy accolades. A room where they could let their guard down. A teacher who was happy just because they showed up. A person who knew a bit of their story.

Aaron and Patrick. Brad and Carla and Renee. David and Sarah and Eddie and Gus and Vicki and Krista and a hundred more. I think of their daily *hellos* and *thank yous*. Their grit. Their determination to face their struggles with grace and humor. I taught them writing and math. They taught me how to persist. How to suffer the world's frustrations and offer only kindness in return. In my heart, I remember them all with love, a message I would write across the sky in letters that would soar a thousand feet high.

Why I Let Him Touch My Hair

TYRESE L. COLEMAN

I sat beside a white boy in a dead bar. Alone, he slurped beer, watched football. Hair yellow like an unpeeled onion, no signs of sun on his skin. A typical white boy. No match for me, yet, I started it, impressed him with what I knew white boys liked: Metallica, tits, *Seinfeld*. He was nice. Bored, I guess. We talked for a while. Both in our twenties, both southerners. I desired his attention because he didn't give it freely. He spoke anxiously. An awkward laugh followed every statement, every eyeball-dash at my cleavage, each concerned glance upward at the wild black kinks springing from my head, and then, each nervous scan behind him, around the room. His fear empowered me.

*

In fifth grade, I fought a white boy beside a stack of gym mats. He touched me down there. I looked like a china doll, my aunt said, fingering my jet hair. Sizzled-straight, it framed slender shoulders, stuck against my skin by hair grease and sweat. She favored me, they all favored me. Lighter than my cousins, my honey complexion drew their wrath. *White girl. Think you cute.* Headaches from pulled hair. Arm scratches from fighting. I fought him, at least tried. We never played together. Yet he chased me around the gym, cornered his prey. We were children, just children, and maybe to him, that was what children did. But there was authority to his touch, an exerted right, his God-given right to me. Because I was pretty. He said I was pretty. For a Black girl.

*

Another laugh, another glance around. My new friend took in my hair again, so I asked him what he thought about it. He said it was cool. I scooted closer to him, my cleavage slow dancing in his eyes—up, down, out, in—with every breath. I offered: Do you want to touch it? We had an audience, another Black woman beside me. I ignored her. Her disapproving stare should've told me something, the way she shook her head to herself. I offered: Do you want to touch it?

*

A white man used to visit my grandmother. He was married with kids my age. He drove a red truck, flying down our dirt road like it was his. I'd get home from school or playing and see his truck in the yard. The rule: *don't go in that house when that truck in the yard*. Middle of the day, face red with sweat—I remember him flushed and always smiling—brown mullet glued against his neck. He'd walk right on in the house, no knocking or nothing, as if it were his. I grew up in front of him. By thirteen, he looked at me funny, but most grown men did. Now, he'd come, and I'd leave, or I'd stay, and he'd give my grandma the money *right in front of me*.

Wenches: what we were called during slavery.

And without me seeing it, I knew he did that every time—every time, he gave my grandma money like she was his.

*

In college, I let the white boys I worked with see my tits.

We were friends. The bar was slow. I wasn't the only girl flashing my breasts that day. It was alright.

My title: *the* Black girl. The only one, surrounded by white boys. The conversation: the color of my nipples. Were they coffee-colored with large areolas? Were they saggy *National Geographic* tits? I laughed. We were friends.

It was alright because of that time that drunk guy called me a nigger, and they threw him out. Cool because they liked rap, were from Baltimore or Philly, their boy was Black.

White boys who talked about the Asian hostess's sushi.

White boys who said they'd never date a Black girl, even if she was pretty for one, or their friend first.

White boys who wanted to party with my Black girlfriends after work— three, four in the morning. And when I said no, they're sleeping, white boys who demanded I wake their nigger-asses up.

White boys who refused to apologize. But we were friends, though.

Now, at a different bar, a different white boy extended a shaky hand toward me. I lowered my head. Who knows what I expected being petted would feel like. His touch was surprisingly soft. He rubbed my hair, only bending the ends.

Done, he cried, "I did it!" His accomplished smile. My power disappeared. If it had ever existed to begin with.

Thanatophobia

CHRISTEN NOEL KAUFFMAN

The first thing I learn about death is the way a dustpan can sever the head of a snake. The way my mother wields the sharp edge, brings it down just behind the jaws. I watch as the mouth opens and closes, pulses in a sunspot disk in the grass. I ask if it knows what comes next—if the memory of mice and fat frogs still spark a connection between cells. The separation of the body is an inconsequential state, and I want to take the head into my room. I want to touch the tip of its nose and see if it knows what I am.

*

I'm told there are angels in the rafters of our house, in the corners of my room, and lurking in the hall. Picture god as a hero of war. Picture light and dark on the battlefield of a girl's hip bone. *You know what side you're on, so why be afraid?* When they tell me to look for angels, I ask if it's all the same. If the branches and the roots are all just the tree growing out from my parietal lobe. I search biblical texts for how scientists differentiate wrens from bees. I look for similarities in wings and measure the width of six spindled legs. I wonder if their god could tell them apart.

*

Physicists claim energy is transformed when a heart stops. Consider how the universe was formed with a finite set of hands. No more could be created with the birth of every star; our hydrogen atoms a memory of where it all began. I sleep on my grandmother's roof to feel the beginning of trees. The rise of a sapling where nothing else will grow. I whisper into its leaves for days into weeks. Draw a circle in salt to protect the shallow-fingered core. I still can't prevent the disfigurement of leaves or the retraction of roots into a thin and falling stem.

Church conjures ways to control the way it ends, count the ways I can step into light. The world is lost in the belly of a whale. See how we sit there all in a row, chins tucked down for a dead and living son. They say that god is a thunderclap, lightning touch on the back of my neck. God is a chef with his hands in our bowls. *Make me something new.* Make me malleable. Replace my thoughts with the creation of sun. Draw me into straight lines that aren't afraid of the dark.

*

A box can become the shape of a tomb. Hatchlings sleep in a mound of down and exposed skin, wings tucked against their ribs in a makeshift nest. Every morning I slip worms into their open beaks, only to watch the thick bodies inch back up toward escape, the baby birds incapable of holding the live food down. Their beaks close in hungry, feeble attempts, the worms' bodies dangling from one side. I instinctively know how their breathing will begin to slow. How I'll cradle their limp heads, marbles in my palm. How I'll hold my breath until my heart pounds in my ears. How I'll find pinfeathers under my bed for months after they're gone.

*

When my father says my aunt *has passed*, my room is uncomfortable black. The heart is a weak and mistaken machine. Her heart—a drawing with disconnected lines. I want to ask where dead birds go and how long it takes for the body to become a shell. How once I pressed my shoe to a cricket's head and listened for the hollow snap. But my father is not a house with open doors, and for months I wake up screaming in the dark. *Night terrors are normal*, they say. *Tuck her back into bed. When she dreams she sees her face, tell her the earth is a broken wheel, and we were all made for sky.*

*

At sixteen, I hear voices whisper my name. Once, a shadow outside my door. A psychic says I can hear *the other side*. How nothing is ever gone if we search hard enough. Listen: every knock is a vibration through the oldest pine. You can whisper at one end of a lake and the sound will glide above the surface, spread its fingers at unimaginable speeds into the expanse, the energy dispersing until words meld into multi-layered moans. Put your ear to the water. The muffled memory of a baby's birth. An egret's last words in the dark.

*

Because I'm unsure of what happens next, I cling to the things I can control. I say prayers in the shape of my grandmother's mouth. I pull wishbones from the cavities of birds. I ask my mother if I can be baptized again, to let me submerge in an unhindered cleanse. I make confessions of shadows and the way I catch my breath, but she says the church won't allow this again. That god is a flood who only swells once. How I have been filled and *isn't that enough?* When I tell her how an opossum was dead in the field, she asks if the legs were curled in a run. If its teeth were still exposed in a smile.

*

We find a garter snake on the road, its tail bloodied and curved to one side. My sister and I retrieve a small box that we fill with dried grass, leaves, and dandelion bones. I pick up the thin body, trace its stripes with the tip of my thumb, nestle it into the soft bed. We leave the box on the back porch and in the morning the snake is gone. I feel abandoned by its will to move. This lesson in how nothing wants to die. I imagine it has turned into other things, metamorphosed into a great blue heron or the hoof of a deer. I remember how energy is an invisible cloud rolling from one life to the next: the snake, then the tree, then my mother's soft blonde hair.

*

The doctor's office is a white box. I answer questions about the phases of the moon. How the earth spins in the spiraled arms of its galaxy, far from the center like a wayward child. I tell him how I opened myself for a man, watched a chicken devour her own eggs, and how sometimes I know I am the product of a billion dying stars. That I feel these molecules decaying faster than the speed of sound. Faster than how a train can dismantle the head of a bear. I tell him my fear of the dark, my fear of losing connection to the trees, the absence of all this light. I know what it means to be unheard.

*

I hold my dog on the day she dies. Her long slender nose in the crook of my arm. The weight of her feels like a question of time, how once we were new in an unfenced yard. I keep her for hours at the base of an elm, remember her paw in the palm of my hand. I know she's gone but I still feel her breath, still feel her hum down the length of my spine. I dig her a grave the way a god might create. Give her a home in the movement of clay. I stay with her in the dark the first full night and hear the pond carry voices from the porch.

*

If energy is never created or destroyed, then the whales could have once been hatchlings in the grass. The tallest felled oak. I dream of the way a voice can sound close. It erupts and then spreads like the first prevailing wind. One point to the next without knowing why. If there are two sides to this, then the bridge must be sea. I wake up each night screaming questions into black—*someone tell me where the failed saplings go.* Where these thoughts are kept in an optimistic sky. How my moans will drift when even moons can disappear.

*

A child begins to bloom and I'm consumed by her round head, the perfect placement of the sun. Each finger encapsulating an infinite system of stars. Our roots connecting in a disordered tangle of touch and sound. My nights are filled with new ways to fear. How the heart is an imperfect vessel for love—something that can stop should never mark time. But sometimes I can feel how a moment is enough. The tree is the bud and the bird and the grass. When I remember that death is an uncracked shell. That fear is the thief of a million cocoons. How this girl is the water I whisper across. If they hear me so soft on the other side.

Of a Confession, Sketched from Ten Vignettes

LATANYA McQUEEN

I.

It begins with:

A feeling, unrecognized.
An unasked Question.
The fear of calling both into being.

II.

This is a story between a woman and a man, but first, we must deal with the question of names. If this were fiction, we could use a pseudonym for the other, maybe an anagram of their name, but this is not fiction. The endeavor, this one, is true.

Yes, the act of unnaming enables a desire for clarification, but specificity proves fraught. What could be said that would not lead a reader through a process and error of discovery? What could be said that would not make one go searching in an attempt at winnowing down to an answer?

If you knew, what would it matter?

Instead, we will strip this down to the abstract, including only the necessary particulars. This is a story between two people where one has fallen for the other, and a story that deals with the aftermath of the realization.

This is a story that could encompass many of us. A story that could also, perhaps, describe you.

III.

The conflict encapsulated in four sentences:

A woman once loved someone who didn't love her back.
A woman loved someone who didn't love her.

A woman loved someone.

A woman loves.

IV.

If this is about a woman's attempt at confessing her feelings for another where A (the inciting incident) leads to B (rising action) resulting in C (climactic moment), then:

> (A) is the recognition of the feeling, leading to (B), the grappling with what she should do, if she should tell him and what the risk is in saying, leading up to her attempts, over and over, to get at the heart of the thing, while each time failing to say, until, until, until— (C)?

V.

Three previous attempts at confessing:

Attempt 1

"I care about you," she tries to say, but care doesn't quite get to the root of it. A person can care for friends. Parents. They can care about a neighbor. Yet, to her, there is something more revealing in the word. She cares about his happiness. She wants him to be happy. With or without her.

Attempt 2

"I feel close to you," she thinks, but this too, is not quite right, but for her—she is not one for closeness. She lives a life of comfortable detachment because that is how one stays safe, unhurt, but she feels close to him. Somehow, he has broken that barrier and she is not the same.

Attempt 3

"I miss you," she says after a brief time apart, but what she means to say is she misses him in the after—after he recognizes her yearning and inevitably pulls away. Already, she misses the time before she ever told him, back when she could dwell in the possibility of what has not happened, but could.

VI.

"I think you need to pick a boat and get in it," a friend suggests. "Tell him, no more hedging. Say it bluntly. Say it plain."

"But there is a risk in doing that, though."

"Yes, there is always a risk. There is always something at stake in the confessing of a desire."

"I don't know if I can do it."

"Well, what is to be gained in telling? What do you even want? Because if you're able to answer that for yourself, it might be best to just say nothing at all."

VII.

Perhaps it could be like it was when we were children. A ripped notebook sheet. A pencil. Scrawled markings over the blue-lined paper. A question formed—simple, direct, followed with a check box next to a choice of answers.

If only it could be that simple. To write:

I like you. Do you like me too (please check one)?

☐ Yes   ☐ No   ☐ Maybe

VIII.

We have not worked ourselves toward an answer but she has considered the potential possibilities:

- She tells him, and he does not feel the same.
- She tells him, he does not feel the same, and she realizes afterward that actually she mischaracterized her feelings and does not feel what she originally thought.
- She tells him, he says he does not know how he feels, and the two of them are left in a dreary limbo until one of them or both decides to pretend the situation never happened.
- If they are friends and she tells him and he does not feel the same, she has to now live with a friendship that is not the same as it once was.

IX.

She has not envisioned a possibility where he does feel the same. It feels impossible he ever could, and therein lies the crux. She knows the path this will take but hopes for a different potentiality anyway. This is what is to be gained, she thinks, because so many of us would do anything for just the hope of a desire, and while she does not know how long she can temper her heart, she understands that confessing will inevitably lead to moving on rather than having to remain in the lingering unrequitedness that has surrounded her life.

X.

But what if he could, and what if knowing was as simple as asking a question, and what if this essay was merely that question in disguise? What if this was her—my—attempt of asking if it could be possible, if he—you—could?

If I were to ask it now, if it were to end like this, with saying it bluntly, with saying it plain—

"Do you think?"
"Could you maybe?"

—what, then, would you say?

The Heart as a Torn Muscle

RANDON BILLINGS NOBLE

Overview

Your heart was already full, but then you saw him and your heart beat code, not Morse but a more insistent pulse: Oh, yes. That's him. That one.

Not The One (The One you already have—and deeply love), but of all the people in that large room far from home, he was the one for you. And your heart stretched more than it should have, tore a little, and let him in.

Symptoms

- Swelling, bruising, or redness. The feeling that your lungs contain a higher percentage of oxygen and have somehow grown in their capacity to respire. A heightened sensitivity to glances, postures, gestures, attitudes, and casual remarks from observers. A propensity to blush.

- Pain at rest. General restlessness. An inability to sleep. Fever dreams. Sleepwalking. Conscious walking: out of your bedroom, out of doors, into the moonlight or an unmown field shrouded in mist and ache (or fantasies of same).

- Pain when the specific muscle is used. When your heart beats to force blood through your femoral arteries, to your iliopsoas muscles, your sartorius muscles, your peroneus muscles, each expanding and contracting to force your legs to walk away, from him, from thrill, from all the promise and potential of an alternate future.

- Inability to use the muscle at all. Lethargy. Apathy. Malaise. Especially after having walked away from the one in question.

Self-Care

- Apply ice: cool it. The early application of heat can increase swelling and pain.
- Note: Ice or heat should not be applied to bare skin. Always use a protective layer—latex only as a very last resort. Clothing is better or, better still, distance: several feet, a separate piece of furniture, a wall, or a building. Ideally: a state line, a continent.
- Try an anti-inflammatory such as herbal tea or a pro/con list. Cool showers and brisk walks in bracing air may help. Do not take depressants in the form of alcohol or otherwise. Avoid stimulants: caffeine, chocolate, Cheetos.
- Protect the strained muscle from further injury by refusing to jump into anything. Avoid the activities that caused the strain and other activities that are painful.
- Compression. Hold yourself together.
- Elevation. Rise above.

When to Seek Care

If home remedies bring no relief in twenty-four hours, call your youngest and most bohemian friend.

If you hear a popping sound, signifying a break from your primary relationship, the one (The One) you truly know and truly love, call your closest and most trusted friend.

Exams and Tests

Your youngest and most bohemian friend asks,

Are you going to run away together, tryst in motels, meet up in Paris, open a PO box, wear a trench coat, give each other code names, assume another identity?

Would he be up for a threesome?

Want to use my place?

Says, It's so romantic.

Says, Tell me everything!

Your closest and most trusted friend asks,

What do you mean, "met someone"?

Have you thought this through?

Is this choice supporting, adding to, enriching, complicating, marring, degrading, not even leaving a blip on the screen in the way in which you will see your life in the years to come?

What will you be left with? Regret? Memory? Or absolutely nothing?

Says, Time wounds all heels.

Says, Don't fuck up.

Recommended Reading

Anna Karenina by Leo Tolstoy

The Bridges of Madison County by Robert James Waller

Time Will Darken It by William Maxwell

The Lone Pilgrim by Laurie Colwin

Mrs. Dalloway by Virginia Woolf

"The Littoral Zone" by Andrea Barrett

The End of the Affair by Graham Greene

No horoscopes. No tarot cards or tea leaves. If you must, you may steep yourself in stories of passion and price. Years from now you can indulge in what-ifs. But for now, right now, put your hand to your chest and feel what beats. The only muscle you can't live without needs to stay whole.

On Beauty Interrupted

MARSHA McGREGOR

Once in search of something pleasing and green to shear for a jar on my windowsill I walked through the swath of yard that lies between a tangle of aggressive grapevine draped over locust trees and the smudged boundary of grass that leaches into woods.

In the span of one second I heard the sweet staccato notes of a chickadee and smelled the humid overripeness of a bank of wild briar roses in July and nearly stumbled, in my summer stupor, over the fetid carcass of a partially eaten groundhog.

The groundhog was stunning in its half-devoured state, half skeleton, half fur-covered flesh, as if its predator had been interrupted by urgent business elsewhere. Standing there with my pruning shears I felt elasticized, spinning in a vortex of birdsong/roses/corpse that unraveled my notion of beauty in spite of or because of the groundhog's ragged flesh, its astounding death mask, its teeth bared mid-snarl as if hurling epithets at the beast that brought it down. I use the word *beauty* too often, though I am no longer sure what beauty is. That is the contradiction of beauty for me, that something paralyzing can still in a primitive way evoke admiration and awe, like death and love entwined.

Late Bloom

CAITLIN MYER

Saturday night in San Francisco. Spring air gentles under my skirt, into
my sleeves. I step across Twenty-Fourth Street to meet friends at the corner bar. Inside, a young couple's tangled legs show under the curtain of
a photobooth, the hem of her skirt sparking in the flash. They are young
enough to be my own kids, if I'd ever had any.

My drink sweats on the bar.

I can get up now and walk in front of a car, I think.

No, not car.

Train is better.

BART trains scream fast underground. I have been stuck on a train while
a body was cleared from the tracks. I am sitting quietly on my barstool
but my body is alive with the shriek of an oncoming train.

Are you okay? asks Dawn.

I smile sweetly at her.

No, I say.

I am on Prozac for menopausal moodswings, but this is new. I finish
my drink and go. I don't step in front of a train, but the image won't leave
my mind.

When I wake the next morning my whole body feels like it has been
yanked inside out, organs splayed, blood swamping the sheets. My brain
can't process the sunlight coming in the window, it's still throwing up this
picture of a train. I am close to the beach, there are no BART trains out
here, but I picture the train running parallel with the shore.

I go back to sleep.

My housemate, Mischa, calls upstairs. *Housemate* is temporary. Six
years ago I packed up, sold, or gave away everything I owned and became
a nomad. I can work from anywhere. Have been traveling the world since

then, all my things in a single suitcase. I stay with friends, or rent a room, or dog sit. Mischa has provided me shelter, and I must put on a face for his sake. Dawn is making brunch for us at her place. I can't disappoint either of them. Dawn will be wearing her favorite, hilarious throwback of an apron and making something delicious. It takes everything I have to pull on my clothes.

A BART train screams through my head.

I sit on Dawn's couch while drinks are being mixed. I need help. I need to go to the ER, but I must be careful how I present myself. I don't want to be committed. At this particular point in time, the only thought more unbearable than the train in my head is being confined to a mental facility. I spent time in one, back when I was a teenager. But the ability to go outside is part of what has kept me alive this long. And, not incidentally, I am a freelancer. I can't afford to miss a day of work. As long as I have to go on living, I have to work.

I stand up and tell Dawn and Mischa I'm taking the bus to the ER.

Don't be silly, they say, after their shock, after their questions. We'll take you.

What I am experiencing is called intrusive thoughts. I know the term, and I use it at the ER. Intrusive thoughts and suicidal ideation are potential side effects of Prozac. I have been on Prozac for two and a half weeks. I am narcotized, swaddled in muslin, sleeping far too much. It is decidedly unpleasant.

I am on Prozac because I'm almost forty-nine years old and menopause has kicked up terrifying mood swings. A few weeks before the ER, I go to a walk-in clinic for help. I think hormone replacement therapy (HRT) will do the trick. The doctor asks what I mean by mood swings and I point at my eyes as they suddenly fill with tears.

Oh, honey, she says. That's hormonal, alright.

But she won't prescribe HRT. Too much risk, she says. Prozac is preferred these days.

Prozac seems an odd choice to me, but she is reassuring.

You can always go off it if there are problems, she says.

And then the train thoughts.

In the ER, I have to surrender all my things. I give my purse to Dawn.

She and Mischa go out for brunch and get good and drunk. Later, when I'm released, Mischa will take an Uber to pick me up.

I'm set up on a chair in a hallway. I am in elephantine scrubs, like the other patients here. I had to put everything into a plastic bag that was sealed and taken away, my notebook, my bra, my socks. One man lurks in the doorway of his room, shuffles out, holding up his scrubs like a debutante lifting her skirt, shuffles back. Two tranquilized men in two rooms snore grandly in stereo.

The nurse takes a chair in front of me, meets my eyes.

You seem very clear about what's happening, he says. Promise me you won't make an attempt on your life, okay?

This sounds like goodbye, but it's many hours still before I'm released.

*

I was ten years old. My mother stood in her black slip and a halo of Chanel No. 5 in front of the bathroom mirror. She leaned in, lips stretched over teeth while she brushed mascara along her lashes. Her hand shook. Sweat wetted her curls, dripped down her cheeks, jaw, neck.

Time for my distemper shot, said Mom, laughing down at her mascara wand.

She meant HRT. Back then it was delivered monthly at the doctor's office. Shots for menopause, pills for bipolar disorder, for depression, for energy, for sleep, for concentration. Mom was a walking pharmacy. None of it stopped her months-long depressions, lumped in bed all day all week all year.

*

Some women glide through menopause and barely notice. They get a little hot now and then and that's it for these empresses of The Change. Then there are women like me. One friend's hot flashes were so intense she threw up. Another woman's friends stopped speaking to her for years, until she was through it and back to herself. My sister tells me she used to burst into tears at the mall, in the car, anywhere.

Maybe menopause is to blame for the shock of rage that rushes into me when I see a bumper sticker: *Believe in mountains*. I want to slug the owner of that car. It feels involuntary as a hot flash.

*

It's the July before Prozac, before the ER, and I'm at an artist's residency in Arizona. I've dragged myself out of the room to get dinner. Two women who live in my dorm call to me from the shade of a tree.

Our dorm is haunted, says one.

It's La Llorona, says the other.

La Llorona, the ghost who sobs eternally for the children she murdered.

I heard sobbing coming from room 6, says the first.

Nobody lives in room 6, says the second.

Oh, I say. *I* live in room 6.

They look at me.

I'm La Llorona, I say. I laugh.

La Llorona is too apt. My body murdered my never-were children before they could exist. I haven't had a period in twelve years, ever since my uterus was taken. My ovaries were left inside me to dumbly pump out hormones, telling my body to make life, make life, make life.

But my body is death. Death bloomed from me in a river of blood until the hysterectomy dammed it up. A week after my hysterectomy, my mother died. Later, my marriage died. No romance since has survived in my harsh environment.

One night, in room 6, I dream I'm nursing the lifeless carapace of a baby, light as rice paper.

*

In my nomadic life, I can't stay in bed, not like Mom did. There is no bed that is truly mine. There's no one in my life like my father, ready to bring me food. I get up and work or I starve. That simple.

There is, of course, a lower rung of depression, the one where starvation doesn't matter so much. I have not yet descended to that rung. It's possible that getting out of bed, getting outside, helps keep me from that lowest rung.

It's likely I just haven't found the bottom of the chemical candy bowl, not yet.

I'm depressed, but it's a simple depression. Not clinical, I tell myself. Not capital-D Depression. I'm not Mom. My heart is aching over a former lover, that's all. Over the family life I can't seem to make. Anyone would be depressed.

Maybe a little menopausal. Arizona in July with hot flashes. Of course I'm depressed. Next I'll go someplace cold.

*

When Mom was manic, she could feel herself spiraling away. I walked her to the park, hoping grass and trees would calm her.

I'm fragmenting, she said.

I was twenty years old. I took her wrist in my hand, placed my fingers on her pulse.

She placed her fingers on my pulse. She breathed heavily.

We can't sit here, said Mom. There are demons in this park.

I took her hand to help her up, and we looked for a demon-free place to sit.

*

After Arizona, I go to Iceland for the winter. There are three hours of daylight every day. The sun doesn't clear the horizon at all for at least a week. It stays just behind the slope of the volcano, skims across the edge of earth, then dips into darkness. Three hours of sunset, the sky close and painted in celestial colors.

I sleep more than usual, but it's understandable. The dark tells my body it's time to sleep.

It's not depression anymore, or not as much. My heart opens out into sky as I tromp through knee-deep snow. On Christmas Day, like every day, I take a walk. I don't know anyone here, and the town is desolate. Today I wander, get as lost as possible on a mile-wide island. I find myself in the cemetery.

This is what Icelanders do on Christmas, it appears. Downtown was ghosted, but there are families here and there in the cemetery. The crosses are adorned with lights. When the snow melts, I'll see extension cords snaking around the headstones. But for now the beauty is almost unbearable, these glowing bulbs in the twilight. My spirit feels too big for my body.

If it were depression, I wouldn't be able to get myself out of bed when the wind kicks in my front door, walks heavily through the house. If it were depression, I wouldn't want to go out into the gale, where my hat whips off my head, and I rise with the wind, feel myself become a giantess—a goddess—grown to match the scale of Icelandic sagas.

*

When you create narratives to make sense of your life, you choose which parts to tell, which parts are significant, which self is yours. In reality a life is shattered glass, pieces missing and scattered. You can place each piece to make a harmonious design, but its essence will always be chaos.

Here I'm writing a narration that will lead you irresistibly to a conclusion that I nevertheless resisted until it bit into my soft abdomen, ripped me open. You may wonder how I managed not to see. But you see the story I'm assembling in hindsight, the one that makes the ending inevitable. Before then, I had a whole other story.

*

Back in the United States, and something feels different. I am angry. No, afraid. No, inconsolable. A list of grievances against my friend Andras grows in my head. I take long walks and stage arguments with him. I'm talking to myself like an asshole with a Bluetooth headset, but I have no Bluetooth. I put my fingers to my lips, unsure if I'm speaking out loud. And then I forget how I must look, plunge back into obsessive righteousness. I win every imaginary argument; I stun him into silence.

This is not what happens when I actually talk to him. The anger masses inside my chest and I lose track of what I meant to say.

Are you sure this is real? Andras asks.

He is gently trying to suggest that maybe, maybe, my mind is skittering away on its own trip.

This is real, I say. My feelings are valid. Just because I'm a woman doesn't mean I'm hysterical, I say.

Either Andras is right and I'm crazy, or my best friend is a misogynist asshole, trying to gaslight me. This is not an argument that is possible to win.

*

I was twenty-two and cleaning the sink because I smelled mildew.

I don't smell anything, said my boyfriend, Malcolm. You're imagining it.

Isn't that a sign of manic depression, said Malcolm.

Manic depression usually shows up in your twenties, said Malcolm.

I knew it was entirely possible that I was bipolar. Mom was inside me; she whispered from every cell in my body. But the way he said this made a sick fear in my stomach. I am not my mother. I will not be like *that*. He said these things and he meant to hurt and it worked. I was shaking while I scrubbed, but I laughed.

I read that women have a sharper sense of smell than men, I said.

That's bullshit, he said.

My vision began to black at the edges. I saw the sink in the very center of my view. Nothing else.

So, I said. Trying to sound light, joking. My voice went tight. So you know better than researchers who have devoted their lives to studying this one thing because, why? Because you know better?

Because it's bullshit, he said.

*

I am in Nepal, before Arizona, before Iceland, before Prozac. I am changing for bed when I hear a harsh whisper over my left shoulder. Shush, it says. I freeze where I am. There is nobody here. No. It was nothing. The sound of pajamas shushing over socks.

I know that is not how that sounds.

Someone is in my room. Or I am hallucinating. Both possibilities sicken me.

I look over my shoulder and the floor of the room tilts upward, shakes itself, and the blood horror that rises in me is real as a just-sharpened blade. I crouch, then go face-down on the floor, holding on with both hands.

Down here with me is a fly.

The fly walks easily along the tilting surface, up and over my hand. Striations along the length of its wings, a delicate veining. Fly wing, leaf, hand. The noise in my head stops, shut off like a choir when the director closes his hand. Fly and me. Floor just floor. I am lying on my belly. My nose almost touching those faerie wings, I will not let my breath disturb this insect savior, winged angel, meditation. Fly wings, fly eyes, busy fly legs.

You and me, Fly. Show me the way.

I was thirty-one years old, engaged to be married. Dad called from the hospital.

You mother has overdosed, he said.

He asked me to go to her room, gather up all the medicine bottles, and bring them to the ER. My fiancé stayed in the waiting room while I went in. I handed the box to the doctor. The doctor started reading the labels. Each one prescribed by a different doctor.

She's taking all of these? he said.

Dad nodded.

The doctor stared at us for a moment before shaking his head. We're going to have to pump her stomach, he said. I don't think you want to see this.

Dad and my fiancé and I sat in the waiting room while the doctor and nurse worked over Mom. There was a half wall separating us from the ER. We could see around it if we stood up and took two steps to the left. We stayed where we were. There were terrible throat sounds on the other side of that wall.

Dad talked with me about the quality of the light coming in through the glass block windows, how it moved on the white tiles.

Do you see, said Dad, drawing a design in the air.

I see, I said. It's graceful.

*

The San Francisco ER told me to go off the Prozac and gave me exactly five Ativan. I use them as sparingly as I can, but now I'm down to just one.

I am timing my mood swings. I can feel one as it ratchets up, like an ancient rollercoaster cranking to the top of its run. It slows at the top. And then I'm plunging. Adrenaline dumps into my brain and the meat behind my ribs knots tight. I want to run away but there's nowhere to run. I want to shout at someone. Anyone. I want to take their fucking head off. I want to use my teeth, feel bone and gristle in my mouth.

I often cry. Not tender tears. Something craven, terrified, spilling over. As I walk down the street, sit in a restaurant over lunch, in front of my laptop. Anywhere.

And then it's gone. I mean gone, no aftertaste, nothing. I'm back to baseline depressed. I check my watch. Three minutes.

Two minutes of relative relief, and then I feel the rollercoaster cranking up again.

Every five minutes, all day.

Is this what menopause is like? Why did nobody tell me?

*

The overdose didn't kill Mom, not then. The hospital wanted to keep her and wean her off the meds, but Dad took her home the next day. My parents felt there was some security, some hope for Mom inside all those pill bottles. But the medications killed her, slowly and then all at once. My father keeps a note from her in his Mom scrapbook.

> *Dear P—*
>
> *I love you so much. But I am so tired, so ill, so depressed. I have lived for more than too long—Please make it possible for me to go—*
>
> *I don't know—can't you tell me how I can get away? Just slip away in my sleep—*
>
> *I'm so sorry. Please help me*

What is this? I asked.

The handwriting was crowded and spindly, lines sloping upward until the last three words. *Please help me* pitched steeply toward the bottom right corner of the page, no punctuation at its end.

Your mother wrote that maybe two months before she died, said Dad. His blue eyes were wet.

Her kidneys gave out, and then she died.

*

So okay, yes, I'm cracking up. Fragmenting, like my mother.

It costs me greatly to admit this. After years with Malcolm, fighting him to hold onto my reality, fighting anyone who tried to tell me I didn't have a right to my own space, my feelings, my anything.

Now, but. I have to accept that my reality doesn't match the world outside my head.

In the meantime I get up and work every day, though I can't vouch for the quality of my work. I get to appointments on time, or nearly on time. I dress myself and go for walks. Five, six-hour walks. If I keep moving, I can almost keep pace with the fear.

*

I am in a psychiatrist's office. I have paid him an amount I cannot afford.

I'm holding, white-knuckled, to the story I've spun: my instability is just menopause. I need something to bridge my body's mourning period, maybe as long as ten years, but there will be an end date, and afterward I'll have new power, the terrifying strength of the crone.

He asks very targeted questions about my personal history, family history, suicide attempt at age sixteen.

He asks if I got a diagnosis then.

My diagnosis was Teenager, I say. But somehow, the shape of his questions makes me question myself.

Hm, he says. Most teenagers don't attempt suicide.

He asks about more recent suicidal ideation, before the Prozac. I don't tell him about the night I was having dinner with a friend and had to fight the urge to get up from the table and walk in front of a bus. I don't tell him because maybe it will mean something more than menopause. I don't tell him because I'm embarrassed.

It doesn't matter that I've left this detail out.

Any periods in your life when you didn't need very much sleep? he asks.

Yes, I say. I remember when I left my husband, was living with a new boyfriend. I worked at the boyfriend's gallery space late into the night, then got up at 5:00 a.m. to run.

And during this time, were you more impulsive than usual? More sexual?

I hesitate. I don't want to pathologize this time in my life, the real connections I made, if only briefly.

High-risk behavior? Several sexual partners?

Yes, I say finally. I don't say sometimes several at once.

Did you spend money you didn't have?

Like now, I think. I don't say that out loud, either.

Yes, I say.

And were you unusually productive, creative? he says.

Oh, it was beautiful. I loved the whole world. This was me at my most potent, the truest me. I saw connection running from my fingertips to the strap I held on the bus to my fellow riders to the street outside. I was a genius of universal love. I could not be a mother, but I could mother the world.

That would be a hypomanic state, he says.

Pretty classic bipolar disorder, he says.

I nod.

What I want to say is WHAT. What I want to say is, Take that back. I'm afraid to take in the next breath.

He has neatly dismantled my story in ten dry minutes.

Friends of mine have said they were relieved to get a diagnosis of bipolar. I am not. My hands are numb. I'm shocked. I shouldn't be shocked. I've been watching myself for signs all my life. But I managed to avoid knowing what those signs are.

My internal narrator said I'd gotten away clean. I'm nearly fifty. Most bipolar disorder is diagnosed in your twenties, like Malcolm used to say.

There are a number of women, says the psychiatrist, who have mild or moderate bipolar, high functioning. They don't know until it's uncovered in menopause.

Menopause ends. Bipolar never does.

My entire sense of myself has been violated, I am hollow and fragile as the rice paper baby in my dream.

*

Medication, then. Not Prozac. Something, says the psychiatrist, who I hate, who I love, something to even out those moods.

But I love my hypomanic states, I tell him.

Most people do, he says.

I don't know if he knows, if anyone can know. I thought this was me, so much a part of myself as to be undifferentiated from the body, the voice, the story that makes me me.

Your very self, then, nothing more than chemicals in your brain, sloshing over their boundaries.

I have—or had—a gift for ecstatic appreciation. I love like love can crack open the universe. A walk in the park and all the gods walk with me, pass me by in the guise of a monarch butterfly, grasshopper, gray squirrel.

All these gushes of love, this ecstasy, transcendence, cosmic beauty. Nothing more than chemical surges. Gone.

*

I am taking a pill every day now. I try not to think of my mother, the fifty pills she took every day, her slow suicide. Just one pill. It promises to dampen my Olympian moments. But I live. And here it is, a minute later, and I live. Every morning I take a diamond-shaped pill and every day I do not fantasize about walking in front of a train.

Once I was a goddess, or I held a potential goddess inside me. Now I am only human, but for today I am alive, by violent grace.

The Last Cricket

STEVE EDWARDS

Blame it on October. A nor'easter blows rain for three straight days and the gleam of blackened tree trunks lifts every summer thought from my head. On one of the last warm days, I find myself by an open window after dark and the only sound in the woods back of the house is wind rustling the leaves, the clack of bare branches.

I've missed it.

Again.

My intention every year is to listen for the last cricket, the explosion of silence after its ridged wings have struck their final chirp. I imagine it as somehow akin to Bashō's temple bell whose sound, after the bell has stopped ringing, comes pouring out of the flowers. I have no reason for wanting to mark the occasion other than a poetic temperament, a feeling that the mindfulness required of such a task is its own reward.

The idea to listen for the last cricket arrives in September when the calls are at their most frantic, midnight a wall of sound. Sometimes I toy with the idea of camping out the night it seems most likely they'll stop. I imagine myself keenly attuned to the crickets' hypnotic lull, aware that if I fall asleep, even for a minute, I could miss it. The novelty appeals to me. The invention of such an inconsequential drama. Clearly, it would make no difference to anyone whether I succeeded or failed, or if it took me years to accomplish. The achievement would be mine alone. Sometimes to up the ante, I imagine years of failed attempts until maybe one night, when I'm an old man—stumbling, bearded, blind, bereft of all hope—and a zen-like oneness with the woods sets in. From nearby, under the bark of a rotten log, I hear the teeth of a cricket wing crackling the air. And I listen, knowingly, as the world resolves itself in silence.

It's easy, of course, to think so fancifully when the crickets are going gangbusters. A time of abundance props up the fiction you'll always have enough. In September you can plan anything. The sun's shining, the trees are full of apples. The first stars of frost on the lawn feel as far off as real stars, wintergreen and blinking. In September the crickets deliver to me every lost dream of childhood, make whole the boy I once was, lying awake all night, listening to them—that boy's love and loneliness, his insomniac mind after a late baseball game, replaying every last impression: the smell of cut grass in the outfield, the oil darkening the mitt he absently jabs a fist into while waiting for a pitch, the coolness oozing from the deep woods beyond the parking lot. That boy's parents are young and strong, and time hasn't carved lines into their faces or grayed their hair. That boy's grandparents smile, blink, and breathe. To have him back is to have innocence restored if only for a moment. The melancholy of that sings to me. I want to rise to it like the last cricket's call and inhabit a quiet big enough to contain my contradictions—that I'm different from who I once was and yet also the same, that all the noise I make in this life doesn't die with me because, in the end, it was never mine but rather some small part of a discordant harmonizing to which I hummed along for a night, a season. Nothing is inconsequential. *Nothing*. But somehow I always forget. October comes along with its dazzling, razor-edged contrasts—warmth and cold, light and dark, color and gray—and other stories start singing. By the time I remember my intention to listen for the last cricket, it's too late. Come the spring, perhaps I'll listen for the first.

Craft Essays

Success in Circuit

Lyric Essay as Labyrinth

HEIDI CZERWIEC

with thanks to Karen Babine for delightful turnings

> We create passages for a reader to move through, seeing and sensing what
> we devise on the way. And when the reader's done—levitation! She looks
> down and sees how she's traveled, sees the pattern of the whole.
>
> —Jane Alison, *Meander, Spiral, Explode*

My first experience of a labyrinth was the movie of that name, one I
watched repeatedly on a nascent HBO, a beautiful and disturbing fairy
tale in which a nascent teen girl (Jennifer Connolly) must travel to the
heart of the labyrinth to retrieve her infant brother from the Goblin King
(a provocatively dressed David Bowie). Of course, that labyrinth was
actually a maze. Or maybe not.

But currently, I'm in a bee-filled garden, drinking ice-cold cider and buzzing with Karen among piles of books. We're spending a summer afternoon
talking around and around the issue of mode—what it is and how it affects
movement—specifically, momentum in the lyric essay, what drives it
forward so that you end in a different place than you begin. I'm trying to
articulate how—rather than a piece advancing by plot, with narrative or
story moving us forward, and instead of logic advancing the argument of
a piece—there are essays that are circuitous, nonlinear, that spiral around
a central concept or incident or image, accruing meaning as they move.
No forks, no false moves, no misdirection, only perhaps a pleasant disorientation as the writing twists and turns. It occurs to me that such an
essay might be described as a labyrinth. *To turn, turn will be our delight /
Till by turning, turning we come round right.* Like Daedalus we construct
both the meander and the thread to follow it, disorientation by design.

When I think of the labyrinth, aside from Bowie I think of Borges, a master of the lyric essay form, though I don't want to evoke the Garden of Forking Paths. While many conflate a labyrinth with a maze, they are not the same thing, and I want to amaze but not lose you. A maze is a puzzle that puts all choices of path and direction with the walker. There are many dead ends. In a labyrinth, the only choice is whether to enter. A labyrinth is defined by its circuits, its singular, unicursal path solved merely by walking. The way in is the way out, a *via negativa*.

If this were a maze, we would need Ariadne's *clew*—a ball of thread and source of our word *clue*—to follow. But this is a labyrinth, and if the way in is the way out is the way through, then in a well-constructed lyric essay, we don't need a clue. Or, rather, the path *is* the clew, the thread unspooling. When I say "thread," it is important to remember that while Daedalus designed the walls that define the structure, it is the path—the white space, the *via negativa*—that gives a labyrinth its capability, an artistic space to move through, to engage with—both the literal white space employed in fragmented lyric essays, but also the figurative white spaces, the lyrical lateral leaps in logic across which we bound faithfully, propelled by the prose. *To turn, turn will be our delight.* This affinity for the lyric, for poetic prose, comes from its source in *verse*, which means *to turn*, its recursive language spiraling but not out of control. The careful writer keeps that path open, if not always apparent—an intention that can be traced, though not always at first reading. There will be clues. The author means to lead, not lose you.

While the lyric essay may follow the labyrinth, Karen and I are prisoners in a maze, and our discussion resembles Borges's garden, with forks we do not follow, false turns, retracing our steps. What is mode, and how is it different from form or shape? Is essay (noun) a form but essay (verb) a mode? Is there pure lyric in prose? Must there always be movement, and does it have to be forward? Can it be recursive so long as it's not redundant? Can I have another piece of rhubarb Bundt cake? Who's doing this well, and what do they call it? Who decides taxonomy—the writer or critical reader? But I have taken notes and am returned to tell you all.

Brian Doyle made a great Daedalus, and would concur that by turning, turning we come round right. Karen and I are now discussing his "Joyas Voladoras," how it's not linear but has a path through it. Labyrinthine. I am reminded that there's a moment as you near the center of the labyrinth where you turn, are turned, back—sent spiraling to the outer circuits, left wondering if you've lost the thread, clueless. In his essay, we start with the speed of a hummingbird's heart, its beauty giving way to its brief beating. Then we move sideways, turn toward consideration of other hearts—those of whales and birds and worms—before eventually wending to the human. In verse, in poetry, there is a term for a rhetorical turn called the *volta*. Just before the heart of this circuitous essay that beats so bright and briefly, we reverse course and zoom out, turn back to human scenes which seem unrelated before, like a thousand volts, we are sent straight to the heart of the essay, the labyrinth's center. But Doyle has prepared us, unspooling that thread throughout for us to follow across the white space of his paragraph breaks and subject leaps, an intention that can be traced.

There must be a path to follow, a negative capability inherent in the design. When I was a young, inexperienced artist, I got the Chartres labyrinth, a cathedral floor design, tattooed on my back by a similarly young, inexperienced Daedalus. Tattoos, like lyric essays, are best crafted by someone with control of its elements, someone who can balance intuition with technique, lest the structure collapse. While I loved the experience of getting that tattoo—the meditative humming as the stylus traced its design in black ink—and while I loved the tattoo at first, twenty years later it has turned into a muddy mess—identifiable, but the path is gone, the thread lost. Recently, I went to a consultation for a new tattoo, the new artist and I again each of a similar age but now with the skill of years of practice. After we settled on the new image and its placement, talk turned to my other tattoos. It made her sad I hated my labyrinth tattoo, though she was not responsible. She offered to fix it, not by re-inking the labyrinth, as I assumed, but rather the inverse: to trace its obscured path, what makes the pattern possible to traverse, in white ink, redefining and reclaiming it. Her stylus would emphasize that white space, that *via negativa*, so I could feel positive about the tattoo once again. Her turning would be my delight, her intention traced in white. Talking about Doyle's essay reminds me of my appointment, and when I tell Karen about this revelation, this revolution, she says, *you have to write this essay.*

When I do so, when I turn to research, I find that a darker metaphor for the labyrinth's path is Christ's Harrowing of Hell, symbolic of his breaking death's prison. This, in turn, is reinterpreted as the Road to Jerusalem, inscribed in medieval cathedrals like Chartres, a substitute for those pilgrims who would walk Christ's path but could not make the trip. Either way, the labyrinth is reenacted as a journey inward, through physical and metaphysical space, in order to return transformed.

At the end of *Labyrinth*, the girl Sarah meets the Goblin King at the center and solves his puzzle by declaring, "You have no power over me." This might suggest that the maze maker possesses no real power, that it's all a lovely fraud. What it actually reveals is that this maze was, in fact, a labyrinth: that its process was not the physical path but an interior journey that leads Sarah to this realization.

But that space must be meaningful—you want the reader to be a willing pilgrim within its patterns, not a prisoner—otherwise they might just strike across the floor's pattern, fly away, escape. Like a literary Lazarus, an undead Daedalus, I am returned to tell you all the clew to the lyric essay: a labyrinth that uses its repetitions with variations, its circuitous patterning, to delight and disorient but lead us, turning and leaping, in its ritual dance around its center.

Finding Your Voice

MARINA BLITSHTEYN

one edict I heard growing up as a budding writer was find your voice

I was told everyone has one, all writers anyway, and that my life's mission would be hunting it

it takes a long time to sound like yourself, Miles Davis said

then in college when I was tortured about my pre-med track or just succumbing to my english major inclinations (that is, overthinking and poverty) the department head at the time told me to find your bliss

that's not it, I thought, not to a post-soviet hell-bent on suffering

it's find your voice isn't it

but one of my voices, out loud, is crude, a learned reaction to otherwise daintiness

I swear like a sailor, or so I'm told, but I've never met a sailor

it's mostly tv english, popular music I cut my teeth on, rated r movies I've seen growing up (too often, too soon)

and another is mimicking poetry english, poetry capital p—to signify ye olde english traditions, chock full of commas or, if I'm feeling especially rebellious, no consistent punctuation at all whose voice was I hearing then, as Eudora Welty suggests at the end of her essay "One Writer's Beginnings"

and which writer?

Welty says it's not her:

"It is human, but inward, and it is inwardly that I listen to it. It is to me the voice of the story or the poem itself."

for her it's directional, inward, but also ultimately it doesn't matter what it is, it is that way to her

I've long held that what resonates with me in a text is a recognition of self or sameness, a familiarity because it is about me
albeit a narcissistic way of reading, I have assumed it is the only way, the only way it makes sense when something strikes your psyche and stays with you, and who can predict what stays with you anyway

Derrida said cut into a text wherever you want, he gave me permission in college, so I bestow that onto my students, I tell them it's yours, whatever it is, it is your way, at least to you

there's nothing outside this text but yourself, the subtle difference between a word and a world is I

at least that's what we landed on at the end of the lesson today, having all read Welty's essay together for the first time

teaching, for me, has felt like a hybrid animal of my 2 voices

the talker/performer in me that relishes english and lavishes my mastery of it

and the introspective (inward) poet cat that sniffs around word-sounds and word-images in the hope of making some meaning

today for example we started where Welty started, in a room, in the word
"room"
what is it about it, I asked
let's get weird, I pressed

and then one student, there's always invariably one, said it reminds her
of the word "cuckoo" later on and then the word "moon" in the middle

ah, the alphabet

we talked a bit about it, I was stunned to hear that with technology some
kids don't know it, they just know how to give voice commands

whose voice could that possibly be, I said to myself

in middle school I dreamed about the alphabet, 2 strands of it, like dna,
interlocking precisely at the m/n junction, a zipper that's gone off the
rails in the middle

I woke up knowing intuitively that m/n is the exact heart of that string
of letters I've adopted as my own

the o then occupies a unique space, in the helix as in Welty's essay:

"In my sensory education I include my physical awareness of the *word*.
Of a certain word, that is; the connection it has with what it stands for. At
around age six, perhaps, I was standing by myself in our front yard waiting
for supper, just at that hour in a late summer day when the sun is already
below the horizon and the risen full moon in the visible sky stops being
chalky and begins to take on light. There comes the moment, and I saw
it then, when the moon goes from flat to round. For the first time it met
my eyes as a globe. The word 'moon' came into my mouth as though fed
to me out of a silver spoon. Held in my mouth the moon became a word.
It had the roundness of a Concord grape Grandpa took off his vine and
gave me to suck out of its skin and swallow whole, in Ohio."

let's be poets, I said to my class
think outside the room

then gradually, 2 speakers in, the light shone through the clouds on a girl in the back

she riffed off the *oo*s in moon, and then spoon, and then likened it to seeing the moon
you know like when you're a kid in a car it looks like the moon is following you, she said
I knew
she said the word was a grape she was swallowing whole
the *oo*s like the sun and moon that split by the end of the passage, "in Ohio"

I said it might sound strange but all this is within the cosmology of the text, as readers we assume it's by design, like we're reading the patterns inside, like astrologers studying the stars, the *oo*s

it was a magical moment, the kind all teachers want to manufacture in a class, you only get one or 2 a semester, and it's been so long since I had one

their attention was rapt, they were laughing at my jokes, but also they were watching the essay for clues, for a voice speaking to them about what's important and what's interesting

it occurred to me too that the student's last name was Oo, it was almost unbelievable, or inevitable, I almost ended class right then

I said sometimes when you're reading it's like a magic happens, like we're witches
sometimes it feels like you're onto something

something else is in the room when you're with another person, my therapist once said

it was there, in that room, our room, a presence or a voice, speaking through us, or we were speaking it we were reading collectively, and bearing witness to the reading process

hours after, still teeming with that class, I thought about that girl's last name, how it prepared her and alerted her to just these sorts of sub-lingual mysteries

I imagined by eighteen already a lifetime of people commenting on her last name, the 2 o's standing out on a roster
it struck me too, but maybe this was all in preparation for attention
she could see the *oos* clearer, she was alert to their eccentricities in a way that the other readers weren't

everything prepares us to read, and for Welty, even before she had lan-guage, all rooms were reading, ready to be read in

all rooms had 2 moons in them, and cuckoos, and spoons and the round-ness of grapes

only now, outside of chaste classrooms, can I read that last passage with the sexual subtext intact
the skin of the grape, the sucking, the moon in her mouth

all day I've been stewing in that passage without even knowing it, and then I come home and in the process of coming I'm writing, I'm coming to writing, as Cixous wrote

it feels like my voice but directed, not inward, but outward, at a student or at a reader

I tell my students just write like you talk, imagine a friendly reader is there with you

it looks like the room is quiet now but something is speaking to me in english, I write it down to unmoor it and hear what it says

Lying in the Lyric

CHELSEY CLAMMER

I know I can make this all poetic and shit, can find some metaphor to wrap this essay up in—give it some pretty pauses and illuminating illusions. Or, hell, I can wallow in the sorrow of the story that I'm not quite sure I want to tell you yet with some soft, long sounds, avoiding words with *k*, with that hard *c*, sidestepping the cackle of the stark *ch*.

Instead, I can soak in the *l*'s and *s*'s, meander my way around some *w*'s and hit an *r* or two to give certain ideas and sentences more emphasis.

Right?

There.

Some one-word paragraphs.

Beautiful.

And here's _____.

An incomplete sentence.

I know the poetic pretense here can proficiently populate the reader's inner parenthesis with some self-deflecting linguistic tricks, can expose myself not through sentienting but swaying, as in persuading sentences, traversing into the categorical territory of "vulnerable" as I raw myself out with words such as *emotive, mawkish, expostulate, lugubrious*—the ones that are big hits on the GRE vocabulary test.

Then I can throw in a triplet of asterisks

Now, in this post-uber-lyric-ized moment, I find that to be a futile task.

Because there's no lyric or lovely, no poetic way to say I've been lying to you lately.

*

According to its popular opinion-ed definition, there shouldn't be any prescribable form to the lyric essay. That would defeat the purpose of a lyric essay's elemental and unconventional innovation. Though I could tell you about the characteristics I have come across—which may at some point include the term *vulnerable*, or more likely *brave*, and how I have started to despise the exaltation of that latter concept in regard to writing nonfiction. One could say that in order to gain readership, one could take a traumatic (read: vulnerable) experience and transform it into a type of art, could dress it up with lyric language and bring poetry to the pain in order to honor it. But that's not being vulnerable. That's called being deflective and pretty.

*

Here, I will begin to address *you*, because you could be the person I'm lying to, and while you most likely are not that person—I am, after all, admitting to a lie and therefore am hoping you don't read this—if you do read this then I'll hope that you, like all you readers, assume I am not addressing *you*, but the general "you" as a literary device to bring you (the reader) more into this confessional essay.

It makes you a part of this.

Part of ~~pain~~ art is sharing.

You'll be more receptive to my lying if I can find a lyrical way to admit all of this. My command of language can bring you into a more conceptual space—how I can distract you with beauty, because what I have to tell you is ugly.

So far, I think this is working.

We are now a third of the way into this essay and all I've really done is make a vague (yet so vulnerable!) admittance that I have been lying to you lately. The subject of said lie is still silent, because I'm still clearing my throat.

And now I'll add in a beautiful quote in order to give you an image not of me doing that thing I'm lying about, but to ricochet away from, to delay, my confession.

"I live between mountains and take my smallness, like a pill, upon waking." —Catherine Pierce

The lie is not that I haven't been taking my medication.

The lie is not that I wake up angry each day because I'm still alive.

The lie has nothing to do with my body.

That's a lie.

It's time to lay this all out for you, because if I take this any further, the suspense in this essay is going to fizzle.

If it hasn't already started to.

*

Elements of a lyric essay: Metaphor. Research. Memoir. Pace. Poeticism. Odd concepts. Fragments. Surprising verb and/or noun-turned-verb (i.e., a noun verbed). Surprising structure. Surprising imagery. Unconventional associations. Juxtaposition. A declarative and/or witty and/or telling title. Subtle humor via wordplay. Quirky way of looking at and addressing the theme(s). At least one paragraph so elusive that even the author isn't quite sure of what she's trying to say.

*

Mandatory elusive paragraph:

"Lie" is a word of which I've learned how to live, live with. With this word tucked into my pocket—into my little pocket of my lie-filled world— I've created a cornerstone of my life based on living myself into the corner of a liar identity, an identification with (the) (")lying(").

*

Actually, I'm not certain I'm anti-fizzling. Don't I want all of this to go away? Don't I want to keep up the lie and continue to fade into each day? Don't I want you to think that everything's fine, that of course I've been eating, and so of course isn't it true that I don't want you to discover that lie for as long as I can lay it down in the air between us?

We have arrived at the setup of the lie.

Yes, I've been eating. True story. But at thirty-two years old, I have yet to figure out how to not un-swallow.

Lately, each day, I've been puking.

Always, every second, I've been hating my body.

Shame prompts lies. Everything's fine. Here, look at this beautiful line:

Tell me then what will render the body alive?

That's not actually my line.

It's Jorie Graham's.

But it is my question.

*

You can't prescribe a lyric essay. There is no "take two fragments and call your asterisks in the morning" of the next chunk of white space offered. Something just dawned on me. I tell my freelance clients that, when you have no clue what the hell to do next in your essay, or even if you have no idea what the hell you're actually *doing* in an essay, then lyric the shit out of said essay. Get all hybrid-ish with it (which, though phonetically identical, is not the same as a European person under the influence of marijuana, a "high British" person). Scoot yourself into a hermit crab's shell and see if thinking about your vulnerabilities (read: confessed lies) in the form of a job application brings some awesomeness to your essay.

Name: Bulimic.

Previous work history: Clinical Director of the Surplus Food Non-digestion Department.

Education: BA in Sound Muffling.

*

I could end this on an apology. I could end this with a plea. I'm going to end this quietly, sneaking off to a space where I can be alone and do my thing and hopefully you can't hear me.

This is called muffling. Hushing. The let's-move-on-already-ing.

And now I need a metaphor or a statement that will tie this all together, that will circle back to the beginning, because my life is a cycle (fill empty fill empty fill empty fill) but all I can feel now, post-revealing, is the stark separation of mind and body because of my shame, because of sharing. Now I can only hear the harsh sounds of *k*, of *c*, of *ch*, and even of *q*. I question the chasm created by killer li(n)es.

*

One should mention *hiding behind form.* Or, to not have every essayist hate me for such a statement, one should instead mention *content shaping into form.* Or *complex content contemplated through an unconventional structure.*

*

I must admit, I don't know much about face-to-face confessions. I deal with the world through my words. Though I know that feel of *vulnerability* when letting go, when letting it all out. A laundry-drying cliché of sorts. Though perhaps a more apt word to use in this specific essay is *purge*.

You'll still love me, trust me, now that I've told you all of this?

Right?

There.

Some one-word paragraphs used for prevention and protection from facing you.

Beautiful.

And here's _____.

THIS:

A switch in point of view and now I can hide behind you.

You admit a lie. You know you need to stop doing this. You don't know if you're talking about the lying you need to quit or the puking. You just know you need to stop doing something. You don't know how to stop doing anything. You are addicted to everything. You don't understand how you became such a hot mess, though you wonder if it has anything to do with how you dress the ugly realities of your existence with creative sentences. You refract, though hopefully not repel. You realize every sentence in this paragraph begins with *you*. You know that's not okay. But (!) it works so well to hide in writing, to let the conversation curve around vulnerability and into craft. What a great point of view we have going on here. Let's talk more about that. Let's look at juxtaposition and pacing out a fragmented narrative arch.

Let's get over it.

Be done with it.

Chance Operations

for Merce Cunningham

The Operations

Use the imperfections in a piece of paper to plot points in space for each dancer. Then overlay the pieces of paper to see where dancers might meet (*Suite for Five*, 1956).

Make a solo according to a square-root system, with seventeen phrases of seventeen counts each (*Doubles*, 1984).

Merce Cunningham famously used chance operations to generate dances. While many believed this use of chance was akin to chaos or improvisation, that the dancers were just making things up as they went along or doing their favorite steps, Cunningham in fact devised each movement, then used tightly controlled and elaborate chance procedures to combine them, creating order rather than chaos. Once established, a dance's structure was almost always followed strictly.

List every possible separate movement for head, hands, arms, torso, legs, feet. Flip a coin to see which movements are done at the same time: one with the feet like a pas de bourrée, some small motion for the hands, turn of the head. "Throw two coins to find the order" (*Untitled Solo*, 1953; *Changeling*, 1957).

Use the chance processes of a game of solitaire called Canfield to determine the sequence of movements in a dance called *Canfield* (*Canfield*, 1969).

In making a dance film, use chance to determine the camera positions, how many close-ups, middle-range shots and back shots, etc. (*Coast Zone*, 1983).

True indeterminacy rarely entered into the performance itself. In *Dime a Dance* (1953), audience members paid a dime, then picked a card from a deck, designating which part of the dance would be performed next. Sometimes Cunningham allowed dancers to determine the tempo at which they completed a phrase. For *Canfield*, he played the card game before each performance and this ordered the dance's sections, which were posted in the wings for the dancers to see. In only a few dances (see *Field Dances* and *Story*, both choreographed in 1963) were the dancers "free to find the movement and speed within their own range, to do it as often as they [wanted] and to complete it or not." To change a sequence of movements, to fragment movements or sequences.

Draw a circle—that's the stage space. A line goes from every one of six exit or entrance places to every other and is associated with a sequence of movements. To this, apply chance procedures to determine direction; tempo; whether movement is done in the air, across the surface, or on the ground; duration; shape of the space, whether covered in a straight line or circularly; number of dancers; whether they perform together or separately; whether they complete the action on or off stage. In addition, the size of different stages will extend or shrink the total time of the dance (*Summerspace*, 1958).

It doesn't matter which section comes next. Flip a coin (*Sixteen Dances for Soloist and Company of Three*, 1951).

Make sixty-four dance phrases "because that's the number of hexagrams in the *I Ching.*" Divide the space into sixty-four squares, eight by eight. A phrase chart and a movement chart, each in sixty-four distinct units. Toss pennies to figure out which phrases are done at the same time, toss to see how many dancers do each phrase, toss to see in which square-space the phrases are done and then the next phrase done in a different space or the same. "What it amounted to was a *continual change*" (*Torse*, 1976).

Here, I have ten paragraphs, their order determined through the rolling of a twenty-sided die.

Expansion

Cunningham's chance operations sometimes resulted in movements that were impossible to do—even for Cunningham himself, and chance methods led many to expect the dances to be "non-human" or mechanistic. But he used them anyway.

- Because the self is a given: it will always be there, always expressed. "We give ourselves away at every moment," Cunningham wrote. "Our racial memory, our ids and egos, whatever it is, is there. . . . We do not need to pretend that we have to put it there."

- Because our "times" are a given anyway. How, Merce wrote, "can one be expressive of anything else?"

- Because the self is also a habit, and "chance methods" are a way to free the "imagination from its own clichés." By composing this way, Cunningham felt he was "in touch with a natural resource far greater than [his] own personal inventiveness could ever be, much more universally human than the particular habits of [his] own practice." Chance allows one to escape the self.

- Because modern dance in the 1940s and 1950s was "stiffened by literary or personal connection."

- Because, in fact, the challenge of facing the impossible is exhilarating. At Black Mountain College in 1953, Merce found rehearsing *Untitled Solo*—a piece he'd constructed using chance methods—so difficult that he finally "sat down in despair." David Tudor, who had been playing Christian Wolff's accompanying piano music during every rehearsal, said, "Well, it's clearly impossible, but we're going right ahead and do it anyway."

- Because the impossible makes the unpredictable possible. Because "if you use chance, all sorts of things happen that wouldn't otherwise." Because it "shows you something you didn't know before." Because "some other possibility appears and your mind opens" "as if jabbed by an electric current."

But of course Cunningham's dances are immediately distinctively his—the arm held across the body just so, the tilt of the torso, the impossibly lovely extensions, the complex interweaving movements of different dancers on and across the stage—and yet they convey nothing about him personally. Or if they do, in some small way, it seems interesting but hardly essential. It would be silly to say *Inlets* exists purely because Cunningham grew up in Centralia, Washington, near Puget Sound. In fact, you could say instead that Cunningham was drawn to coves or bays because there, as in his dances, "nature makes a space and puts lots of things in it, heavy and light, little and big, all unrelated, yet each affecting all the others."

And so the use of chance leads not to something inhuman but to a particular notion of the self grounded in the physical body. "What is fascinating and interesting in movement," Merce said, "is, though we are all two-legged creatures, we all move differently, in accordance with our physical proportions as well as our temperaments. It is this that interests me. Not the sameness of one person to another, but the difference, not a corps de ballet but a group of individuals acting together."

- Because, as an artist, "You must try, constantly, to make it difficult for yourself."

Chance and Writing

Sometimes writers announce a new story, poem, or essay as the most personal and vulnerable piece of writing they've ever written, suggesting that this link to the self—a self defined by pain, bound by personality, family, and history—is an indication of the work's quality.

But when I'm writing, I sometimes feel like Martha Graham lamenting inside her purple cloth tube—imprisoned by my self. Even when I'm not writing directly about my secular Jewish heritage, my femaleness, my straightness, my whiteness, my kids, my lack of money-Bohemian-Manhattan-1960s upbringing, my artist parents who fought all the time, my union-leader grandmother, my summers in Maine and before that my summers traveling the desert Southwest in the back seat of the junker car my father bought because he knew it would last exactly as long as our trip, I often feel trapped by my own habits, predilections, and personal taste. As Donald Barthelme said, the artist "is one who, embarking on a task, does not know what to do. . . . Without . . . the possibility of having the mind move in unanticipated directions, there would be no invention." Perhaps chance operations can serve as an opening to invention I can't yet imagine.

Chance forced Cunningham to find new ways to bridge the space and time between discreet movements. Down on the ground, then up in the air. How does the dancer get from one to the other? Things that seemed impossible become necessary and therefore possible.

Perhaps in planning a story, I too might list discreet states of being: a woman has a baby, a woman has no baby, a woman has five grown children, a woman lives in a castle, a woman lives in a shoe. Chance could determine an unfamiliar order, leaving me to figure out how the woman gets from one to another.

But unconstrained by the physical body (burdened or loved by gravity, tethered to the forward motion of time), nothing is impossible on the page, and the parallel with Cunningham's methods dissolves. In writing, any gesture can follow any other gesture, and so the pressure to invent is much less urgent.

Instead, I might submit the very choice of topic to chance. Camels, for example—I don't think I know how to write about camels. But I can already see that facing random subject matter won't be enough for me to escape my own habits, limitations, and fears. I want chance to bring me to a moment of despair like the one Cunningham experienced when rehearsing the impossibly difficult solo he'd created for himself and then for it to bring me to the moment when he went on anyway.

Quotes by and about Merce Cunningham
come from the following sources:

Carolyn Brown, Merce Cunningham, Laura Diane Kuhn, Joseph V. Melillo, Thecla Schiphorst, David Vaughn. "Four Key Discoveries: Merce Cunningham Dance Company at Fifty." *Theater* 34, no 2 (Summer 2004): 107.

Merce Cunningham. *Changes: Notes on Choreography*. New York: Something Else Press, 1968.

Merce Cunningham. "The Impermanent Art." In *Merce Cunningham: Fifty Years*, edited by Melissa Harris. New York: Aperture, 1997, pp. 86, 87.

Merce Cunningham. Interview, "Choreography and the Dancer." In *The Creative Experience*, edited by Stanley Rosner and Lawrence E. Abt. New York: Grossman Publishers, 1970, p. 177.

Merce Cunningham. "Space, Time and Dance." In *Merce Cunningham: Fifty Years*, edited by Melissa Harris. New York: Aperture, 1997, pp. 66, 67.

Merce Cunningham, in conversation with Jacqueline Lesschaeve. *The Dancer and the Dance*. New York: Marion Boyers, 1990, pp. 20–22, 80, 81, 127.

Merce Cunningham, quoted in Calvin Tomkins. *The Bride and the Bachelors: Five Masters of the Avant-Garde*. New York: Penguin 1976, p. 260.

Merce Cunningham, quoted in David Vaughan. *Merce Cunningham: Fifty Years*. Edited by Melissa Harris. New York: Aperture, 1997, pp. 69, 78, 221.

David Vaughan. *Merce Cunningham: Fifty Years*. Edited by Melissa Harris. New York: Aperture, 1997, pp. 73, 109–10, 169.

Also:

Donald Barthelme. "Not-Knowing." In *Not Knowing: The Essays and Interviews of Donald Barthelme*, edited by Kim Herzinger. New York: Random House, 1997, pp. 11–12.

This work was produced with support from the Merce Cunningham Trust, the Velocity Dance Center, Seattle, and the University of Washington's Helen Riaboff Whiteley Center.

On the EEO Genre Sheet

JENNY BOULLY

On Interviewing

When I was on the job market, I was asked repeatedly to define *nonfiction*. I knew I could venture into one of two courses: I could give the traditional textbook definition, or I could say what I really felt. If I said what I really felt, then I knew I wouldn't get a campus visit; I wouldn't get the job. If I gave the textbook definition, it would make the interviewers feel that I was on their side, that I was a safe candidate, that I would be someone the chair and dean approved of. Because I have a natural inclination to be rebellious, I always chose to go the road of the untraditional. The interviews then became centered less on my qualifications and more on my transgressions. Some interviewers felt that I was misguided, that I needed counseling, and they would use the space of the interview to do just that. You see, they aimed to tame me, and it became their goal to do that before the next candidate arrived. It wasn't about what I could offer but rather about what they could fix.

On Former Students

One of my goals as a teacher of nonfiction is to totally destroy every held belief a student has about essays and nonfiction. I expect my students to essay fiercely and obsessively. I want to see, truly, what new thing they will unleash into the universe. One student wrote quite beautifully. She wrote so poetically, but what she wrote wasn't verse. It was essaying; it was essayistic; it was an essay. Many of my students did this over the years, but this one did it quickly and passionately. I met her later, randomly, on a street corner in the West Village. She said that she was depressed; her new teacher wouldn't let her write; her new teacher told her she was writing poetry and the class wasn't a poetry class. She asked her teacher if a prose poem could be nonfiction, and the teacher said no. I told her, why don't you quite discreetly slip her a copy of Pope's "An Essay on Man"?

I kept thinking about my former student and all her talent being crushed by a teacher who could have been in the room interviewing me, asking for my definition of nonfiction.

On Being Mixed

Once, when I was twenty-two, I worked in a mall in Roanoke, Virginia. I worked at several stores in the mall. I needed the money. I could go from part-time shift to part-time shift and not even have to leave the mall. One day, on break, a local came up to me and asked if I was "mixed."

On Being Mixed 2

So, it seems that I am mixed. I am quite mixed. I am more mixed than many, many people I know. My father grew up knowing only that he was half Cherokee, half white. We've never known where his white ancestors came from; he became a ward of the state when he was eight, and so much of his history was lost. My mother is Thai, but she has curly hair, as do I, which leads me to think there must be something else lurking in there.

In terms of what I write, it seems that my writing is also mixed. I am sometimes called a poet, sometimes an essayist, sometimes a lyric essayist, sometimes a prose poet. My second book was published under the guise of fiction/poetry/essay. I find these categorizations odd: I have never felt anything other than whole.

It seems to me that the inability to accept a mixed piece of writing is akin to literary discrimination. I think of the Equal Employment Opportunity (EEO) data sheets: choose the genre that you feel most accurately describes you.

Please Be X, Y, or Z

I want to know why what is often "other" ends up being labeled as poetry. I think it's equivalent to forcing me to check the ethnicity box on the EEO data sheets. Which ethnicity most accurately describes me? Does this mean to myself or to other people? Other people who meet me for the first time always ask me if I'm Spanish. When they ask me where I'm from, I always say Texas. So that confirms for them that I'm definitely of Hispanic descent. I never say that I am from Thailand. I was born there, but I can't say I'm from there. From, to me, denotes a forming of awareness and identity and memory. Most of these happened for me in Texas.

When I was younger and when I dated, my dates were always very uneasy about asking me about my ethnicity. You could see it in their hesitating restaurant decisions, their waiting to see if I'd order in a language other than English if taken to an ethnic restaurant. And then always, inevitably, I'd be asked if I'm Spanish. When I said no, they'd invariably be disappointed. The two most disappointed dates: the Spanish analyst who worked for the government and the boy who had just broken up with his Spanish girlfriend—I don't know what they were hoping to find in me.

Poetry as Refuge

A refuge is where unwanted animals go. It is also where some of my submissions to journals end up. Some intern or graduate student has dropped my submission into the poetry pile; in a way, that person has made it possible for my submission to live. It would not have lived in the nonfiction pile. There, it would have starved to death, or it would have been eaten alive. Once, I got a rejection slip from a nonfiction editor saying, "I'm not sure how to take this. I don't know what this is." That particular journal was solely a nonfiction journal; my submission, therefore, had nowhere else to go.

On the EEO Genre Sheet

I'm not sure which genre I would select. I guess, being who I am and doing the type of work I do, I would have to choose many. Do I choose "other" (if the option is even there) and write in a selection (if there's even a write-in space)? Isn't having to choose, being forced to choose, also essentially an act of bias? Being told that there simply isn't an easy category for you, you just don't fit in, you destroy the natural order of things. The term "other" also immediately connotes an agenda: if you don't fit into one of our predetermined categories, well, you aren't playing the game correctly. You are an other. You will always be an other. You will get thrown into a slush pile marked "origin unknown."

Coda

And so, in the literary world, I find that I spend a lot of time trying to keep everyone from becoming disappointed in me.

I may look like an essay, but I don't act like one. I may look like prose, but I don't speak like it. Or, conversely, I may move like a poem, but I don't look like one.

Do I bend genre? Or does genre bend me? I think it's the latter. I have always been the same person: I have always been made up of three things. My birth may be fictional; I may be from poetry; I might now be living in essays. I cannot see these three things as separate parts of my identity; rather, they form to make one being. I may be the product of fiction, nonfiction, and poetry, but they come together to form one entity. To be told to choose is to be told that you disrupt the neat notion of where things belong, that you don't belong.

What's Missing Here?

(A Meta Lyric Essay)

JULIE MARIE WADE

"Perhaps the lyric essay is an occasion to take what we typically set aside between parentheses and liberate that content—a chance to reevaluate what a text is actually about. Peripherals as centerpieces. Tangents as main roads."

Did I say this aloud, perched at the head of the seminar table? We like to pretend there is no head in postmodern academia—decentralized authority and all—but of course there is. Plenty of (symbolic) decapitations too. The head is the end of the table closest to the board—where the markers live now, where the chalk used to live: closest seat to the site of public inscription, closest seat to the door.

But I might have said this standing alone, in front of the bathroom mirror—pretending my students were there, perched on the dingy white shelves behind the glass: some with bristles like a new toothbrush, some with tablets like the contents of an old prescription bottle. Everything is multivalent now.

(Regardless: I talk to my students in my head, even when I am not sitting at the head of the table.)

"Or perhaps the entire lyric essay should be placed between parentheses," I say. "Parentheses as the new seams—emphasis on letting them show."

*

Once a student asked me if I had ever considered the lyric essay as a kind of transcendental experience. "Like how, you know, transcendentalism is all about going beyond the given or the status quo. And the lyric essay does that, right? It goes beyond poetry in one way, and it goes beyond prose in another. It's kind of mystical, right?"

There is no way to calculate—no equation to illustrate—how often my students instruct and delight me. HashtagHoratianPlatitude. HashtagDelectandoPariterqueMonendo.

"Like this?" I asked, with a quick sketch in my composition book:

$$\text{Poetry}^{\text{LyricEssay}} \qquad \text{Prose}^{\text{LyricEssay}}$$

"I don't know, man. I don't think of math as very mystical," the student said, leaning—not slumping—as only a young sage can.

"But you *are* saying the lyric essay can raise other genres to a higher power, right?"

Horace would have dug this moment: our elective humanities class spilling from the designated science building. Late afternoon light through a lattice of wisp-white clouds. In the periphery: Lone iguana lumbering across the lawn. Lone kayak slicing through the brackish water. Some native trees cozying up to some nonnative trees, their roots inevitably commingling. Hybrids everywhere, as far as the eye could see, and then beyond that, ad infinitum.

You'll never guess what happened next: My student high-fived me—like this was 1985, not 2015; like we were players on the same team (and weren't we, after all?)—set & spike, pass & dunk, instruct & delight.

"Right!" A memory can only fade or flourish. That palm-slap echoes in perpetuity.

*

"The hardest thing you may ever do in your literary life is to write a lyric essay—that feels finished to you; that you're comfortable sharing with others; that you're confident should be called a lyric essay at all."

"Is this supposed to be a pep talk?" *Bless the skeptics, for they shall inherit the class.*

I raise my hand in the universal symbol for *wait*. In this moment, I remember how the same word signifies both *wait* and *hope* in Spanish. (*Esperar.*) I want my students to do both, simultaneously.

"Hear me out. If you make this attempt, humbly and honestly and with your whole heart, the next hardest thing you may ever do in your literary life is to *stop* writing lyric essays."

My hand is still poised in the *wait* position, which is identical, I realize, to the *stop* position. Yet *wait* and *stop* are not true synonyms, are they?

And *hope* and *stop* are verging on antonyms, aren't they? (Body language may be the most inscrutable language of all.)

"So you think lyric essays are addictive or something?" *Bless the skeptics—bless them again—for they shall inherit the page.*

"Hmm . . . generative, let's say. The desire to write lyric essays seems to multiply over time. We continue to surprise ourselves when we write them, and then paradoxically, we come to expect to be surprised."

(*Esperar* also means "to expect"—doesn't it?)

*

When I tell my students they will remember lines and images from their college workshops for many years—some, perhaps, for the rest of their lives—I'm not sure if they believe me. Here's what I offer as proof:

In the city where I went to school, there were twenty-six parallel streets, each named with a single letter of the alphabet. I had walked down five of them at most. When I rode the bus, I never knew precisely where I was going or coming from. I didn't have a car or a map or a phone, and GPS hadn't been invented yet. In so many ways, I was porous as a sieve.

Our freshman year a girl named Rachel wrote a self-referential piece—we didn't call them lyric essays yet, though it might have been— set at the intersection of "Division" and "I."

How poetic! I thought. *What a mind-puzzle—trying to imagine everything the self could be divisible by*:

I / Parents I / Religion I / Scholarships I / Work Study I / Vocation I / Desire

Months passed, maybe a year. One night I glanced out the window of my roommate's car. We were idling at a stoplight on a street I didn't recognize. When I looked up, I saw the slim green arrow of a sign: *Division Avenue.*

"It's real," I murmured.

"What do you mean?" Becky asked, fiddling with the radio.

I craned my neck for a glimpse of the cross street. *It couldn't be—and yet—it was!*

"This is the corner of Division and I!"

"So?"

"Just think about it—we're at the *intersection* of Division and I!"

The light changed, and Becky flung the car into gear. There followed a pause long enough to qualify as a caesura. At last, she said, "Okay. I guess that *is* kinda cool."

*

Here's another: I remember how my friend Kara once described the dormer windows in an old house on Capitol Hill. She wrote that they were "wavy-gazy and made the world look sort of fucked."

I didn't know yet that you could hyphenate two adjectives to make a deluxe adjective—doubling the impact of the modifier, especially if the two hinged words were sonically resonant. (And "wavy-gazy," well—that was straight-up assonant.)

Plus: I didn't know that profanity was permissible in our writing, even sometimes apropos. At this time, I knew the meaning of the word *apropos* but didn't even know how to spell it.

One day I would see *apropos* written down but not recognize it as the word I knew in context. I would pronounce it "a-PROP-ose," then wonder if I had stumbled upon a typo.

Like many things, I don't remember when I learned to connect the spelling of *apropos* with its meaning, or when I learned *per se* was not "per say," or when I realized I sometimes I thought of Kara and Becky and Rachel when I should have been thinking about my boyfriend—even sometimes when I was *with* my boyfriend. (He was majoring in English, too, but I found his diction far less memorable overall.)

*

"The lyric essay is not thesis driven. It's not about making an argument or defending a claim. You're writing to discover what you want to say or why you feel a certain way about something. If you're bothered or beguiled or in a state of mixed emotion, and the reason for your feelings doesn't seem entirely clear, the lyric essay is an opportunity to probe that uncertain place and see what it yields."

Sometimes they are undergrads, twenty bodies at separate desks, all facing forward while I stand backlit by the shiny white board. Sometimes they are grad students, only twelve, clustered around the seminar table while I sit at the undisputed, if understated, head. It doesn't matter the composition of the room or the experience of the writers therein. This part I say to everyone, every term, and often more than once. My students will all need a lot of reminding, just as I do.

(A Post-it note on my desk shows an empty set. Outside it lurks the question—"What's missing here?"—posed in my smallest script.)

"Most writing asks you to be vigilant in your noticing. *Pay attention* is the creative writer's credo. We jot down observations, importing concrete nouns from the external world. We eavesdrop to perfect our understanding of dialogue, the natural rhythms of speech. Smells, tastes, textures—we understand it's our calling to attend to them all. But the lyric essay asks you to do something even harder than noticing what's there. The lyric essay asks you to notice what isn't."

{   }
What's missing here?

I went to dances and dried my corsages. I kept letters from boys who liked me and took the time to write. Later, I wore a locket with a picture of a man inside. (I believe they call this *confirmation bias.*) The locket was shaped like a heart. It tarnished easily, which only tightened my resolve to keep it clean and bright. I may still have it somewhere. My heart was full, not empty, you see. I was responsive to touch. (We always held hands.) I was thoughtful and playful, attentive and kind. I listened when he confided. I laughed at his jokes. We kissed in public and more than kissed in private. (I wasn't a tease.) When I cried at the sad parts in movies, he always wrapped his arm around. For years, I saved everything down to the stubs, but even the stubs couldn't save me from what I couldn't say.

*

"Subtract what you know from a text, and there you have the subtext." Or—as my mother used to say, her palms splayed wide—*Voilà!*

I am stunned as I recall that I spoke French as a child. My mother was fluent. She taught me the French words alongside the English words, and I pictured them like two parallel ladders of language I could climb.

Sometimes in the grocery store, we would speak only French to each other, to the astonishment of everyone around. It was our little game. We enjoyed being surprising, but the subtext was being impressive or even perhaps being exclusionary. That's what we really enjoyed.

When Dee, the woman in the blue apron with the whitest hair I had ever seen—a *shock* of white, for not a trace of color remained—smiled at us in the Albertson's checkout line, I curtsied the way my ballet teacher taught me, clasped the bag in my small hand, and murmured *Merci*. My good manners were not lost in translation.

"Lyric essays are often investigations of the Underneath—what only seems invisible because it must be excavated, brought to light. We cannot, however, take this light-bringing lightly."

When I was ten years old, my parents told me they were going to dig up our backyard and replace the long green lawn with a swimming pool. This had always been my mother's dream, even in Seattle. She assumed it was everyone else's dream, too, even in Seattle. Bulldozers came. The lilac bushes at the side of the house were uprooted and later replanted. Portions of the fence were taken down and later rebuilt. It took a long time to dig such a deep hole. Neighbors complained about the noise. Someone came one night and slashed the bulldozer's tires. (Another slowdown. Another setback.) All year we lived in ruins.

Eventually, the hole was finished, the dirt covered over with a smooth white surface. I remember when the workmen said I could walk into the pool if I wanted—there was no water yet, just empty space, more walled emptiness than I had ever encountered before. In my sneakers with the cat at my heels, I traipsed down the steps into the shallow end, then descended the gradual hill toward the deep end. There I stood at the would-be bottom, where the water would someday soon cover my head by a four full feet. When I looked up, the sky seemed so much further away. The cat laid down on the drain, which must have been warmed by the sun.

I didn't know about lyric essays then, but I often think about the view from the empty deep end of the dry swimming pool when I talk about lyric essays now. The space felt strange and somehow dangerous, yet there was also an undeniable allure. I tell my students it's hard what's under the surface. We don't always know what we'll f.

That day in the pool, I looked up and saw a ladder dangling i. right side-wall. It was so high I couldn't reach it, even if I stretched arms. I would need water to buoy me even to the bottom rung. For symmetry, I thought, there should have been a second ladder on the left-side wall. And that's when I remembered, suddenly, with a shock as white as Dee's hair: I couldn't recall a word of French anymore! I had lost my second ladder. *When did this happen?* I licked my dry lips. I tried to wet my parched mouth. *How did this happen?* There I was, standing inside a literal absence, noticing that a whole language had vanished from my sight, my ear, my grasp.

*

I live in Florida now. I have for seven years. In fact, I moved to Florida to teach the lyric essay, audacious as that sounds, but hear me out. I think "lyric essay" is the name we give to something that resists being named. It's the placeholder for an ultimately unsayable thing.

After ten years of teaching many literatures—some of which approached the threshold of the lyric essay but none of which passed through—I came to Florida to pursue this layered, voluminous, irreducible thing. I came to Florida to soak in it.

"That's a subgenre of creative nonfiction, right?" *Is it?*

"You're moving to the subtropics, aren't you?" *I am!*

On the interview, my soon-to-be boss drove me around Miami for four full hours. The city itself is a layered, voluminous, irreducible thing. I love it irrationally and without hope of mastery, which in the end might be the only way to love anything.

My soon-to-be boss said, "We have found ourselves without a memoirist on the faculty." I liked him instantly. I liked the word choice of "found ourselves without," the sweet and the sad commingling.

He told me, "Students want to learn how to write about their lives, their experiences—not just casually but as an art form, with attention to craft." (I nodded.) "But there's another thing, too. They're asking about—" and here he may have lowered his voice, with that blend of reverent hesitancy most suited to this subject—"*the lyrical essay*." (I nodded again.) "So, you're familiar with it, then?"

"Yes," I smiled, "I am."

Familiar was a good word, perhaps the best word, to describe my relationship with this kind of writing. The lyric essay and I are kin. I know the lyric essay in a way that feels as deep and intuitive, as troubling and unreasonable, as my own family ties have become.

"Can you give me some context for the lyrical essay?" he asked. At just this moment, we may have been standing on the sculpted grounds of the Biltmore Hotel. Or: We may have been traffic-jammed in the throbbing heart of Brickell. Or: We may have been crossing the spectacular causeway that rises then plunges onto Key Biscayne.

"Do you ever look at a word like, say, *parenthesis*, and suddenly you can't stop seeing the parts of it?"

"How do you mean?" he asked.

"Like how there's a *parent* there, in *parenthesis*, and how parentheses can sometimes seem like a timeout in the middle of a sentence—something a parent might sentence a child to?"

"Okay," he said. He seemed to be mulling, which I took as a good sign.

"You see, a lyric essayist might notice something like that and then might use the nature of parentheses themselves to guide an exploration of a parent-child relationship."

I wanted to say something brilliant, to win him over right then and there, so he would go back to the other creative writers and say, "It's *her*! We must hire *her*!"

But brilliance is hard to produce on command. I could only say what I thought I knew. "This is an approach to writing that seeks out the smallest door—sometimes a door found within words themselves—and uses that door to access the largest"—I may have said *hardest*—"rooms."

I heard it then, the low rumble at the back of his throat: "Hmm." And then again: "Hmm."

*

Years before Overstock.com, people shopped at surplus stores—or at least my mother did, and my mother was the first people I knew. (She was only one, true, but she seemed like a multitude.)

The Sears Surplus Store in Burien, Washington, was a frequent destination of ours. Other Sears stores shipped their excess merchandise there, where it was piled high, rarely sorted, and left to the customers who were willing to rummage. So many bins to plunge into! So many shelves laden with retaped boxes and dented cans! (*Excess* seemed to include items missing pieces or found to be defective.) Orphaned socks. Shoes without laces. A shower nozzle Bubble-Wrapped with a handwritten tag—AS IS.

I liked the alliterative nature of the store's name, but I did not like the store itself, which was grungy and stale, a trial for the senses. There were unswept floors, patches of defiled carpet, sickly yellow lights that flickered and whined, and in the distance, always the sound of something breaking.

"We don't even know what we're looking for!" I'd grouse to my mother rather than rolling up my sleeves and pitching in. "There's too much here already, and they just keep adding more and more."

I see now my mother was my first role model for what it takes to make a lyric essay. The context was all wrong, but the meaning was right, precisely. She handed me her purse to hold, then wiped the sweat that pooled above her lip. "If you don't learn how to be a good scavenger," my mother grinned—*oh, she was in her element then!*—"how do you ever expect to find a worthy treasure?"

*

Facebook Post, February 19, 2016, 11:58 a.m.:
Reading lyric essays at St. Thomas University this morning. In meaningless and/or profound statistics—also known as lyric math—the current priest-to-iguana ratio on campus is 6 to 2 in favor of the priests. Somehow, though, the iguanas are winning.

An aspiring writer comments: ♥ Lyric math ♥ I love your brain!
I reply: May your love of lyric essays likewise grow, exponentially! ♥

*

Growing up, like many kids who loved a class called language arts, I internalized a false binary (to visualize: an arbitrary wall) between what we call art and what we call science. "Yet here we are today," I tell my students, palms splayed wide, "members of the College of Arts & Sciences. Notice it's an ampersand that joins them, aligns them. Art and science playing together on the same team."

When they share, my students report similar divisions in their own educational histories. They say they learned early on to separate activities for the "right brain" (creative) from activities for the "left brain" (analytical). When they prepared for different sections of their standardized tests, they almost always found the verbal questions "fun," the quantitative questions "hard."

"Must these two experiences be mutually exclusive?" I ask. "Because I'm here to tell you the lyric essay is the hardest fun you can have." They laugh because they are beginning to believe me.

My students also learned early on to assign genders to their disciplines of study—"girl stuff" versus "boy stuff." They recount how the girl stuff of spelling and sentence-making and story-telling, while undeniably pleasurable, was treated by some parents and teachers alike as comparably frivolous to the boy stuff, with its ledgers and numbers and chemicals that burbled in a cup. In the end, everyone, regardless of their future majors, came to believe that boy stuff was serious—*meaningful* math, *salient* science—better than girl stuff, and ultimately more valuable.

"It's not just an arbitrary wall either," they say, borrowing my metaphor. "You see it on campus too—where the money goes, where the investments are made." I'm not arguing. My students, deft noticers that they are, cite a leaky roof and shingles falling from the English building, while the university boasts "comprehensive upgrades" and "state-of-the-art facilities" in buildings where biology and chemistry are housed. They suggest we are living with divisions that cannot be ignored. They are right, of course, right down to their corpus callosums.

*

"So," I say, "one mission for the lyric essayist is to identify and render on the page these kinds of incongruities, *inequalities*, and by doing so, we can challenge them. We can shine a probing light into places certain powers that be may not want us to look. Don't ever let anyone tell you lyric essays can't be political."

The students are agitated, in a good way. They're thinking about lyric essays as epistles, lyric essays as petitions and caveats and campaigns.

"To do our best work," I say, "we need to mobilize all our resources—not only of structure and form but even the nuances of language itself. We need to mine every lexicon available to us, not just words we think of as 'poet words.' In a lyric essay, we can bring multiple languages and kinds of discourse together."

Someone raises a hand. "Is this your roundabout way of telling us the lyric essay isn't actually more art than science?"

I shake my head. "To tell you the truth, I'm not sure if the lyric essay is more art than science. I'm not even sure the lyric essay belongs under the genre banner of *creative nonfiction* at all."

"Well, how would you classify it then?" someone asks without raising a hand.

"*Mystery*," I say, and now I surprise myself with this sudden stroke of certainty, like emerging from heavy fog into sun. Some of my students giggle, but all the ears in the room have perked up. "I think lyric essays should be catalogued with the mysteries." I am even more certain the second time I say it.

"So, just to clarify—do you mean the whodunnits or, like, the paranormal stuff?"

"Yes," I smile. "*Exactly.*"

Meditations

ORIGIN mid-16th century: from Latin *meditat-* 'contemplated', from the verb *meditari*, from a base meaning 'measure'; related to **mete**

The lyric essay may make no argument at all—not as such. Rather, it may worry away at a single image by talking around it. This type of essay may wander through time, collecting sensations and memories in a long glittering train that the reader can't help seeing again long after reading.

Talea Anderson, "In My Brother's Shadow"

*

My body holds a record of trauma. The snail-trail-shaped scar on my cornea. The burn in my lungs when I can't draw a full breath. While the body remembers trauma as a physical occurrence, our brains work to fragment it, pulling it apart in a way that's associative, not linear. When I first tried to write my own trauma, I tried to force it onto the page linearly, biographically, therapeutically. Doing so didn't honor this personal history or present it authentically. Segmented and braided essays give space and structure to the internal logic of trauma. They allow the narrative to split and converge with a fluidity that replicates the emotional experience of trauma in a way that traditional forms resist. Lyric language itself is a vehicle built for the transportation and expression of this trauma; it allows the writer to transform pain into beauty on the page in a way that replaces the original experience with a new one: the act of writing those moments. The body remembers, but the lyric essay finds a new structure to hold it.

Aimée Baker, "Beasts of the Fields"

*

Memoirists come to their work with a sense of tremendous vulnerability, but to outside readers—particularly to family and friends—our
position is one of power. How can the author complicate the implicit
authority of their narration? How can we question, in real time, our own
reliability? This flash piece juxtaposes a firsthand experience with spec-
ulating another person's take on the same set of actions. Both versions
are factually accurate. Although it'd be easy to claim the first version is
the "real story," perhaps the latter version captures something the former
won't admit. I'm interested in what it looks like, formally, to surrender
power on the page. And, for all its tallgrass prairie beauty, Kansas can
get lonely in winter.

Sandra Beasley, "Depends on Who You Ask"

*

I once found an empty emerald-colored balloon resting on a chair at a
birthday party, its color so bright it begged to be inflated. Being a child,
I struggled to fill its latex parameters with the air my small lungs could
offer. I heaved in and out, my head increasingly fuzzy and light, as though
I might fly away with the balloon into another realm. When it was filled,
just before I might have lost consciousness, I realized I could not properly
tie the balloon closed. I let it go. It flew in ways I did not expect—it veered,
it darted, it coiled in its own time and music. It became something both
recognizable in its essential purpose and something that existed beyond
the constraints of form. It looked, to me, to be free.

Dorothy Bendel, "Body Wash: Instructions on Surviving Homelessness"

*

The spirit of the lyric essay is twinned in my mind with Robert Bly's *Leaping Poetry*, recalling those leaps in thought which bridge the unconscious
with the conscious and are a kind of grandchild to Pope's *What oft was
thought, but ne'er so well express'd*. The way an idea is packaged in a lyric
essay, as opposed to anything more academic or traditional, takes that
commitment to personal emotions championed by lyric poetry and teaches
the reader through emotional and informational leaps. I'm reminded of
the Hunter/Jumper horseback-riding style I grew up practicing: Hunters
were judged on style and an elegant progression around a logical course.

Jumps were positioned in straight lines, curves were gentle, there was a measured answer that horse and rider were expected to arrive at, and the judge could assess how well they completed this set task. This is a traditional essay. In contrast, the jumpers' course was full of sharp turns and options, and the goal of a speedy and clean round encouraged creative choices and risk taking. The lyric essay takes these kinds of creative leaps and can sometimes unseat a reader with jarring revelations. "Time and Distance Overcome" by Eula Biss was my most memorable introduction to these jarring leaps which cemented both image and information in my mind as I "discovered" information along with her. With the lyric essay, it isn't only what we often thought but lacked elegant expression for, but new revelations, things that we often needed to think and know but lacked the connections between dots. The lyric essay both pushes us to leap and rewards the leap.

Layla Benitez-James, "Nausea"

*

i came to it late, admittedly, out of the confines of poetic form, in grad school, god forgive me, bored of perfecting the line i picked up maggie nelson's *bluets* at the old st. mark's bookshop, god rest its soul, classified under poetry. it was a gift, a revelation, a relief. ever since, teaching the essay mostly, mostly in comp, i've come to it in the hélene cixous way of coming to writing—gendered, exiled, porous, but then unsexed, rooted in language, poetics.

lately i've been thinking of essays in terms of their states of matter (i'm planning on writing a lyric essay on this): some essays aspire toward solidity, some end up more fluid, and some are a gas. lyric essays are a gas, the more poetry the better, the more fog in its streets, room for the reader to stretch out, make connections, be unsure. or just breathe. it shows trust in the reader, in abstraction, in multiplicity, in the future.

i love lyric essays for their ongoingness, their digressions, just a mind in love with itself, in the george oppen way, "consciousness // which has nothing to gain, which awaits nothing, / which loves itself." that stanza ends without period. if in oppen's *of being numerous* "we are pressed,

pressed on each other," the city a solid mass, writing that moves like poetry can offer relief from that. if in lyric poetry we are "obsessed, bewildered // by the shipwreck / of the singular," writing that moves in prose can offer us the chance to be numerous. either way, as he says, "speak // if you can // speak." this also ends without period, without ending. at least grammatically. it opens up into time. to open time.

Marina Blitshteyn, "Finding Your Voice"

✳

An essay that begins with the self, searching for the self—that's often the start of the lyric essay, yes; however, the self in this search reaches outward for the real stuff of the world. The lyric essay allows the self to encompass or become encapsulated within another structure in order to reorient the self to the mysteries, conundrums, complexities, ironies, wonders, or mishaps of existence. A lyric essay is always trying to find its way out of what it thinks it knows.

Jenny Boully, "On the EEO Genre Sheet"

✳

I wrote "Manual" as a segmented lyric essay because the material asked me to. The sickening night and bleary days surrounding it were so dense; the story demanded room to breathe. I had unsuccessfully tried to write "Manual" in other forms over the last decade. By breaking the subject into discreet parts and adding mundane ancillary topics like making toast and ticks, I finally found clarity in the muddled mess of memory, emotion, and trauma.

I wanted to explore the shooting but also its effect on my parenting. I also wanted to consider race and the attendant privileges of white domesticity. And I wanted to think about hands and the work they do: the hands of mothers when they tend to their children, their empty hands when they can't fix what has gone wrong, and the different hands that hold guns.

It was important to me to tell this story in part as a tribute to Leroy's life. I was not his friend but felt a sharp intimacy with him as I watched him struggle, emotionally anguished, and then be gunned down. My second-story vantage point offered a unique clarity of the unfolding scene. And for years, I carried that with me. I saw, and I knew, and I couldn't make sense of it. Thirty-five bullets were discharged that night, thirteen tore through his body, and twenty-two missed, hitting the surrounding walls, flying off in the air, and entering the neighboring apartment. This egregious and reckless waste of young life continues to haunt and enrage me.

Amy Bowers, "Manual"

*

Most of what I know about the lyric essay came from my time spent in a writing workshop focused on the genre led by poet Mary Ruefle. She began the workshop by saying, "Remember, the only thing that matters is you're alive on earth." I can't say exactly why, but this felt like mystical knowledge, and I took it to mean that while writing lyrically, one should make space for an almost exclusive focus on the sensory experience of now. What does your nose tell you about being alive? What do your teeth tell you? The parts of your fingers holding the pen? Give those parts of yourself, that are just as active as your mind and heart, the option—the responsibility—of voice. If you are to write lyrically, you must trust that what matters will speak. In any case, this is how I understood the thing. And so, before and while I wrote the first draft of "Thanks, but No," I let go of any logical intention and followed the way my initial image traveled through my body. I can still remember the physical experience of those words landing on the page, and how I felt while writing them: awake, alert, alive.

Emily Brisse, "Thanks, but No"

*

I took a course in graduate school called "The Art of the Essay" with memoirist Kathleen Finneran. One of our assignments that semester was to read the entire body of work of a single essayist, then write a critical piece in response to this essayist's work as well as a creative piece inspired by it. I chose lyric essayist Brenda Miller, who, as far as I can tell, coined the term *hermit crab essay* in the first place. (See *Tell It Slant*, coauthored by Miller and first published in 2004.) As I read Miller's body of work (five essay collections, two books on craft and the writing process, plus additional online publications), I studied the way she plays with form to get at difficult emotional experiences and complex relationships: a miscarriage, depression, breakups, health scares, an abusive relationship, step-parenting, and spiritual pilgrimage, to name a few. Her work gave me permission to play with form as I searched for ways into my own material, which seemed like a big hairy mass of "don't go there" at the time. Hermit crab essays subvert expectations while defining their own rules of engagement. They invite the reader to dissociate right alongside the writer, or to dissect a given moment, phase of life, or frame of mind. Hermit crab essays allow the reader to be a voyeur, or allow the writer to be someone else, someone two steps removed from the page. Adopting already existing documents, guides, lists, or other artifacts as a container for the material at hand can be a form of play too. In any case, the result often gets to the heart of what a writer can't or won't say in any other way.

Elizabeth K. Brown, "Informed Consent"

*

A confession: I can't say I know exactly what a lyric essay is or isn't, only that I know the feeling a good one evokes. My nonfiction writing background has been the opposite of lyric; I spent the first twelve years of my professional life as a daily newspaper reporter. I've always admired the writers of pieces whose "nut grafs" (journalism lingo for the So What paragraph of a piece of newswriting) lie in the associative space breaks of a braided essay, or the subversive formality of a hermit crab. But I had never considered myself among them.

Case in point: My contribution to this volume began as two unrelated pieces I never imagined braiding together—except for in an act of last-minute desperation. On the eve of my visit to poet Karen Leona Anderson's creative writing seminar at Saint Mary's College in Maryland, I hastily combined the two failed essays, a travel narrative and a short medical memoir, because the resulting hybrid aligned with the seminar's topical focus. I wrote DRAFT over each page, an apology, and swallowed a sense of dread when I took my seat at the table. Her undergraduate class lovingly workshopped my Frankenstein's monster of a DRAFT. That they saw so much in it, even when it was clearly unfinished, kept me going through many rounds of revisions.

I began to understand lyricism in fine-tuning between showing, telling, and something in lyric writing that is neither. Each rewrite, each reader (there were many more after those twenty-some writing students), helped me calibrate between those modes of exposition, scene, and the ineffable spaces between them. To (badly) paraphrase Wisława Szymborska's iconic line, their hearts pound inside this essay—because the sum of their experiences, associations, and emotional resonances have formed its circulatory system, and given me the courage to construct writing around what is neither shown nor told.

Angie Chuang, "Scars, Silence, and Dian Fossey"

*

The lyric essay is an act of observation, then exploration. Each word an engagement with the reader. To write the lyric essay is to both excavate and create the poetics of an experience. And to read one is to breathe at the intersection of witnessing and transformation. Which is to say, the lyric essay is the magical side effects of word-nerdery.

Chelsey Clammer, "Lying in the Lyric"

*

I am fascinated by the idea of deliberate ambiguity, the concept of Hemingway's "Iceberg theory," where a piece of writing is intentionally does not reveal what the story is about, allowing the reader to make that determination. I am fascinated with all the ways I can hint at the "thing": through the title, through imagery, through language, through structure. A good lyric essay gives you more and more every time you read it, no matter how short it is. I imagine that each time my reader sticks their head beneath the waters around the iceberg, they glimpse a ragged ridge, see how wide it spreads beneath the water, but come up for air before finding out all of the truth. You cannot stay under water long enough to see the whole thing. Which is why you go back, risk another dive, another dive, another dive.

Tyrese L. Coleman, "Why I Let Him Touch My Hair"

*

I think my lyric craft essay in this anthology embodies what I mean by lyric essay, but it is negative capability, hyperlink, lateral leaping. What Rilke's "Der Panther" describes as "the movement of . . . powerful soft strides / . . . like a ritual dance around a center" (trans. Stephen Mitchell). If Hermes created the lyre to salvage beauty from death, then the lyric essay is, literally, an attempt to stave off loss by transforming it into art.

Heidi Czerwiec, "Success in Circuit: Lyric Essay as Labyrinth"

*

I had written the four sections of "The Boys of New Delhi" as four stand-alone flash essays. But for the longest time, they didn't feel done. No matter how much I tinkered, not one seemed ready for publication. Ultimately, it made sense to club them together, to convey how one's vulnerability, and the people who prey on it, can change throughout one's life but never really disappear. I also wanted the sections to end abruptly to echo how such conversations continue to live on in one's mind. They are fragments, with no memory of what happened the day before or after, existing merely in the singular moment of their creation. Hence the decision to neither summarize nor make sense of them via one neat concluding paragraph but end the essay on a sharp break.

Sayantani Dasgupta, "The Boys of New Delhi: An Essay in Four Hurts"

*

The lyric essay offers an on-ramp to saying something that can't be said. By exceeding the bounds of traditional "essay," you can find release from the constraints associated with high school's ruled paper, its reek of BO, the undersides of desks lichened with bubble gum. Instead you'll find the freedom of walking on a high wall at night when your parents didn't know your whereabouts.

It's a film, a dream, the sky over a field, condensed into a small space. It should exist only as long as the bubble can sustain its own weight. Instead of being a structure, the lyric is the *idea* of a structure that frees us to express what we really need to say.

The dictionary definition of *lyric* includes "exuberant, rhapsodic." The lyric essay invites revelry in language, its rhythm, the lush taste of the perfect word. It's less focused on scene or reason and more tuned to the sensory impressions around an episode or epiphany. Less "what happened?" and more "what's the mark it left, and how does the scar feel?" It doesn't always have to be scarfs of birds and grass dancing in the breeze; it can be taut and quick, it can be funny.

Lyric is a luscious form of essay—like a dream, like looking at a painting. I think of staring at Jules Bastien-Lepage's *Joan of Arc* until the ghostly saints feel very clear and then flicker away. Even more than other essays, the lyric needs to avoid the maudlin and the trite; it needs to be especially new.

The lyric lets your mind's eye focus while another part of your brain pries open the vault of emotion and experience. Through its lens, you can stare into unsayability until you circumvent it. Coming out the other side, you may, in fact, say something. What you say may not be the thing you couldn't say, but instead you may say something more vital.

Susanna Donato, "Classified"

*

In name, a lyric essay resembles the contradictions of a Jerusalem artichoke. The tuber's not from Jerusalem, nor an artichoke exactly. Depending on its venue (farmers market, farm to table, grocery store), the root vegetable takes other names: sunchoke, sunroot, earth apple.

In structure, a lyric essay may also resemble a Jerusalem artichoke. The sunflowers entice the senses, conjuring something like beauty. Anchored in soil, their rugged roots are useful, nurturing, even tasty.

In my case, a lyric essay resembles what's sometimes called poet's prose. Close attention to form, to sentence and paragraph rather than image, figure, and line (though these linger), abides. Language remains its subject. In this interrogative, process-based writing, I foreground my life as a reader. For this reason (among others), a lyric essay may be more pleasurable to write than a poem. It eludes lyric's historical baggage, skirting what the scholar Gillian White calls "lyric shame," not to mention the seasonal squabbles of the poetry business.

But I'm scrubbing the knobby sunchoke too heartily. In my case, a lyric essay has been where the fragments of failed poems gathered into a story. A poem that flubbed its lines. A poem that wanted to stretch its legs. A poem greedy for sentences *and* white spaces.

Two poets' lyric essays showed me the way. The Puerto Rican poet Victor Hernández Cruz describes U.S. Latinx writers and performers reinventing English: "Worlds exist simultaneously, flashes of scenarios, linguistic stereo; they conflict, they debate, Spanish and English constantly breaking into each other like ocean waves." In a lyric essay, poem and prose constantly break into each other.

The Arkansan poet C. D. Wright had a similar notion of her languages meeting and, often as not, failing to. "I poetry," she proclaims, "I also arkansas." Then, "Sometimes these verbs coalesce. Sometimes they trot off in opposite directions." How can one tell the difference? Wright suggests a sensitive instrument: the nose. "When it begins to stink," a poem should be composted.

In my case, the lyric essay has helped me write with urgency about coparenting a daughter in an era of ecological catastrophe and the retrenchment of white supremacist heteropatriarchy. Minus heightened stakes, a lyric essay is diminished from something you *need* to write *in this form* to mere exercise. I remember that, when kept too long in the fridge or pantry, a Jerusalem artichoke gets slimy.

Michael Dowdy, "Elementary Primer"

*

Many when they hear the term *lyric essay* assume it means the prose is lyrical. It can be, but it isn't necessarily. I think this is because *lyric* is associated with poetry and music, which often is considered lyrical. To me, a lyric is self-expression in creative format. Just as song lyrics can be about any topic, set to different beats, tones, and timbres, and written for any genre of music, so too can the prose in a lyric essay be written in any number of formats. The words in the essay are the lyric, and the form and structure it takes is the composition.

Laurie Easter, "Searching for Gwen"

*

"In one's moments," writes Kenneth Burke, "one is absolute." The lyric essay is a moment—an attitude, a posture, a strut. In its patterns and sequences it mimics the fragmentary wholeness of our perception of life. Like the eyes on the back of a butterfly's wings returning our gaze. Like an octopus changing colors as it dreams.

Steve Edwards, "The Last Cricket"

*

The lyric essay is, at its heart, an act of generosity. It doesn't pronounce, as Thoreau did, on how one should live one's life. It doesn't say goodbye to all that, as Didion did, or argue against joie de vivre, as Lopate does. Most often, it eschews the polemical altogether, offering up instead the artifact. It says *look here* more often than *listen to me* and collects more than it digests. The lyric essay—and in this, it is more akin to the poem than to its prose relations—offers the reader the material form which to make meaning, rather than the meaning itself. For this reason, I especially favor the collage essay. A literary Cornell box, the collage gathers together its pieces and places them in a particular order, but it leaves the work of seeing those pieces in that order, and making sense of it all, to the reader. It invites us in; it says, *take a look around and tell me what you think*. It is, I think, the most conversational essay form in that it always assumes the reader will answer back, will do that work of assembling and reassembling its bits into something larger. And I love this collaborative spirit, both as a reader and a writer. Because I don't know anything, but I have seen some things, many of them beautiful, and I would love to show them to you and know what you see when you look at them.

Sarah Einstein, "Self-Portrait in Apologies"

*

It must contain evidence of a rich interiority that can sustain a narrative articulated with poetic phrasing. It does not require a journey though it may have one, often in the guise of a labyrinth gestured toward. Its shapeliness should belie a tight concentration of images, ideas, and thoughts, held together by a clear intelligence and clarion language. It must inhabit the in-between space, resisting both the classification of essay and that of poetry, while keeping easy pace with both.

Ru Freeman, "The Sound of Things Breaking"

*

Lyric essays *can* be so slippery to define, which made me terrified of them. Without a definition, how do you know if you are doing it right? They are essays, meditations on a subject—that definition is easier. But what does *lyrical* mean, really: Musical? Poetic? Songwriters will tell you they are not poets, poets will tell you they are not songwriters. Perhaps the lyric essay must be both. Like song lyrics, the essays make you see connections between things that seem to have no connection. Like poetry, they evoke emotions through words and patterns. As a nonfiction writer, I'm tempted to say they must also be true. But like the lyric essay, truth can be slippery to define.

Kristina Gaddy, "Intersectional Landscapes"

*

Often, I find there's a particular bias toward creative nonfiction, an impression that suggests an act of vanity, a mirror held up facing toward one's self. It's seen as *look at me*, rather than the *see with me* it actually is. Even among writers, I notice an unspoken disdain, an implied *oh, you write that?* that I don't see with poetry or fiction writers.

I was drawn to the format of a single-sentence essay after reading Jaquira Díaz's essay "Reflections, While Sitting in Traffic." Initially, I'd written the piece with that structure, though once I sat with the essay more in later revisions, I found myself incorporating the Twelve Steps into the piece; for a time, I considered restructuring the essay (as, say, an enumerated piece). Though one-sentence essays aren't terribly uncommon, I eventually opted to stick to it, less to pay homage to Díaz, and more to do justice to the stream-of-consciousness narrative, using commas and semicolons and conjunctions to convey pacing, cadence, and so on. As a lyric essay, I wanted to strike a balance between that and what was happening while still attempting to tell a good story.

Which amounts to, essentially, nothing. There's more I could say, of course: I could bring up the parallels and overlapping qualities of lyric essays and prose poems. I could say something about lyrically inclined imagery and an attention to language on a syntactical level. I could even mention narrative—how I later went to therapy and Got Better (which is hardly relevant here), or how I Moved On (a half-truth at best) and Persevered with Grace and Determination (eh, not really).

Certainly a lyric essay contains elements of the foregoing, but what *is* a lyric essay? Truthfully, I've no actual answer. I find with lyric essays, with essays that center around a narrative, things are different than other forms of writing. I lend myself to the lyric essay, yes, to tell a good story, but also in that I'm looking for something. *Essay*, after all, means "to try, to attempt."

It is never look *at* me. It is look *for* me. It is holding up a mirror facing away from oneself and hoping someone will see themselves in it. As I write this, I'm sitting in the student union, on my lunch break, and I'm just about out of time. Outside, perhaps a hundred feet from me, is the campus bus station. I can almost hear the *thrum-hiss-exhale* of the buses rumbling by like a sputtering heart, like weighty knocks at a door. What is it I can't stop looking for, that I can't put into words beyond *this happened to me, something of me is missing, have you seen it?* Look for it in these words. Tell me I'm not alone in this. Let me know when you find it. Let me know where I went.

An autumn breeze slips its fingers through the gaps in the branches of nearby trees, tugging and stirring the leaves.

Daniel Garcia, "Re: Sometime after 5:00 p.m.
on a Wednesday in the Middle of Autumn"

The lyric essay is first and foremost an essay; that is the noun in the phrase. The adjective conveys the style: lyric. The lyric essay's foundation resides in memory, experience, reflection, and fact, but its expression foregrounds poetic prerogatives of prosody and figurative language, while celebrating connotation, denotation, and the essences embedded in individual words.

My perhaps dogmatic conception of the lyric essay raises questions. Does something different arise when the noun becomes the adjective and vice-versa? Is the prose poem the lyric essay's opposite, its antagonist? Or fraternal twins, not identical but close enough to make some people pause? Is their relationship similar to how all squares are rectangles, but not all rectangles are squares, where all lyric essays are prose poems, but not all prose poems are lyric essays? Or is there a more fundamental distinction between the two?

I write lyric essays and not prose poems because I embrace the challenge of writing within truth's quagmire. Yes, we recreate dialogue and generate description from the blurry, shifting recollections of memory. The power—and dare I say, the fun—of writing lyric essays is in working within the parameters of truth while explicitly engaging with lyricism in its various forms. Most attempts to weave these strands together struggle. When they don't, they shine.

Nels P. Highberg, "This Is the Room Where"

*

What I like about the lyric essay is its versatility, the way you can braid themes and genres and linger on the sound of each word. When I write I often start with an image or series of images, usually a few snippets of memory or a scene from something I've read, and then follow those threads wherever they go.

Kelsey Inouye, "A Catalog of Faith"

*

As a poet, the lyric essay allows me to write pieces that are language centered while still playing with narrative and research in a way I often don't feel I can with poetry. When I was getting my MFA, there was a poem I wanted to write that included so much personal narrative, and I wanted to incorporate moments in time that weren't linear and create this wandering map of an event in my life. I didn't realize until later that I was writing my first segmented lyric essay. I've since fallen deeply in love with the lyric essay, and it serves my need to pull moments and gathered information together in fun and surprising ways. The lyric form has given me a way to expand my ideas into prose without sacrificing my aesthetic as a poet.

Christen Noel Kauffman, "Thanatophobia"

*

The flash lyric essay is more than a moment of mediation or a scene of action or one long glittering sentence, though the best of the genre can be a mixture of all three. Often the flash form reveals something about the malleability of space-time and collapses memories and events from the writer's life into a dynamic—sometimes unstable—vortex of language and image and association.

Christopher Linforth, "The Punch"

*

I've had many conversations about form, especially when discussing my lyric memoir *The In-Betweens*, which features my essay "My Mother's Mother," published here. In regard to form, I think memoir, in particular, operates a lot like memory. So when writing, I started with what I could remember—what I could see, what I experienced with my senses, or what my grandmother experienced, when retelling her story.

In "My Mother's Mother," there are cornerstones that hold up the story, which are grounded in images: the white apron with a black smudge, the plantation house, the big sturdy trees, and the constant reference to lynching. And then, I built the arc around that—what the images themselves could tell and how I brought that to fruition.

Sometimes when writing flash memoir, I feel as if I'm just arranging and rearranging photos and allowing them to do the work. I believe "My

Mother's Mother" exemplifies that process because it is written as a series of moments that, when formed into a narrative, tell the fragments of my grandmother's life, of her history, and maybe the untold stories of others.

Davon Loeb, "My Mother's Mother"

*

I write lyric essays as an extension of my poetic self. I find myself turning to them when I want to unravel myself from a tight poetic line. My favorite lyric essays pull me into the ocean of language.

Casandra López, "Fragment: Strength"

*

I love short prose that exists on the blurry boundary between lyric essay and prose poetry. I'm not interested in answering "What is a lyric essay?" or "What is prose poetry?" as much as I'm interested in examining what readers expect when they approach a piece as a lyric essay or as a prose poem. How do genre labels set up readers' expectations, and why does that matter? I've tested this with my college students for several years, and this is what I've found: When my students approach a text as a poem, they usually focus more on sound play, imagery, and figurative language. When they approach a short prose piece expecting it to be an essay, they are more attuned to details about the speaker, location, time period, and other aspects of context. I believe the genre label—even more than the title or anything else in the piece—has the power to shape what details readers notice and how they're able to receive and interpret the piece as a whole.

Katie Manning, "Nevermore"

*

There is something profoundly healing in discovering a sideways slant into personal story, inventive frameworks that push against traditional narratives and remind me of the discipline and freedom found in John Coltrane's jazz or Jackson Pollock's paintings. Braided, segmented, flash, and my personal favorite, the hermit crab essay, offer a way to confront erasure, transform traumatic fragments of memory into a cohesive whole and reshape the ugliness of trauma into something beautiful. As a woman of color and as a divergent thinker, the lyric essay helped me discover my voice.

Rowan McCandless, "Practical Magic: A Beginner's Grimoire"

*

Lyric essay invites me to enter the music of language, and therefore the music of unexpected meaning. Lyric essay grants me the long, long sentence, the odd choice of punctuation, the headlong beginning, and the ending that with other genres might seem truncated, even alarming. The process is no less rigorous than other writing, no less disciplined. Yet at its essence, it feels like climbing onto a raft and allowing the river to take me wherever it's going. When I return to other genres, I remember that ride down the river. I carry forward that current of exploration.

Marsha McGregor, "On Beauty Interrupted"

*

Even now, the definition of the lyric essay seems slippery to me, as it is a genre that is constantly changing the conventions of what it is or is supposed to be. The term *essay*, first used by the philosopher Michel Montaigne, comes from the French word *essai*, meaning "trial" or "an attempt." For Montaigne, the essay was the writer's *attempt* at examining his or her own views on life and the self. The lyric essay pushes further, moving beyond content to challenge the boundaries of what the overall form can do.

LaTanya McQueen, "Of a Confession, Sketched from Ten Vignettes"

*

I actually don't think of a lyric essay as the genre that arrives when nonfiction and poetry "have a baby." Instead I'm proud of the lyric essay as prose that has become familiar with the spatial, sonic, and formal strategies of poetry that other proses tend to ignore. Essays ask questions, and lyric essays do this primarily by *situating in relation*. The implied or literal gaps that define lyric essays invite the reader to participate, not in answering a question, but in expanding and specifying the ask. What is missing or *blank* in a lyric essay invites (or requires) the reader to insert what they've brought with them—a subjective experience—to build transitions, or bridges, across disparate sections. In this way, lyric essays have the power to make their readers complicit.

In a visual (lyric) essay like "Vide," white space that traditionally reads as vacant and that in lyric essays invites the reader's signature becomes active, to offer more direction. Following the tradition of the essay, visual essays are self-aware, and visually so. The shapes they take aim to play with a reader's perception and experience across time. As in examples of concrete poetry, shaped prose invites the audience to act as both reader and viewer and to see the shape in different ways as they move through the text.

At first glance, "Vide" may read like an abstract waveform, but as a reader progresses she may begin to perceive a coastline or, as she moves further, to see the shape of a body falling from a tall rock and into water. By the end, the shape of the text might ultimately appear more like the essay's final image—a stream of bats flying away from the viewer and toward the horizon. Which image is the one she can't unsee? This depends on the reader.

Sarah Minor, "Vide"

*

The Lyric Essay, Interviewed

INTERVIEWER: Are you hard to define?

THE LYRIC ESSAY: Scarily Yes

INTERVIEWER: Let's try to describe you a bit, then, by getting to know something of your habits and preferences. Do you have a favorite whiskey, for instance?

THE LYRIC ESSAY: Classy Rye I

INTERVIEWER: Me too. Do you play any musical instruments?

THE LYRIC ESSAY: Yas Sic Lyre

INTERVIEWER: Fascinating. I didn't know anyone still played a lyre. Are you a writer as well? Do you write anything?

THE LYRIC ESSAY: A Lyrics Yes

INTERVIEWER: Boxers or briefs?

THE LYRIC ESSAY: Lacy Yes Sir

INTERVIEWER: Hmmm! Okay, one last question. Are you to be believed? Are you telling the truth?

THE LYRIC ESSAY: Scary Lyes I

INTERVIEWER: I've heard that. And I've heard that you don't lose much sleep over it, that you are just fine blurring the boundaries between language and experience. Is that correct?

THE LYRIC ESSAY: Ya Cry Less I

Dinty W. Moore, "Frida's Circle"

*

A lyric essay elevates language, the music of the language, and form to the same level as narrative. I think of it as a baggy poem.

Caitlin Myer, "Late Bloom"

*

L-Y-R-I-C-E-S-S-A-Y

Slice. Lace. Ease. Lyre. Crease. Crass. Say. When asked to define or reflect on terms, my restless brain tends toward a Boggle of the mind. A stubborn tendency to express through language the notions found in between, outside of, within. The spaces between life and death, past and present, memory and remembering. The wing of a moth in the wind might appear aloft, or it may appear as dead. The lyric essay allows for poetry, nonfiction, ambiguity, and multitude as much as it allows for imagination and wonder.

Lyric contains *cry*, which can occur at the extremes of human emotion— joy and sadness, meditation and madness. *Lyric* contains *icy*. Something liquid in a solid form.

Case. Ace. Rice. Year. Early. Rise—Yes. The lyric essay is an affirmation. An homage to language for the sake of language or, rather, for the sake of meaning over narrative, over experience, over overt definition. An assertion of the senses. An avowal of substance.

Jericho Parms, "Immortal Wound"

*

I once heard Pam Houston compare the lyric essay to juggling: it was a challenge, a particular art form, she said, to throw as many balls up into the air as you could, to keep them rotating with clocklike precision and never drop one of them. Then there's that singular moment when the juggler finishes her act and manages to catch all the balls in one hand: THE END, all the orbs dropping at once, in one open palm, *thunk, thunk, thunk*.

Then, at NonfictioNow in Reykjavik, Lacy M. Johnson talked about the importance of the segmented essay—the fragmented narrative—for women writers in particular. Our lived experiences are often traumatized, jumbled; we are rarely allowed to move forward in straight, chronological lines. Of course, our essays resemble broken windows, shards of glass. How else should we tell our stories?

Every time I sit down to shape a new essay, I think about Pam's and Lacy's words. Like the former, I still very much enjoy the play of the lyric essay, the magic of launching those balls into the air, making them spin together. And like the latter, the form, for me, is an organic choice—I don't select it unless it is the appropriate container for my subject. And it so frequently is the *only* choice because I'm almost always fighting the box that cultural standards have built for me to live inside; I'm almost always questioning norms regarding justice, love, identity, ownership, good art. I have to bust that coffin into tiny pieces.

Over time, I've also come to my own metaphor for the lyric essay: I'm chasing rabbits. In the beginning, it would appear that I've caught the strong scent of the idea I'm hunting on the page, but then I find myself jumping down a tunnel, and soon it forks, and so I burrow in a new direction, and then another, until I'm not sure which course leads up and which down. It gets darker and darker, and just when I think the essay has gone completely mad, the rabbit leading me to a dead end, or even a trap, I see a light in front of me, a pinprick, and then brighter, brighter, until I burst through into the fresh air again. The rabbit is gone, of course, such a quick little thing, but it was always the chase the essay needed, not the kill.

Leslie Jill Patterson, "Against Fidelity"

A flash essay is a solid, rounded stone. It is self-contained; you can roll it around in your palm, warming it with your attention. Soon, you'll notice little inclusions, cracks, a spot of rougher texture. The closer you look, the more you can see.

Sarah Perry, "Satellite"

*

A while back, an editor I worked with challenged the use of the term *lyric essay*—"shouldn't that be a term someone *else* applies to your essay?" I know what he meant—"lyrical," inflected a certain way, sounds like a vanity applied to oneself. As in, "I write 'illuminated' or 'ethereal' or 'authentic' essays." I never felt completely at home with the term, though indeed it was something others did apply to my work. "Lyric" suggests that sound, pulse, rhythm (music), and form (leaps, juxtapositions, turns) have prominent places in prose. If that's the case, then the "lyric" impulse is seeded into many forms of prose. I write essays—a capacious form, and one I like keeping whole and therefore mysterious as a category. Oppression, shit, ecological ruin, loss of biodiversity, our core tethering to all our kin—all these "subjects" have ways of singing into the unutterable.

"Yeah, they often sound like poems" is my other favorite response.

Lia Purpura, "Loss Collection"

*

To paraphrase U.S. Supreme Court Justice Potter Stewart, who defined his threshold test for obscenity as "I know it when I see it," I know a lyric essay when I read it. Lyric essays are evocative, and as much art as they are prose. I am sure it's a lyric essay that I'm reading when I want to lay down in it and fall asleep like Dorothy and her cohorts did in the field of poppies outside the Emerald City.

I tend to write more traditional essays. But occasionally, I'll break out with a lyric essay or poem, especially when I feel the essence of a being, location, or circumstance, or as Lawrence Ferlinghetti said about writing poetry, when I care to make public my private solitude.

Amy Roost, "The Wait(ress)"

*

I primarily write poems, but now and then the right margin calls me and I find myself extending the line outward, all the way to the eastern seaboard of the page. This asks me to focus on the unit of the sentence rather than the line. Sentences change my priorities. Music becomes more of an undercurrent than a primary concern as it is in poems. Sentences let more in—and by *more* I guess I mean narrative details and the forward motion of a plot and even argumentation. Poems strike me as representative of a compressed moment of being. Even if they have narrative elements, it is narrative as remembered or considered in a charged present tense. The sentence allows for sequencing, causality: this happened, then that happened, and that led to this. In poems, everything happens at once. Past and future are an agreed-upon illusion. I go to a lyric essay with material that demands temporal sequencing, that gains volition from linear development, even if that linearity includes backroads and rest stops.

Yes, everything I've said thus far is arguable. There are numerous examples of lyric essays that inhabit a moment of being, and poems that primarily rest in plot. For me anyway, the division between a lyric essay and a poem is a barely there wedding veil, a membrane as thin as a ghost. It's a borderline that wavers and that I can't get my mind around; thus, it allows for mystery, like a foggy night, a country road, and low-beam headlights. The lyric essay is not so much marginal as in between. It's the stepchild who spends a lot of time in her room, no matter the house, playing with horse statues.

One thing each genre has in common with a traditional essay, and this, too, is arguable, is that all three can be said to have a thesis. Even a poem. Maybe especially a poem, if poems, indeed, are the most theoretical. There is something to be proved, a reality or surreality to be established, an idea to be enacted, an experience from which the writing must render the tallow. The choice of genre for me, especially line versus sentence, is all about the nature of the thesis. What I mean is less about its intellectual tenor than its texture, and therefore the texture of the language one needs in order to serve it, and whether that texture is best unfolded via linear time, or quick-blooms in the present moment.

The DNA that links my first genre, poetry, and my second, the lyric essay, is that word—*lyric*—characterized by a single speaker, an expression of deep feeling, and attention to music. I love that the lyric essay, that hybrid, or better, that two-headed wonder, can hold poetry's urgency and intimacy while maintaining the essay's traditional commitments. Because the lyric essay is so impossible to accurately define it allows its practitioner space to re-invent its borders. In that regard, it enhances the writer's authority. *It's a lyric essay because I say it is. It's a poem, despite the fact that it looks like prose, because I say it is.* The baby's name determines the way the baby is received.

Another link between poetry and the lyric essay is silence. I'm not speaking here of the need for silence as a condition of creation, which is also true for some of us, but the archetypal silence, the solitude, the privacy, out of which the individual voice emerges and sings. There is no shortcut to it, no way to avoid its loneliness, which lives at the very heart of the lyric, whether essay or poem. The mother of song is silence. The lyric writer endlessly breaks her, and like a prodigal, endlessly returns.

Diane Seuss, "Gyre"

*

For me, even though fiction and nonfiction share the same craftsman's toolbox, the processes couldn't be more different. Fiction is like molding with clay. If I need material, I just grab a handful of plot or images and glom it on. Sequence, details, meaning—I can choose from any to form designs that suit the narrative. Nonfiction is like chiseling through granite. Beneath, a form waits—but getting to it requires a different kind of labor. And hopefully, buried even deeper, there's some form of connective tissue, the elusive threads I need to discover to give resonance to this event lifted from the randomness of my life.

And at the end of it all, the confession all writers understand, the knowing I can't offer truth, only experience. My memories fade by the year, and in my head, warped filters, lenses crafted by personal mythologies and the humblings and humiliations that have been my truest teachers. So here's my experience, imperfect, spotty, yet rendered as honest and naked as I can conjure.

Curtis Smith, "I'm No Sidney Poitier"

*

Lyric and Essay

Lyric: structure similar to the structure of a lyric poem, which is to say that (primarily) the repetition and variation of image, idea, and emotion—rather than (primarily) narrative or logic—provide armature and engine.

Lyric: language deliberate as the language of a lyric poem or as the progression of notes in a Beethoven quartet, which is to say that placing a period and then starting the next sentence with *But* creates a suspension, which is to say that an alliteration of *s*'s may appropriately describe little waves when they touch the shore, which is to say a well-placed semicolon acts as a pivot point.

Essay: true, which is to say if I wrote about imagining my father while visiting the Harvard Museum of Natural History and decided, instead, to write about my father actually being there with me at the Harvard Museum of Natural History, I would write fiction instead.

Maya Sonenberg, "Chance Operations"

*

A lyric essay is almost more concerned about what is not said. The restraint and negative space give room for imagination, for questions that are too terrifying to give form, for ghosts, for breath and gasp and sigh.

Eric Tran, "Prophecy"

*

If an essay is the mind on the page, a lyric essay implies a particularly musical mind at work or a mind thinking through the medium of music and its imagined shapes. This means surprise and pattern making. It means that, while narrative may show up, neither the wave nor the triangle nor the male orgasm are the lyric essay's chosen shapes. Instead, the reading experience is patterned with mini explosions that surprise or confuse or madden us. The author was talking about the *Nutcracker* and now she's imagining her mother as a mouse?! We were reading about pain and now we're contemplating chickens and absolute zero?! Like a volta at the end of a poem, these careening turns in the essay's road are meant to disorient us, to make us forget what we expect from prose. But they must also build one upon the next, echoing or refracting or colliding so that meaning accumulates more than it is constructed, so that we spin around a story instead of rolling one on the page. Until we reach the end and have to reckon with what has just happened. Before it dies, the lyric essay should give us something: a feeling, an understanding, a satiated exhaustion. Because lyric or not, it is still an essay, and a good essay always convinces the reader that she has entered someone else's mind and spent a little time there, listening to the music play.

Sarah Viren, "Mash-Up: A Family Album"

*

The lyric essay reminds me of lily pads slathered across the surface of a pond. As a child, I was enamored of lily pads I saw at Camp Long—their shimmery green beauty, the intermittent flowers (purple, yellow, pink, and white) that blossomed among them like aquatic ellipses. *The pond's punctuation*, I might have said, but didn't.

Imagine my surprise when I learned lily pads were not merely floating atop the water but were actually tethered to the bottom of the pond through an intricate system of stems, tubes, and stoma. Lush and dense, pleasing to the eye, often placid on the surface but always carefully, even painstakingly, organized on the underside: well, you see the metaphor, don't you?

Sometimes people ask me what it's like to *write* a lyric essay, and that's harder to describe. Still, I try:

I say it's like assembling a puzzle—only the box you start with is full of pieces you have to cut yourself and the cover of the box is blank until you draw the picture that goes there.

Regardless, a giddy feeling comes over me whenever a lyric essay is nigh, not unlike the feeling I used to have as a child spreading the contents of a puzzle box on the dining room table, then propping the lid as pictorial guide. With a lyric essay, though, you're making incisions into a plain sheet of cardboard, cutting shapes from the alphabet itself—carving out the most particular words.

And while the pieces you cut are fragments, true, their edges are precise, and while you cut the language into shapes, you also have to draw the ways they'll fit together. To make a lyric essay is to toggle: between parts both essential and ancillary—you won't know which are which at first—in pursuit of an elusive whole. So you switch back and forth, from box-knife to Cray-Pas, from cutting to coloring, preparing the pieces while also devising their sequence and arrangement, the larger thing they'll add up to—that (hopefully) unified, (preferably) enthralling gestalt.

What I don't say, or rarely, is that I fell into that pond at Camp Long trying to scoop up a lily pad in my hand. (Such resistance where I thought the leaf would be light and soft, an easy grab!)

What I don't say, or rarely, is that I was very poor at puzzle assemblage overall but was drawn to the *idea* of the jigsaw: making something on the table that resembled something on the lid, though they were different textures, those pictures—like, I might say now, life and art.

As I'm writing this, someone could peer over my shoulder and insist, "You need to cut the lily pads or the puzzles because the two don't go together." But I won't. I think lyric essayists are obstinate in certain ways, especially about the kinds of things that "go together." Instead, I'll draw a cover on the puzzle box, shimmery green, lily pads slathered across its surface . . .

Julie Marie Wade, "What's Missing Here?"

*

I don't know what *lyric essay* has become. I never knew what *lyrical essay* meant, and I almost don't want to think about it, because I suspect it speaks to the fact that a writer's love of words and sentences is, for some readers and some outlets, optional. I try to hold *lyric essay* tight, but it grows, morphs, and squirms out of my hands.

I use a different term now, *exquisite vessel*, which occurred to me when I was thinking about the role of materiality in Native essayists' approaches to form. Think of a basket, its shape determined by what it should hold: berries, water, camas. Clams without water or sand. An essay, too, is a beautiful and useful container. For me, this is not a metaphor but a shared lineage. Cosmologies and axiologies shape relationships between beauty, meaning, utility, and purpose.

I like *exquisite vessel* because it brings to mind the Coast Salish and Klickitat baskets I've held. Even as I study the details of the weave, I can see the entirety of the basket's shape. Anyone is welcome to use this term, but I have no expectations that they will. I'm used to Indigenous knowledges being seen as niche rather than the foundations they are, embedded in and emerging from the land that every square inch of the United States settles into. Settler colonialism is nearly too large to envision whole. Anyway, I would rather look at this: split root against split root, over and over and over, a process I recognize and a term I feel. *Exquisite vessel* can't do what *lyric essay* does in situating me within a literary tradition and beckoning to readers. Okay. Find me on the mountain with a basket tied to my waist, one hand in a bush, pulling berries into my palm the way I was taught.

Elissa Washuta, "Apocalypse Logic"

*

Put simply, the lyric essay is shaped like the inside of my head. I say that because lyric essays move between poetry and prose and even image, and so does my writing, and so does my imagination. The lyric essay amplifies associational forms, the primacy of the image, the poetics of prose, emotional intensities, repetition and cyclical time, and the free-flow of form untethered from a unified voice or singular narrative strategy. The lyric essay lets go of the hegemony of plot in favor of the phenomenon of patterns, as reflected in what has become my mantra from Virginia Woolf: "Let us record the atoms as they fall upon the mind in the order in which they fall, let us trace the pattern, however disconnected and incoherent in appearance, which each sight or incident scores upon the consciousness."

Lidia Yuknavitch, "Woven"

Source Acknowledgments

Image credits

Introduction

Braiding V-Technique, by Stilfehler. CC BY-SA 3.0, https://commons.wikimedia.org
/w/index.php?curid=28031958.

Practical Magic

All images except those appearing with captioned credit lines or noted below are
courtesy of the author.

Full Moon as Seen from Denmark, by Peter Freiman. CC BY-SA 3.0, https://commons
.wikimedia.org/w/index.php?curid=6438448.

Publication credits

Etymologies in the introduction, "Meditations," and contributors list come from the
New Oxford American Dictionary, version 2.3.0 (238).

"Apocalypse Logic" by Elissa Washuta was previously published in *The Offing* (November 21, 2016) and *Shapes of Native Nonfiction: Collected Essays by Contemporary Writers*, ed. Elissa Washuta and Theresa Warburton (Seattle: University of Washington Press, 2019).

"Beasts of the Fields" by Aimée Baker was previously published in *Guernica* (February 19, 2020).

"Body Wash: Instructions on Surviving Homelessness" by Dorothy Bendel was previously published in *Catapult* (October 6, 2017).

"Frida's Circle" by Dinty W. Moore was previously published in *Sweet* 3, no. 2 (January 2011).

"Gyre" by Diane Seuss was previously published in *Brevity* 45 (Winter 2014).

"The Heart as a Torn Muscle" by Randon Billings Noble was previously published in *Brevity* 48 (Winter 2015) and *Be with Me Always: Essays* (Lincoln: University of Nebraska Press, 2019).

"Immortal Wound" by Jericho Parms was previously published in *Lost Wax* (Athens: University of Georgia Press, 2016).

"The Last Cricket" by Steve Edwards was previously published in *Orion* (Fall 2020).

"Loss Collection" by Lia Purpura was previously published in *All the Fierce Tethers* (Louisville KY: Sarabande Books, 2019).

"Lying in the Lyric" by Chelsey Clammer was previously published in *Essay Daily* (September 7, 2015) and *Circadian* (Pasadena: Red Hen Press, 2017).

"My Mother's Mother" by Davon Loeb was previously published in *The In-Betweens* (Sefton Park, Australia: Everytime Press, 2018) and in *Split Lip Magazine* on January 14, 2018.

"Nevermore" by Katie Manning was previously published in *MORIA*, no. 4 (Fall 2019) and *28,065 Nights* (New Orleans: River Glass Books, 2020).

"On the EEO Genre Sheet" by Jenny Boully was previously published in *Bending Genre: Essays on Creative Nonfiction* (New York: Bloomsbury, 2013) and *Betwixt-and-Between: Essays on the Writing Life* (Minneapolis: Coffee House Press, 2018).

"Re: Sometime after 5:00 p.m. on a Wednesday in the Middle of Autumn" by Daniel Garcia was previously published in *Gordon Square Review*, no. 5 (November 2019).

"Self-Portrait in Apologies" by Sarah Einstein was previously published in *Fringe*, no. 24 (October 4, 2010).

"Vide" by Sarah Minor was previously published in *Best American Experimental Writing 2020*, ed. Carmen Maria Machado and Joyelle McSweeney (Middletown CT: Wesleyan University Press, 2020).

"Why I Let Him Touch My Hair" by Tyrese L. Coleman was previously published in *Brevity* 53 (Fall 2016) and *How to Sit: A Memoir in Stories and Essays* (Baltimore: Mason Jar Press, 2018).

"Woven" by Lidia Yuknavitch was previously published in *Guernica* (August 2015).

"Late Bloom" is excerpted from *Wiving: A Memoir of Loving Then Leaving the Patriarchy* (New York: Arcade, 2020) by Caitlin Myer.

Contributors

ORIGIN mid-16th century: from Latin *contribut-* 'brought together, added', from the verb *contribuere,* from *con-* 'with' + *tribuere* 'bestow'

TALEA ANDERSON is a librarian at Washington State University with BA degrees in history and creative nonfiction writing. She has published creative work in Walla Walla University's *Gadfly,* Central Washington University's *Manastash,* and *Cobalt.* She was born with congenital cataracts and her recent work often deals with vision loss.

AIMÉE BAKER is the author of *Doe* (University of Akron Press, 2018) and winner of the Akron Prize. Her work has appeared in journals such as *Guernica, The Southern Review, Gulf Coast,* and *Witness.* She teaches at the State University of New York–Plattsburgh, where she is also the executive editor of *Saranac Review.*

SANDRA BEASLEY is the author of four poetry collections—*Made to Explode; Count the Waves; I Was the Jukebox,* winner of the Barnard Women Poets Prize; and *Theories of Falling*—as well as *Don't Kill the Birthday Girl: Tales from an Allergic Life,* a disability memoir. She also edited *Vinegar and Char: Verse from the Southern Foodways Alliance.* She lives in Washington DC.

DOROTHY BENDEL's writing appears in *Catapult, Literary Hub, Electric Literature, American Literary Review, The Rumpus,* and additional publications. See more of her work at dorothybendel.com.

LAYLA BENITEZ-JAMES lives in Alicante. Her work appears in *Acentos Review, Guernica, Poetry London, Waxwing, Revista Kokoro,* and *Asymptote Journal. God Suspected My Heart Was a Geode but He Had to Make Sure,* selected by Major Jackson for Cave Canem's Toi Derricotte & Cornelius Eady Chapbook Prize, was published by Jai-Alai Books in Miami.

Born in the Soviet Union, MARINA BLITSHTEYN came to the United States with her family as refugees. She is the author of *Two Hunters*, published by Argos Books in 2019 with a CLMP Face Out grant. Prior chapbooks include *Russian for Lovers* (Argos Books), *Nothing Personal* (Bone Bouquet Books), *$kill$* (dancing girl press), and *Sheet Music* (Sunnyoutside Press). She is a lecturer in composition and hybrid writing and runs the Loose Literary Canons, a feminist reading group in New York City and over Zoom.

JENNY BOULLY is the author of *Betwixt-and-Between: Essays on the Writing Life*. Her previous books include *not merely because of the unknown that was stalking toward them*, *The Book of Beginnings and Endings: Essays*, *[one love affair]**, *of the mismatched teacups, of the single-serving spoon: a book of failures*, and *The Body: An Essay*. She currently teaches at the Bennington Writing Seminars.

AMY BOWERS is a Florida native currently living in Connecticut with her family. Her writing explores domestic culture, the insect and natural worlds, and manufactured places and spaces. She is currently working on an essay collection about growing up in Central Florida among amusement parks, alligators, and hurricanes. She holds an MFA from Bennington Writing Seminars. Her work has been published in *Bella Grace*, *Mabel Magazine*, PANK *Magazine*, and *Centered*.

EMILY BRISSE's essays have appeared in publications including the *Washington Post*, *Creative Nonfiction's True Story*, *Ninth Letter*, and *River Teeth*. She is a *december magazine* Curt Johnson Prose Award finalist, a Pushcart Prize nominee, and a 2018 recipient of a Minnesota Arts Board Grant. She teaches English in Minneapolis.

ELIZABETH K. BROWN's essays have appeared in *Brevity* and *They Said* (Black Lawrence Press, 2018). Her play, *You Don't Live Here Anymore*, was selected for the A. E. Hotchner Playwriting Festival and will be produced in 2021. Currently completing a master's degree in clinical mental health counseling, Elizabeth has been a writing fellow at the Kimmel Harding Nelson Center for the Arts and holds an MFA from Washington University in Saint Louis. elizakae.com.

ANGIE CHUANG's debut memoir, *The Four Words for Home* (Aquarius Press/Willow Books, 2014) won an Independent Publishers Book Award Bronze Medal. Her work has appeared in *Creative Nonfiction, The Asian American Literary Review, Litro*, and *The Best Women's Travel Writing*. She lives in Denver and is on the journalism faculty of University of Colorado–Boulder.

CHELSEY CLAMMER is the author of the award-winning essay collection *Circadian* (Red Hen Press, 2017) as well as *BodyHome* (Hopewell, 2015). Her work has appeared in *Salon, The Rumpus, Hobart, Brevity, McSweeney's Internet Tendency, The Normal School*, and *Black Warrior Review*. She teaches online writing classes with WOW! *Women On Writing* and is a freelance editor. www.chelseyclammer.com.

TYRESE L. COLEMAN is the author of the collection, *How to Sit*, a 2019 Pen Open Book Award finalist published with Mason Jar Press in 2018. Writer, wife, mother, attorney, and writing instructor, she is a contributing editor at *Split Lip Magazine*. Her essays and stories have appeared in several publications, including *Black Warrior Review, Literary Hub, The Rumpus*, and the *Kenyon Review*. She is an alumnus of the Writing Program at Johns Hopkins University and a Kimbilio Fiction Fellow. Find her at tyresecoleman.com or on Twitter @tylachelleco.

Essayist and poet HEIDI CZERWIEC is the author of the lyric essay collection *Fluid States*, winner of Pleiades Press's 2018 Robert C. Jones Prize for Short Prose, and the poetry collection *Conjoining*. She teaches and writes in Minneapolis. Visit her at heidiczerwiec.com.

SAYANTANI DASGUPTA is the author of *Women Who Misbehave* (forthcoming, Penguin Random House), *Fire Girl: Essays on India, America, & the In-Between*—a finalist for the 2016 Foreword Indies Awards—and the chapbook *The House of Nails: Memories of a New Delhi Childhood*. Her writings have appeared in several national and international publications such as *The Rumpus* and *The Hindu*. She teaches in the MFA program at the University of North Carolina–Wilmington and has also taught in India, Italy, and Mexico.

SUSANNA DONATO's work has appeared in *Electric Literature, Redivider, Proximity, Entropy*, and elsewhere. She was born in the steel-mill town of Pueblo, Colorado, and now lives in Denver. Find her at susannadonato .com/creative or on Twitter @susannadonato.

MICHAEL DOWDY is a poet, critic, essayist, and editor. His books include the collection of poems *Urbilly*, the study of Latinx poetry *Broken Souths*, and, as coeditor with Claudia Rankine, the critical anthology *Poetics of Social Engagement*. He teaches at the University of South Carolina. For more information, visit www.michael-dowdy.com.

LAURIE EASTER is the author of the essay collection *All the Leavings*, forthcoming from Oregon State University Press in fall 2021. Her essays have been listed as Notable in *Best American Essays* and awarded a grant and a fellowship by the Vermont Studio Center. Her work appears in *The Rumpus, Chautauqua*, and *The Shell Game: Writers Play with Borrowed Forms*, among others. She lives off the grid in southern Oregon.

STEVE EDWARDS is author of the memoir *Breaking into the Backcountry*, the story of his seven months as caretaker of a backcountry homestead along the Rogue River in Oregon. His writing can be found in *Longreads, Literary Hub, Orion Magazine, The Rumpus, Electric Literature*, and elsewhere. He lives in Massachusetts.

SARAH EINSTEIN teaches creative writing at the University of Tennessee–Chattanooga. She is the author of *Mot: A Memoir* (University of Georgia Press, 2015) and *Remnants of Passion* (SheBooks, 2014). Her essays and short stories have appeared in the *Sun, Ninth Letter*, PANK *Magazine*, and other journals. Her work has been reprinted in the *Best of the Net* and awarded a Pushcart Prize and the AWP Prize for Creative Nonfiction.

RU FREEMAN is a Sri Lankan and American novelist, poet, editor, and critic whose work appears internationally and in translation including in the *UK Guardian*, and the *New York Times*. She is the author of the novels *A Disobedient Girl* and *On Sal Mal Lane*, a New York Times Editor's Choice Book, and the forthcoming collection *Sleeping Alone* (2022). She is the editor of the anthology, *Extraordinary Rendition: American Writers on Palestine* and *Indivisible: Global Leaders on Shared Security*. She teaches creative writing in the United States and abroad and directs the artists network for Narrative 4.

KRISTINA GADDY is the author of *Flowers in the Gutter: The True Story of the Edelweiss Pirates, the Teenagers Who Resisted the Nazis* (Dutton, 2020) and *Well of Souls: Music, Dance, Spirituality, and the Early Banjo*, forthcoming from Norton in 2022. Her journalism and essays have appeared in the *Washington Post, Baltimore Sun, Baltimore*, OZY, *Narratively*, and *Proximity*, among others. She received her MFA in nonfiction writing from Goucher College.

DANIEL GARCIA's essays appear or are forthcoming in SLICE, *Denver Quarterly, The Offing, Ninth Letter, Guernica, Hayden's Ferry Review*, and elsewhere. Poems appear or are forthcoming in *The Puritan, Harbor Review, So to Speak, Arkansas International, Ploughshares*, and others. A recipient of the Myong Cha Son Haiku Award and winner of a Short Prose Prize from *Bat City Review*, Daniel has received awards and scholarships from Tin House and the Mayborn Literary Nonfiction Conference. Daniel's essays appear as Notables in *Best American Essays*.

NELS P. HIGHBERG is a professor of English and modern languages at the University of Hartford. His literary work has been nominated for a Pushcart Prize and appeared in journals such as *Concho River Review, Riding Light Review, Duende, After the Art*, and *Intima: A Journal of Narrative Medicine*.

KELSEY INOUYE holds a PhD in education at the University of Oxford. Her work has appeared in *Tarpaulin Sky, Ricepaper Magazine*, and elsewhere.

CHRISTEN NOEL KAUFFMAN lives and teaches in Richmond, Indiana, with her husband and two wild daughters. Her essays and poems can be found or are forthcoming in journals such as *Tupelo Quarterly, Cincinnati Review, Booth, Willow Springs*, DIAGRAM, and *The Normal School*, among others.

CHRISTOPHER LINFORTH is the author of *Directory* (Otis Books/Seismicity Editions, 2020). He has published nonfiction in *Hinterland, Dallas Review, Gargoyle, New Madrid, Whiskey Island, South Dakota Review*, and other literary magazines.

DAVON LOEB is the author of the memoir *The In-Betweens* (West Virginia University Press, 2022). He earned an MFA in creative writing from Rutgers University–Camden. Davon is an assistant features editor at *The Rumpus*. His work has been featured at *Catapult, The Rumpus, Ploughshares Blog, PANK Magazine, Creative Nonfiction,* CRAFT *Literary,* and elsewhere. His writing has been nominated for the Pushcart Prize and the Best of the Net. Davon is a high school English teacher, husband, and father living in New Jersey. He can be reached at davonloeb.com and on Twitter @ LoebDavon.

CASANDRA LÓPEZ is a California Indian (Cahuilla/Tongva/Luiseño) and Chicana writer. She's the author of the poetry collection *Brother Bullet,* and her memoir-in-progress, *A Few Notes on Grief,* was granted a 2019 James W. Ray Venture Project Award. She's a founding editor of *As/Us* and teaches at Northwest Indian College.

KATIE MANNING is the founding editor in chief of *Whale Road Review* and a professor of writing at Point Loma Nazarene University in San Diego. Her most recent books are *Tasty Other* (Main Street Rag Poetry Book Award, 2016) and *28,065 Nights* (River Glass Books, 2020).

ROWAN McCANDLESS writes from Treaty One territory in Winnipeg, Manitoba. In 2020 she won a National Magazine Award and in 2018 the Constance Rooke Creative Nonfiction Prize. Her work has appeared in *The Fiddlehead,* the anthology *Black Writers Matter,* and elsewhere. Her first book, *Persephone's Children,* is forthcoming from Dundurn Press in 2021. Discover more at rowanmccandless.com.

MARSHA McGREGOR's literary nonfiction has appeared in *BrainChild, Zone 3, Kenyon Review Online, Fourth Genre, Literary Mama,* and else-where. A Peter Taylor Fellow for the Kenyon Review Writers Workshop and a fellow for the Kenyon Review Writing Workshop for Teachers, she leads writing workshops for literary organizations and library systems.

LATANYA McQUEEN is an assistant professor at Coe College. Her essay collection, *And It Begins Like This,* was recently published with Black Lawrence Press. She is an associate editor for *Story Magazine* and a non-fiction editor for *Gigantic Sequins.*

SARAH MINOR is the author of *Bright Archive* (Rescue Press, 2020), *Slim Confessions* (Noemi Press, 2021), and the digital chapbook *The Persistence of the Bonyleg: Annotated* (Essay Press, 2016). Minor is assistant professor of nonfiction at the Cleveland Institute of Art and video essays editor at *TriQuarterly Review*.

DINTY W. MOORE is author of the theological memoir *To Hell with It: Of Sin and Sex, Chicken Wings, and Dante's Entirely Ridiculous, Needlessly Guilt-Inducing Inferno*, the writing guide *Crafting the Personal Essay*, and numerous other books. He is deathly afraid of polar bears.

CAITLIN MYER is the author of *Wiving: A Memoir of Loving Then Leaving the Patriarchy* (Arcade, 2020). Her work can be found in *Guernica, Electric Literature, The Butter, Joyland, No Tokens*, and on NPR's *The Moth Radio Hour*, among others. She has received fellowships from several organizations, including the MacDowell Colony. She currently lives in Portugal.

RANDON BILLINGS NOBLE is an essayist. Her collection *Be with Me Always* was published by the University of Nebraska Press in 2019, and her lyric essay chapbook *Devotional* was published by Red Bird in 2017. Other work has appeared in the Modern Love column of the *New York Times, Brevity, Creative Nonfiction*, and elsewhere. Currently she is the founding editor of the online literary journal *After the Art*.

JERICHO PARMS is the author of *Lost Wax* (University of Georgia Press, 2016). Her essays have appeared in *Fourth Genre, The Normal School, Hotel Amerika, Passages North*, and elsewhere.

LESLIE JILL PATTERSON teaches in the creative writing program at Texas Tech University. Her prose has appeared in *Gulf Coast, Baltimore Review, Colorado Review*, and *Prime Number Magazine*, among others. Her recent awards include the Richard J. Margolis Award for Social Justice Writing and a Pushcart Prize. She serves as copyeditor for *Creative Nonfiction* and edits *Iron Horse Literary Review*.

SARAH PERRY's debut memoir, *After the Eclipse*, was named a New York Times Book Review Editors' Choice. She is the recipient of a 2020–21 Tulsa Artist Fellowship and was the 2019 McGee Distinguished Professor of Creative Writing at Davidson College. She holds an MFA in nonfiction from Columbia University and has taught at Columbia and elsewhere in New York City. She is at work on a second memoir. Find her on Instagram @sarahperry100 and at sarahperryauthor.net.

LIA PURPURA's *On Looking* (essays) was a finalist for the National Book Critics Circle Award. Her latest collections are *It Shouldn't Have Been Beautiful* (poems, Penguin) and *All the Fierce Tethers* (essays, Sarabande). Her work appears in the *New Yorker*, the *Paris Review*, *Emergence*, *Orion*, and elsewhere. A Guggenheim Fellow, Purpura is writer in residence at the University of Maryland–Baltimore County.

AMY ROOST is a freelance writer and podcaster and an Annenberg California Health Journalism Fellow. She is also the coeditor of *Fury: Women's Lived Experiences during the Trump Era* (Pact Press, 2020) and has bylines in numerous publications including *Narratively*, *The Writer*, and *Guideposts*. Amy lives in San Diego with her husband and weighted blanket, a.k.a. her two cats.

DIANE SEUSS's *Still Life with Two Dead Peacocks and a Girl* (Graywolf Press, 2018) was a finalist for the National Book Critics Circle Award in Poetry; *Four-Legged Girl* (Graywolf Press, 2015) was a finalist for the Pulitzer Prize. *Frank: Sonnets* was published in 2021.

CURTIS SMITH has published more than a hundred stories and essays, and his work has been cited by or appeared in *The Best American Short Stories*, *The Best American Mystery Stories*, *The Best American Spiritual Writing*, *The Best Short Fictions*, and the Norton anthology *New Micros*. His thirteenth book, *The Magpie's Return*, was released last year.

MAYA SONENBERG's story collection *Bad Mothers, Bad Daughters* is the recipient of the 2021 Sullivan Prize in short fiction. Previous books and chapbooks include *Cartographies*, *Voices from the Blue Hotel*, and *After the Death of Shostakovich Père*. Her work on Merce Cunningham has been supported by Velocity Dance Center (Seattle) and the Merce Cunningham Trust. Many thanks to them for their encouragement and backing. She is professor of creative writing at the University of Washington.

ERIC TRAN is the author of *The Gutter Spread Guide to Prayer*, winner of the 2019 Autumn House Rising Writer Prize, which was featured in The Rumpus Poetry Book Club. His work appears in *Poetry Daily*, *Poetry Northwest*, *Missouri Review Poem of the Week*, and elsewhere. He is a resident physician in psychiatry in Asheville, North Carolina.

SARAH VIREN is the author of *Mine*, which won the *River Teeth* Book Prize and the GLCA New Writers Award and was longlisted or a finalist for the PEN/Diamonstein-Spielvogel Award for the Art of the Essay, a Foreword Indies Award, and a Lambda Literary Award. Her writing appears in the *New York Times Magazine*, the *Oxford American*, *Texas Monthly*, and elsewhere and has been supported by the National Endowment for the Arts. She is an assistant professor at Arizona State University, and her next book, *Autobiography of Shadows*, is forthcoming from Scribner Books.

JULIE MARIE WADE teaches in the creative writing program at Florida International University in Miami. Her newest lyric essay collections are *Just an Ordinary Woman Breathing* and *The Unrhymables: Collaborations in Prose*, coauthored with Denise Duhamel.

ELISSA WASHUTA is a member of the Cowlitz Indian Tribe and a non-fiction writer. She is the author of *White Magic*, *My Body Is a Book of Rules*, and *Starvation Mode*. With Theresa Warburton, she is coeditor of the anthology *Shapes of Native Nonfiction: Collected Essays by Contemporary Writers*. Elissa is an assistant professor of creative writing at the Ohio State University.

LIDIA YUKNAVITCH is author of the novels *The Book of Joan*, *The Small Backs of Children*, and *Dora: A Headcase* as well as a critical book on war and narrative, *Allegories of Violence*, and the widely acclaimed memoir *The Chronology of Water*. Her new collection of fiction, *Verge*, was published by Riverhead Books this year, and her forthcoming novel, *Thrust*, emerges from Riverhead in 2021. She founded the workshop series Corporeal Writing in Portland, Oregon, where she teaches both in person and online. She is a very good swimmer.

Printed in the USA
CPSIA information can be obtained
at www.ICGtesting.com
LVHW041336291223
767659LV00004B/527

9 781496 217745